Intelligent Manufactu
Under Challenging C

Intelligent Manufacturing and Design Under Challenging Conditions

Guest Editors

Ling Chen
Yanyan Li
Jinming Zhou
Guoqing Zhang

MDPI

Basel • Beijing • Wuhan • Barcelona • Belgrade • Novi Sad • Cluj • Manchester

Guest Editors
Ling Chen
School of Mechanical Engineering
Sichuan University
Chengdu
China

Yanyan Li
School of Mechanical Engineering
Sichuan University
Chengdu
China

Jinming Zhou
Department of Mechanical Engineering Sciences
Lund University
Lund
Sweden

Guoqing Zhang
School of Mechanical Engineering
Shenzhen University
Shenzhen
China

Editorial Office
MDPI AG
Grosspeteranlage 5
4052 Basel, Switzerland

This is a reprint of the Special Issue, published open access by the journal *Applied Sciences* (ISSN 2076-3417), freely accessible at: https://www.mdpi.com/journal/applsci/special_issues/SLJ3Y0TJ90.

For citation purposes, cite each article independently as indicated on the article page online and as indicated below:

Lastname, A.A.; Lastname, B.B. Article Title. *Journal Name* **Year**, *Volume Number*, Page Range.

ISBN 978-3-7258-8299-1 (Hbk)
ISBN 978-3-7258-8300-4 (PDF)
https://doi.org/10.3390/books978-3-7258-8300-4

Contents

About the Editors

Ling Chen

Ling Chen is a professor at the School of Mechanical Engineering, Sichuan University, China. His research focuses on advanced cutting technology, design and application of major instruments and equipment, as well as innovative design and intelligent manufacturing. He has been involved in the development of high-performance machining systems and intelligent equipment for challenging conditions. His work includes both theoretical investigations and practical engineering implementations, contributing to improved manufacturing efficiency and system reliability.

Yanyan Li

Yanyan Li is a researcher at the School of Mechanical Engineering, Sichuan University, China. Her research interests cover mechanical manufacturing and automation, mechanical electronic engineering, and intelligent diagnosis and control. She has worked on projects related to condition monitoring and fault diagnosis of mechanical systems, integrating sensor technologies with intelligent algorithms. Her contributions support the advancement of automated manufacturing processes and smart maintenance strategies.

Jinming Zhou

Jinming Zhou is a professor in the Division of Production and Materials Engineering, Department of Mechanical Engineering Sciences at Lund University, Sweden. His research interests include cutting tools, high-performance machining, innovative design, wear of materials, process monitoring, and sustainable manufacturing. He has led numerous research projects aimed at improving tool performance and machining efficiency under demanding conditions. His work bridges fundamental wear mechanisms with industrial applications, contributing to more sustainable and resource-efficient manufacturing processes.

Guoqing Zhang

Guoqing Zhang is a professor at the School of Mechanical Engineering, Shenzhen University, China. His research focuses on ultra-precision machining processes and technologies, diamond tools, smart machining, machining equipment, advanced cutting technology, and the design of instruments and equipment for extreme environments. He has been actively involved in developing high-precision machining solutions and equipment tailored for harsh operational settings, including deep-earth and deep-space applications. His work integrates innovative design principles with advanced manufacturing techniques to enhance tool performance and system robustness.

Preface

The depletion of near-surface resources has pushed engineering toward extreme environments—deep earth, deep sea, and deep space. These settings impose high temperature, high pressure, deep uncertainty, and limited maintainability. Traditional empirical design approaches rarely hold up under such harsh conditions, making intelligent manufacturing and intelligent design essential for autonomous operations and remote health management.

This Reprint collects peer-reviewed articles on intelligent equipment for extreme environments. The contributions cover three interconnected threads. The first examines intelligent drilling, coring, and robotic systems for deep coal mines and lunar missions. The second focuses on deep in situ environment reconstruction and high-temperature/high-pressure simulation platforms for fidelity core transfer and tool validation. The third addresses reliability enhancement of critical components through multi-physics optimization, including thermo-electrical coupling, CFD-guided erosion mitigation, and downhole power and signal transmission.

The methodologies and evidence presented here offer a valuable reference for researchers and practitioners in deep underground engineering, deep-sea exploration, and planetary drilling. We gratefully acknowledge all authors and reviewers for their contributions.

Ling Chen, Yanyan Li, Jinming Zhou, and Guoqing Zhang
Guest Editors

applied sciences

Editorial

Editorial: Intelligent Manufacturing and Design Under Challenging Conditions

Ling Chen [1,2], Zengfeng Duan [1], Yanyan Li [1,*] and Guoqing Zhang [3]

1 School of Mechanical Engineering, Sichuan University, Chengdu 610065, China; chenlingscu@scu.edu.cn (L.C.); 2023323020001@stu.scu.edu.cn (Z.D.)
2 State Key Laboratory of Intelligent Construction and Healthy Operation and Maintenance of Deep Underground Engineering, Sichuan University, Chengdu 610065, China
3 College of Mechatronics and Control Engineering, Shenzhen University, Nan-hai Ave 3688, Shenzhen 518060, China; zhanggq@szu.edu.cn
* Correspondence: liyanyan@scu.edu.cn

1. Introduction

As readily accessible resources near the Earth's surface are gradually depleted, the focus of resource development and scientific exploration is increasingly shifting toward extreme environments, including deep earth, deep sea, and deep space [1–3]. In the deep-earth domain, the former Soviet Union's Kola Superdeep Borehole reached a drilling depth of 12,262 m, pioneering ultra-deep drilling at the 10,000 m scale [4]. In recent years, China has also successfully initiated the drilling of multiple 10,000 m-class wells, such as Chuanke-1 and Take-1, with notable indications of oil and gas reported [5,6]. In the deep-sea domain, China achieved in 2023 the first acquisition at the global scale of deep-sea sediment and gas-hydrate samples under a simultaneously preserved pressure of 14.5 MPa and a temperature of 3 °C at a water depth of 1385 m in the South China Sea [7]. In the deep-space domain, the U.S. Artemis program is advancing lunar resource development, while China's Chang'e-6 mission employed fidelity coring to enable in situ sampling and return of lunar materials [8]. Engineering endeavors once regarded as science fiction, such as deep-sea mining, ultra-deep drilling at the 10,000 m scale, and lunar mining, are gradually evolving from demonstration projects into routine applications [9]. However, these extreme physical environments pose formidable challenges in terms of cost, efficiency, and operational safety [10]. Consequently, the intelligent design and manufacturing of equipment for extreme environments has become a pivotal strategy to address these challenges by enabling autonomous decision-making operations, in situ sensing, and closed-loop control, as well as remote collaboration and health management.

The core of intelligent equipment design for extreme environments lies in augmenting the capability to establish and stably maintain controlled "internal working conditions", thereby ensuring equipment reliability and sample fidelity. On the one hand, for deep-earth and deep-sea drilling and sampling, integrated systems combining intelligent temperature regulation and pressure preservation have been developed. For example, coupling an intelligent thermal control system with hollow glass microsphere composite insulation can effectively maintain the in situ temperature of deep cores [11]. In addition, a self-triggered sealing system based on a ball valve and a flip-cover valve has demonstrated stable operation under extreme conditions of 150 °C and 140 MPa, providing support for resource extraction in deep seas and ultra-deep wells [7]. On the other hand, deep-space environments, such as the lunar surface, feature extreme temperature swings from −180 °C to 130 °C together with high-vacuum conditions, making the thermal management of

https://doi.org/10.3390/app16042136

electronic devices a key enabling technology [12,13]. Recent advances mainly include high-efficiency passive heat dissipation techniques, such as phase-change cooling materials and loop heat pipes, as well as radiation heat-transfer optimization designs tailored for vacuum environments, to ensure stable instrument operation under the extreme thermal conditions on the lunar surface [14–16]. Finally, at the level of integrated intelligent design and manufacturing, international efforts have established technical frameworks involving digital twins, multi-physics coupled design, and intelligent control to achieve reliable, efficient, and autonomous operations [17–20].

Based on this foundation, this Special Issue continues to focus on intelligent manufacturing and equipment design for extreme environments, including deep earth, deep sea, and deep space, with the aim of advancing related systems from experience-driven development toward a high-reliability paradigm that is synergistically driven by models and data. The core research topics include the following: the design of intelligent drilling and coring equipment and robotic systems for extreme environments; research on deep in situ environment reconstruction and high-temperature/high-pressure simulation testing methods and platforms; and the reliability enhancement of critical components and multi-physics-based structural optimization under extreme conditions.

2. Overview of the Contributions

To address these challenges, this Special Issue has presented a series of studies spanning the aforementioned scope. The latest contributions can be categorized into the following three areas:

2.1. Design of Intelligent Drilling and Coring Equipment and Robotic Systems for Extreme Environments

The published studies address two representative task scenarios, namely, temporary support advancement in deep coal-mine short-wall roadways and lunar sampling; they have established a system-level design concept spanning "support–rock breaking–sampling–core-tube replacement and storage". For 15–40 m deep coal-mine short-wall faces in integrated drilling–mining operations, where conventional temporary support methods struggle to balance stability and efficiency, Ma et al. proposed a self-propelled temporary support robot that achieves "walking under load" through mutual pushing and pulling between two support units. They developed both a stable-support mechanical model and a load-walking dynamic model. By formulating boundary criteria and equipment–rock interaction mechanisms, they clarified the range of support forces that enables stable load-assisted advancement. Finite element analysis and multibody dynamics simulations were further combined to evaluate structural and floor stresses as well as the critical advancement conditions. In particular, incorporating Stribeck friction markedly improved the predictive accuracy for the required push–pull forces, thereby providing a more reliable analytical framework for the refined modeling and control of heavy-duty equipment under complex contact conditions.

In addition, for crewed lunar sampling missions, Zhang et al. noted that a single sampling mode poses higher risks under harsh lunar conditions and operational constraints. They proposed a dual-mode hybrid coring concept that combines high-frequency percussive penetration with rotary drilling. Key adjustable parameters were reported, including an impact frequency of 0–20 Hz, an impact energy of 5–15 J, and a rotational speed of 0–300 rpm, to accommodate varying depths and media while improving coring efficiency and preserving stratigraphic information. Their design also considered the coordination between handheld operations and lander- or rover-mounted operations, aiming to reduce astronaut workload and enhance sampling safety and stability.

 https://doi.org/10.3390/app16042136

Furthermore, targeting deeper lunar rock sampling, Wen et al. proposed a functional division between a surface core-tube replacement and storage executor and an underground wire-line self-excavating coring robot, referred to as WSC. The surface unit performs core-tube replacement and storage of filled tubes, whereas the underground unit is responsible for in-hole anchoring, thrusting, and combined rotary–percussive rock breaking and coring. A model describing the depth-dependent evolution of anchoring support force was established to guide the power and thrust strategy at different depths. The authors emphasized that anchoring fluctuates markedly in the shallow 0–4 m interval and thus requires real-time adjustment, whereas it becomes more stable at greater depths, enabling higher-power operation. Structural features such as anchoring lock mechanisms, temporary cuttings storage, and automatic cuttings removal were also incorporated to support continuous operation in the absence of drilling fluids.

2.2. Research on Deep In Situ Environment Reconstruction and High-Temperature and High-Pressure Simulation Testing Methods and Platforms

Research in this area has progressed in two collaborative directions: "high-precision reconstruction and maintenance of in situ temperature and pressure environments" and "high-temperature and ultra-high-pressure ground simulation testing equipment for pressure-preserved coring tools." First, Peng et al. proposed the Deep In Situ Environment Reconstruction and Core Transfer System (SERCT), which uses water as a medium for a working condition corresponding to a depth of approximately 2500 m, with 95 °C and ≤70 MPa. To address the control difficulties caused by the coupling of temperature and pressure, they proposed a P–T decoupling control approach based on water's density-equivalent P–T curve interpolation. After decoupling, fuzzy PID dual-mode pressure control and fuzzy PID temperature control based on gray prediction were applied. Additionally, segmented electric heating was used to improve temperature field uniformity. The system emphasizes that temperature and pressure fluctuations due to valve and pushrod movements during core preparation and testing must be controlled within ±3% of the range, thereby providing methodological and system-level support for "fidelity" physical property testing and cross-chamber transfer.

Second, Huang et al. addressed the development and testing requirements for deep pressure-preserved coring tools by constructing an in situ simulation device consisting of a high-temperature and ultra-high-pressure testing chamber and a coring drive module. They provided key specifications, including a maximum working pressure of 140 MPa and a temperature of 150 °C. They further validated through experiments that the segmented testing chamber could stably withstand up to 190 MPa and remain in the elastic deformation stage at 150 °C without leakage. The drive module can provide a stable rotational speed of up to 150 rpm under a 140 MPa sealing pressure. This provides reproducible equipment and validation for conducting pressure-preserved coring simulation tests on the ground and reducing high-risk and high-cost field trials.

Overall, these two studies complement key elements of the deep in situ fidelity testing chain from the perspectives of "temperature–pressure decoupling and stable maintenance control algorithms and process platforms" and "high-temperature and ultra-high-pressure load-bearing and dynamic sealing test equipment platforms," thus laying the foundation for an integrated testing system for coring, transfer, preparation, and testing under extreme environmental conditions.

2.3. Enhancement of Critical Component Reliability and Multi-Physics Structural Optimization Under Extreme Environments

Focusing on this research direction, related findings provide practical frameworks and engineering evidence from three perspectives: thermal–electrical coupling reliability

https://doi.org/10.3390/app16042136

assessment, structural optimization under complex fluid–solid multiphase erosion, and innovative designs for downhole power and signal transmission structures. First, in terms of electronic packaging reliability, Min et al. conducted high-voltage stress tests on semiconductor packaging under data center immersion cooling conditions, revealing the nonlinear growth of heat accumulation and leakage current due to increasing stress voltage. Overvoltage in air environments leads to significant heat buildup and an increase in leakage current, which accelerates device degradation, while immersion cooling enhances heat dissipation, thereby suppressing leakage current growth. These findings provide a basis for design margins and accelerated testing thresholds for packaging under extreme heat dissipation conditions.

Next, in the optimization of key hydraulic components for deep downhole coring systems, Guo et al. focused on the issues of differential motion component sealing failure, jamming, and erosion in in situ pressure-preserved coring (IPP-Coring) systems. They performed a mechanistic analysis of flow field velocity, pressure drop, and vortex structure using computational fluid dynamics (CFD) and proposed synergistic improvements to geometric parameters and outlet structures. By increasing the seat diameter from 30 mm to 40 mm, the maximum flow rate and pressure drop were reduced to 0.55 and 0.2 times of the original, respectively. Furthermore, changing the seat outlet from a right angle to an arc could further shorten the vortex area and reduce near-wall velocity and pressure drop. Particle trajectory and erosion calculations showed that the improved structure reduced the average erosion rate to only 0.42 times that of the original structure. More importantly, field tests verified that the surface erosion of the improved seat outlet was significantly reduced, and the system pump pressure difference was reduced from approximately 0.2 MPa to nearly 0 MPa, demonstrating an effective "simulation–manufacturing–field verification" engineering loop.

Finally, regarding energy and signal transmission in extreme high-temperature and high-pressure downhole environments, Yu et al. observed that deep hard rock coring systems urgently need to transition from "only pressure preservation" to "both temperature and pressure preservation". Achieving active insulation and intelligent control requires reliable downhole power supply and signal transmission, which remains a significant challenge internationally. In response, the authors combined TRIZ's contradiction resolution mechanism with axiomatic design (AD) system decomposition principles to propose an innovative process mapping functional requirements to structural solutions for the conductive center rod. They clarified key requirements for module alignment, contact conduction, and avoiding wire entanglement to improve the stability and manufacturability of connections and transmission under extreme environmental conditions.

Overall, the results presented in this Special Issue focus on three main areas: the design of intelligent drilling and coring equipment and robotic systems for extreme environments, research on deep in situ environment reconstruction and high-temperature and high-pressure simulation testing platforms, and the enhancement of critical component reliability and multi-physics structural optimization under extreme conditions. These contributions form a complete chain from components to systems, from design to verification, providing a transferable methodological framework and engineering basis for the efficient development and safe operation of equipment in extreme environments, while also advancing the engineering application of intelligent manufacturing in harsh conditions, such as deep earth and deep space. In industrial applications, deep mining and geotechnical engineering can benefit from intelligent support systems and condition-preserved coring and testing platforms, reducing the risks associated with dynamic excavation, enhancing stability management, and obtaining more reliable subsurface properties to support disaster prediction and support design. In the energy exploration sector, the optimization of

 https://doi.org/10.3390/app16042136

pressure-preserved coring components and CFD-guided reliability enhancement reduces the risk of failure and improves sample fidelity, thus advancing reservoir evaluation and decision-making. Additionally, laboratory simulation systems reduce reliance on expensive field tests and shorten development cycles, and the fidelity coring analysis of gas hydrates enables the direct quantification of in situ methane, highlighting the value of fidelity sampling in extreme environments. Planetary exploration also benefits from autonomous and human-assisted drilling and coring concepts, which are essential for tasks in environments that are difficult to maintain, with strict limitations on mass and energy. In conclusion, these studies emphasize that the key to deployable intelligence lies in integrating robust design, validation-oriented testing systems, and data-driven optimization into a cohesive workflow, rather than isolated improvements.

3. Conclusions

Overall, the published papers in this Special Issue concentrate on three main areas: (i) intelligent drilling and coring equipment and robotic systems for extreme environments, (ii) deep in situ environment reconstruction and high-temperature/high-pressure simulation testing platforms, and (iii) the reliability enhancement of critical components and multi-physics structural optimization under extreme conditions. Collectively, the contributions form a chain from components to systems and from design to verification, providing methodological elements and engineering evidence for the efficient development and safer operation of equipment in extreme environments—particularly for deep earth and deep space.

From an application perspective, deep mining and geotechnical engineering can benefit from intelligent support systems and fidelity coring/testing platforms to reduce risks in dynamic excavation and improve stability management while enabling more reliable subsurface-property characterization for hazard prediction and support design. In energy exploration, the reliability enhancement and CFD-guided optimization of pressure-preserved coring components can reduce failure risks and improve sample fidelity, strengthening reservoir evaluation and decision-making. In parallel, laboratory simulation systems can reduce dependence on expensive field trials and shorten development cycles. Finally, planetary exploration may benefit from autonomous and human-assisted drilling/coring concepts that address operational constraints under limited mass, energy, and maintainability.

In summary, this Special Issue highlights that deployable intelligence under challenging conditions is most effectively achieved by integrating robust design, validation-oriented testing systems, and data-driven optimization into a cohesive workflow, rather than by isolated incremental improvements. Future research may further focus on the following:

(1) Enhancing robust autonomy and online adaptability under strongly varying conditions and data scarcity;
(2) Strengthening closed-loop integration across "design–simulation–testing–deployment", including deeper coupling between digital twins and physical validation;
(3) Establishing transferable evaluation metrics and standardized validation protocols to enable reproducible comparisons and scalable engineering deployment.

Author Contributions: Conceptualization, L.C.; validation, Y.L. and G.Z.; writing—original draft preparation, L.C. and Z.D.; writing—review and editing, Y.L. and G.Z. All authors have read and agreed to the published version of the manuscript.

Conflicts of Interest: The authors declare no conflicts of interest.

 https://doi.org/10.3390/app16042136

List of Contributions:

1. Ma, H.; Cheng, J.; Wang, C.; Zhang, H.; Cui, W.; Xue, X.; Mao, Q.; Liu, P.; Guo, Y.; Su, H. Research on Temporary Support Robot for the Integrated Excavation and Mining System of Section Coal Pillar. *Appl. Sci.* **2025**, *15*, 4896.
2. Zhang, X.; Zhang, G.; Gao, M.; Wen, Y.; Wang, Y. Design of man-machine synergic lunar coring device and its coring dynamic analysis. *Appl. Sci.* **2023**, *13*, 7961.
3. Wen, Y.; Zhang, G.; Xie, H.; Gao, M.; Zhang, X.; Wang, Y.; Li, C. Design and dynamic analysis of the wire-line coring robot for deep lunar rocks. *Appl. Sci.* **2023**, *13*, 1722.
4. Peng, X.; Li, X.; Yang, S.; Wu, J.; Wu, M.; Wan, L.; Zhang, H.; Xie, H. An innovative system of deep in situ environment reconstruction and core transfer. *Appl. Sci.* **2023**, *13*, 6534.
5. Huang, W.; Xie, H.; Li, J.; Yang, Y.; Li, C.; He, Z.; Li, Y.; Zhang, Z. Development of an In-Situ Simulation Device for Testing Deep Pressure-Preserving Coring Tools under High-Temperature and Ultrahigh-Pressure Conditions. *Appl. Sci.* **2023**, *13*, 3889.
6. Min, K.; Kang, T.; Kang, T.Y.; Pyo, J.-B. Evaluation of Leakage Currents of Semiconductor Packages Due to High-Voltage Stress Under an Immersion Cooling Environment. *Appl. Sci.* **2025**, *15*, 4668.
7. Guo, D.; Li, J.; Wang, D.; Zhang, Y.; Fang, X.; Xie, H. Structural improvement of differential motion assembly in in situ pressure-preserved coring system using CFD simulation. *Appl. Sci.* **2023**, *13*, 4108.
8. Yu, B.; He, Z.; Yang, J.; Wei, Z.; Li, C.; Xie, H. Innovative design of a conductive center pole for an active thermal insulation and coring system in deep rock. *Appl. Sci.* **2023**, *13*, 1242.

References

1. Snelgrove, P.V.; Metaxas, A. Mining of the Deep Ocean. *Annu. Rev. Environ. Resour.* **2025**, *50*, 455–481. [CrossRef]
2. Teagle, D.A. Re-energizing the quest of drilling to the mantle. *Nat. Rev. Earth Environ.* **2023**, *4*, 207–208. [CrossRef]
3. Reiss, P.; Abbud-Madrid, A.; Arm, P.; Bickel, V.T.; Kehl, F.; Kolvenbach, H.; Ligeza, G.; Lomax, B.; Zabel, P. Technologies for prospecting, extraction, and utilization of space resources. *Front. Space Technol.* **2024**, *5*, 1493494. [CrossRef]
4. Lobanov, K.V.; Chicherov, M.; Sharov, N. The 50th Anniversary of the Start of Drilling the Kola Superdeep Well. *Arct. North* **2021**, *44*, 267–284. [CrossRef]
5. Chunsheng, W.; Shaobo, F.; Zhi, Z.; Bo, Z.; Xiaogang, L.; Bao, Z. Key technologies for drilling design of well Shendi Take-1. *Pet. Drill. Tech.* **2024**, *52*, 78–86.
6. Ran, L.; Wenzhe, L.; Jiayin, Z.; Yang, L. Drilling fluid technology for Ultra-Large wellbore in the upper part of 10,000-meter deep Well SDCK1. *Pet. Drill. Tech.* **2024**, *52*, 93–99.
7. Xie, H.; Gao, M.; Zhang, R.; Zhou, H.; Gao, F.; Chen, L.; Peng, X.; Li, X.; Ju, Y. Application prospects of deep in-situ condition-preserved coring and testing systems. *Adv. Geo-Energy Res.* **2024**, *14*, 12–24. [CrossRef]
8. Wang, C.; Zhang, G.; Wang, Y.; Song, L. A Review of Lunar Environment and In-Situ Resource Utilization for Achieving Long-Term Lunar Habitation. *Galaxies* **2025**, *13*, 103. [CrossRef]
9. Wang, C.; Zhou, S.; Shu, X.; Song, H. Deep-sea mining: A potential solution to secure critical energy minerals availability. *npj Ocean Sustain.* **2025**, *4*, 59. [CrossRef]
10. Yao, W.; Tian, C.; Teng, Y.; Diao, F.; Du, X.; Gu, P.; Zhou, W. Development of deep-sea mining and its environmental impacts: A review. *Front. Mar. Sci.* **2025**, *12*, 1598584. [CrossRef]
11. Chen, L.; Qin, B.; Li, Y.; Yang, X. Design and evaluation of in-situ temperature-preserved deep rock coring systems based on analytic hierarchy process. *Adv. Geo-Energy Res.* **2025**, *16*, 8–20. [CrossRef]
12. Chen, J.; Li, R. Advances in Solidification Technologies of Lunar Regolith-Based Building Materials Under Extreme Lunar Environments. *Buildings* **2025**, *15*, 2543. [CrossRef]
13. Van Velson, N.; Diebold, J.; Schulze, D.-P.; Tarau, C.; Anderson, W. Two-Phase Thermal Switch for Lunar Lander and Rover Thermal Management. In Proceedings of the 52nd International Conference on Environmental Systems (ICES), Calgary, AB, Canada, 16–20 July 2023; Paper No. ICES-2023-370.
14. Garmendia, I.; Vallejo, H.; Seco, M.; Anglada, E. Design and fabrication of a phase change material heat storage device for the thermal control of electronics components of space applications. *Aerospace* **2022**, *9*, 126. [CrossRef]
15. Medici, E.F.; Turk, J.C.; Stewart, E.R.; Page, T.; Dobarco-Otero, J.; Quintanilla, G.; Slusser, T.B.; Mittag, Z.W.; Barragan, J.M.; Alvarez-Hernandez, A. Thermal Vacuum Testing of a VIPER Loop Heat Pipe. In *Proceedings of the 36th Thermal and Fluids Analysis Workshop (TFAWS)*; ICES Steering Committee: Copenhagen, Denmark, 2025.

https://doi.org/10.3390/app16042136

16. Gibson, A.S.; Poyntz-Wright, O.; Bishop, A.; Oldfield, M.; Iglesias, A.; Rottmeier, F.; Humphries, M.; Hager, P.B. A Dust-Resilient Thermal Shutter Mechanism for Lunar Radiators. In *Proceedings of the 47th Aerospace Mechanisms Symposium*; Mechanisms Education Association: Los Angeles, CA, USA, 2024.
17. Soori, M.; Arezoo, B.; Dastres, R. Digital twin for smart manufacturing, A review. *Sustain. Manuf. Serv. Econ.* **2023**, *2*, 100017. [CrossRef]
18. Bayat, M.; Dong, W.; Thorborg, J.; To, A.C.; Hattel, J.H. A review of multi-scale and multi-physics simulations of metal additive manufacturing processes with focus on modeling strategies. *Addit. Manuf.* **2021**, *47*, 102278. [CrossRef]
19. Lee, M.-F.R. A review on intelligent control theory and applications in process optimization and smart manufacturing. *Processes* **2023**, *11*, 3171. [CrossRef]
20. Padmavathi, V.; Kanimozhi, R.; Saminathan, R. Digital twin driven smart factories: Real time physics based co-simulation using edge ai and federated learning. *Sci. Rep.* **2025**, *15*, 43373. [CrossRef] [PubMed]

https://doi.org/10.3390/app16042136

applied sciences

MDPI

Article

Research on Temporary Support Robot for the Integrated Excavation and Mining System of Section Coal Pillar

Hongwei Ma [1,2], Jiashuai Cheng [1,2], Chuanwei Wang [1,2,*], Heng Zhang [1,2], Wenda Cui [1,2], Xusheng Xue [1,2], Qinghua Mao [1,2], Peng Liu [1,2], Yifeng Guo [1,2], Hao Su [1,2], Zukun Yu [1,2], Peng Wang [1,2] and Haibo Tian [1,2]

1 School of Mechanical Engineering, Xi'an University of Science and Technology, Xi'an 710054, China; mahw@xust.edu.cn (H.M.); 22205016001@stu.xust.edu.cn (J.C.)

2 Shaanxi Provincial Key Laboratory of Intelligent Testing and Control of Mine Mechanical and Electrical Equipment, Xi'an University of Science and Technology, Xi'an 710054, China

* Correspondence: wangchuanwei228@xust.edu.cn

Abstract: Facing the support challenges of short-wall working face (15–40 m) roadways in the 'excavation–backfill–retention' tunneling method for section coal pillars, traditional equipment struggled to achieve stable, reliable, and efficient support. This paper designed a temporary support robot for the excavation and mining system of section coal pillars to ensure the safety of equipment and personnel in short-wall working faces. The support requirements of the section coal pillar excavation and mining system were analyzed, and a general 'driving under pressure' temporary support scheme was proposed. The working principle of the temporary support robot was analyzed. A mechanical model for the stable support of the temporary support robot was established. The mechanical properties of the surrounding rock were analyzed, and the allowable range of the temporary support robot's supporting force was determined while ensuring the stability of the surrounding rock. Based on the Stribeck friction theory, a dynamic model of the temporary support robot in the driving under pressure state was constructed. The boundary conditions of the dynamic model were set, and the corresponding relationship between the temporary support robot's supporting force and its maximum static friction force was determined. This accurately described the influence of the supporting force and pushing (pulling) force on the movement during the process of driving under pressure. Through finite element simulation, the stress conditions of the temporary support robot and the floor under maximum load were analyzed, indicating that this load condition would not cause damage to the temporary support robot or the surrounding rock. Through multi-body dynamics simulation, the pushing (pulling) forces required for the temporary support robot's movement under different supporting force conditions were obtained, verifying the feasibility of the driving under pressure action under different supporting force conditions. Moreover, the model-predicted and simulated values of the required pushing (pulling) forces during the process of driving under pressure were consistent, validating the accuracy of the driving under pressure dynamic model. This research provides a new theoretical framework for the design and dynamic analysis of temporary support equipment for short-wall working faces in section coal pillar mining, holding significant academic value and broad application prospects.

Keywords: driving under pressure; dynamic model; Stribeck friction; boundary condition

1. Introduction

Based on the development trend of China's excavation and mining technology and the actual needs of coal mining enterprises for solid waste treatment and section coal pillar resources recovery, academician Wang proposed the integrated 'excavation–backfill–retention' tunneling method for section coal pillar extraction [1], which can realize the collaborative operation of "roadway excavation, solid waste disposal, and section coal pillar resources recovery". The new method employs a set of advanced comprehensive mining equipment for short-wall working face excavation, continuously and efficiently filling behind the excavation face. Overall, it replaces the section coal pillar with waste rock, while automatically leaving two side lanes along the filling belt, achieving tunnel excavation, waste rock disposal, and section coal pillar resource recovery.

Temporary support is an indispensable process in roadway excavation, which can ensure the safety and stability of the roof in the area between the drilling head and permanent support [2]. Compared with the permanent support of general roadways, the temporary support strength is far lower than the permanent support strength [3,4]. Therefore, realizing safe and stable temporary support during face section coal pillar excavation is an important engineering problem in integrated 'excavation–backfill–retention' mining.

Currently, most of the temporary support equipment used in coal mine roadway excavation do not rely on the tunneling machine and can realize autonomous movement [5,6]. They can be categorized by their movement method: stepping mobile temporary support, crawler-type temporary support, and translational temporary support. The stepping mobile temporary support moves by mimicking a walking motion using independent units that alternately support, release, advance, and re-support. This adapts to complex geology and offers high strength [7]. The crawler-type temporary support uses a crawler mechanism for continuous support and advancement, improving efficiency. It is ideal for long, uniform tunnels, especially in soft soil [8]. The translational temporary support uses large frames pushed forward; during the pushing process, the support force on the roof is usually maintained. It is simple and suited for regular tunnels with good geology [9].

Regarding the stepping mobile temporary support, Yang et al. [10] designed a novel advanced roadway support with a support height of 2~4 m and a support width of 3.2~4.5 m, analyzing the influence of support timing and location on roof load and deformation. This provided a basis for optimizing the support design and improving the support effect. Mao et al. [11] studied the structural stability of the stepping arch advanced supporting equipment and established the multi-point distributed static model of the top support beam. Structural design optimization was carried out through simulation software to ensure the structure had better stability. Wang et al. [12] proposed a novel approach for roadway excavation, support, and anchoring by utilizing the twin-link stepping mobile temporary support method, it can provide support for roadways that are 3.6 m high and 5 m wide. This method laid a theoretical foundation for implementing the parallel operation mode in underground roadway excavation in coal mines and significantly improved safety and efficiency.

Regarding the crawler-type temporary support. Xu [13] introduced a hydraulic-driven crawler-type tunneling support device designed for a tunneling width of 5.0 m and a support height range of 3.0 to 3.8 m, addressing safety and efficiency issues in coal mine roadway support. Utilizing a hydraulic motor and a four-bar linkage mechanism, the device enhances stability, reduces roof damage, and allows rapid forward movement without lowering the frame, thereby improving tunneling efficiency.

Regarding the translational temporary support, Ma et al. [14] proposed a precise control method based on fuzzy PID for the supporting force of a shield-type temporary support robot and verified the stability of the control system through experiments to ensure the safe and stable support of the surrounding rock during the pushing movement.

In summary, the existing temporary support equipment can only address excavation issues in roadways with widths below 5 m, and there is a high risk of damaging the roof during the support process. There are few reports on temporary support equipment for a short-wall working face with a length of 15~40 m required for the face section coal pillar excavation and mining system. Therefore, aiming at the needs of the face section coal pillar excavation and mining system, this paper designs a self-propelled temporary support robot (TSR). The working principle of TSR driving under pressure is analyzed, and mechanical models of TSR for stable support and dynamic models for driving under pressure are constructed. The stable support state, the boundary conditions of driving under pressure, and the process of driving under pressure are simulated and analyzed to solve the support and driving problems of excavation equipment in short-wall working face tunnels.

This paper is organized as follows: Section 1 designs a self-moving TSR and clarifies its working principle. Section 2 constructs a mechanical model of the TSR during stable support. Section 3 constructs a dynamic model of the TSR when driving under pressure. Section 4 establishes a criterion system for the boundary condition of the dynamic model, and clarifies the mechanism of interaction between the TSR and the surrounding rock under the driving under pressure condition. Section 5 conducts a finite element analysis on the TSR and the floor and simulates the critical value of the boundary condition of the dynamic model for driving under pressure, as well as the process of driving under pressure.

2. Analysis of the Principles of the Temporary Support Robot

2.1. Overall Scheme of the Temporary Support System

The 'excavation–backfill–retention' system of the section coal pillar is responsible for completing the integrated 'excavation–backfill–retention' mining of the section coal pillar, and its scheme is shown in Figure 1. The 'excavation–backfill–retention' system of the section coal pillar includes four subsystems: section coal pillar excavation and mining system, waste-filling system, transportation system, and ventilation dust removal system. Among them, the section coal pillar excavation and mining system includes a cutting robot [15], a scraper conveyor [16], a temporary support system, and platforms with drilling and anchoring equipment [17,18], which are responsible for working face excavation and support. The waste-filling system completes the middle waste rock filling and the natural roadway formation on the left and right sides through the waste-filling robot. The transportation system can timely and smoothly load and transport the cut coal rock to the main transport system and transport the materials used for waste-filling to the designated position according to the requirements so as to provide an effective and reliable guarantee for the continuous work of the entire face section coal pillar excavation and mining and waste-filling. The loader and belt conveyor are essential in the mining face and belong to the transportation system. The loader transfers coal from the mining area to the main belt conveyor or storage, providing flexibility and improving efficiency. The belt conveyor enables continuous, stable transport of coal over long distances, reducing manual labor and enhancing safety. Together, they form the backbone of modern coal mining operations. The ventilation dust removal system is mainly responsible for supplying fresh air to the underground, diluting and discharging harmful gases and dust, providing a safe and healthy working environment for miners, preventing gas explosions and dust hazards, and ensuring the safe production of the mine. Each subsystem operates in parallel and collaboratively, which can realize the safety, high efficiency, and intelligence of the excavation and waste-filling process of the section coal pillar extraction system.

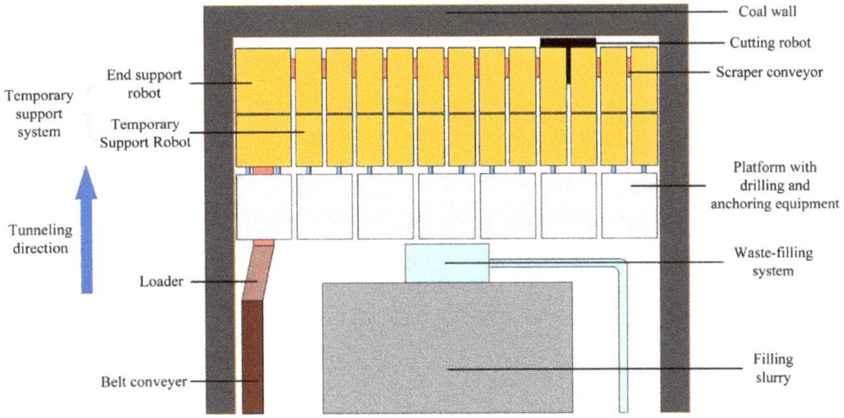

Figure 1. Schematic diagram of 'excavation–backfill–retention' system of section coal pillar.

The temporary support system is a part of the 'excavation–backfill–retention' system of section coal pillar extraction, mainly including the TSR and the end support robot. Considering that the end support robot needs to straddle the scraper conveyor and has a unique structure, this paper only focuses on the TSR. The face of the section coal pillar excavation and mining working face is divided into several sections. The cutting robot cuts a section from left to right for each section. Each section contains a group of two TSRs and a platform with drilling and anchoring equipment (as shown in Figure 1). The working process of each TSR group is as follows: two TSRs wait in the stable support situation for the cutting robot to complete the cutting action of the coal wall in the section. When the cutting work of the section is completed, and the cutting robot is traversed to the next section, the group of TSRs, according to the requirements of the scraper conveyor pushing in the comprehensive working face, and coordinates with the scraper conveyor pushing cylinder of the left TSR by controlling the extension of its scraper conveyor pushing cylinder to form an S-bend in the scraper conveyor pan. When the scraper conveyor pushing cylinder of the group of TSRs reaches the maximum stroke, the group of TSRs drives forward under pressure for a section from left to right in a push–pull sequence. When the group of TSRs completes the driving under pressure action, they jointly pull the platform with drilling and anchoring equipment located in the section forward for a section. All groups of TSRs in the temporary support system complete all the actions from left to right and then enter the next cycle.

2.2. Working Principles of the Temporary Support Robot

The temporary support system needs to provide timely and stable support for the empty top area generated after the cutting robot cuts the coal wall, and also provide a safe working space for personnel and equipment in the excavation and mining working face. To ensure the filling of waste rock and the forming of two roadways, the roof cannot collapse during the tunneling process of the excavation and mining system. Therefore, the temporary support system should avoid damaging the roof as much as possible during the support and driving process [19]. The excavation and mining system requires a temporary support system to provide forward power during tunneling. Therefore, the temporary support system must drive the cutting robot, scraper conveyor, and platform with drilling and anchoring equipment while moving autonomously. The requirements of the temporary support system include support and driving requirements, as shown in Figure 2.

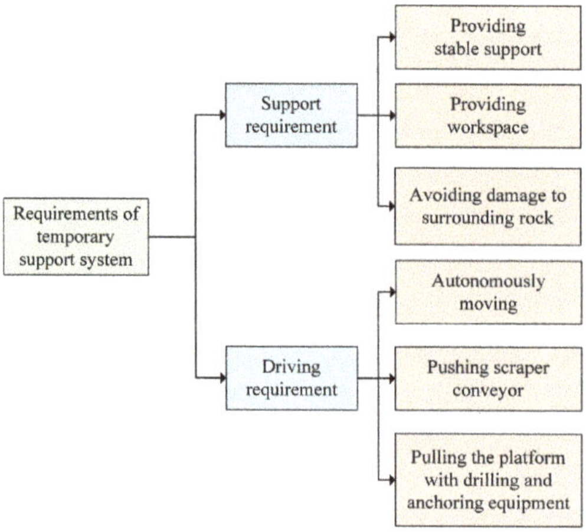

Figure 2. Demand for the temporary support system.

In response to the requirements of the 'excavation–backfill–retention' temporary support system for section coal pillar extraction, this paper designs a novel self-propelled TSR. The TSR mainly comprises two parts: support 1 and support 2, as shown in Figure 3. The driving under pressure process of the TSR involves the collaborative operation of support 1 and support 2. Both can adaptively change the supporting force to the roof while maintaining the surrounding rock stability. When support 1 is driving under pressure, its supporting force decreases, while support 2 is in a steady state, and its supporting force remains unchanged. The moving cylinder uses support 2 as a supporting point, pushing support 1 forward. Then, support 2 is dragged forward by support 1 under the same principle. The two TSRs in the same group rely on the friction with the roof and floor to move the platform with drilling and anchoring equipment forward through the pushing cylinder traction. The TSR adopts the method of pushing the scraper conveyor with the hydraulic support of the comprehensive working face. Multiple TSRs cooperate to complete the scraper conveyor pushing action through the pulling cylinder [20].

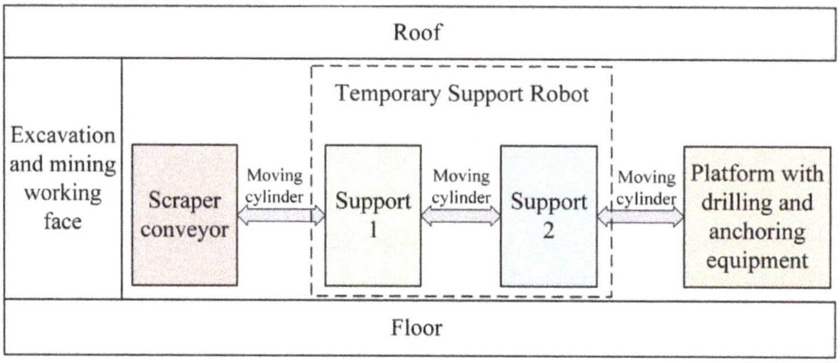

Figure 3. Working principle of the temporary support robot.

2.3. Construction of the Principle Model for the Temporary Support Robot

According to the working principle of the TSR and the structure of the chock-type hydraulic support [21], the principle model of the TSR is constructed as shown in Figure 4. The structural components of the simulation include the top beam of support 1, the base of support 1, the top beam of support 2, the base of support 2, the four-bar linkage mechanism of support 1, the four-bar linkage mechanism of support 2, the support hydraulic cylinder of support 1, the support hydraulic cylinder of support 2, roof, floor, and the moving cylinders. The TSR's top beam is connected to the base through a four-bar linkage mechanism and supporting cylinder [22]. The support hydraulic cylinders of support 1 and support 2 are, respectively, hinged to the corresponding top beams and bases, providing support forces to both support 1 and support 2 [23]. The top beams of support 1 and support 2 make contact with the roof, while the bases of support 1 and support 2 make contact with the floor. The connection method of the four-bar linkage mechanism is hinged. The four-bar linkage can withstand horizontal loads from the rock layer, preventing the bending of the vertical columns. Additionally, it can control the variation in distance between the front end of the top beam and the coal wall within a certain range when the height of the top beam changes, thereby enhancing the control level of the roof.

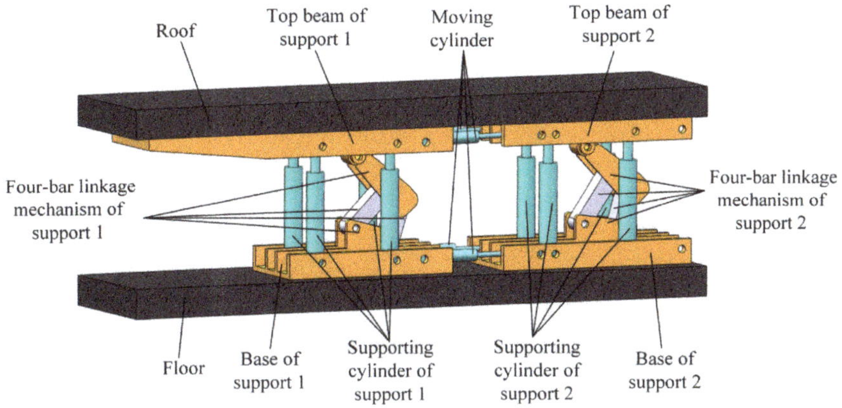

Figure 4. Virtual prototype model of the temporary support robot.

3. Mathematical Model Construction Based on Theoretical Mechanics Methods

3.1. Construction of Stable Support Mechanical Model

In order to analyze the force distribution of the TSR under stable support conditions, a mechanical model of the TSR in a stable support state is constructed based on the principle model of the temporary support robot. In this model, the force on the TSR is simplified to a plane linkage model on the neutral surface [24], as shown in Figure 5.

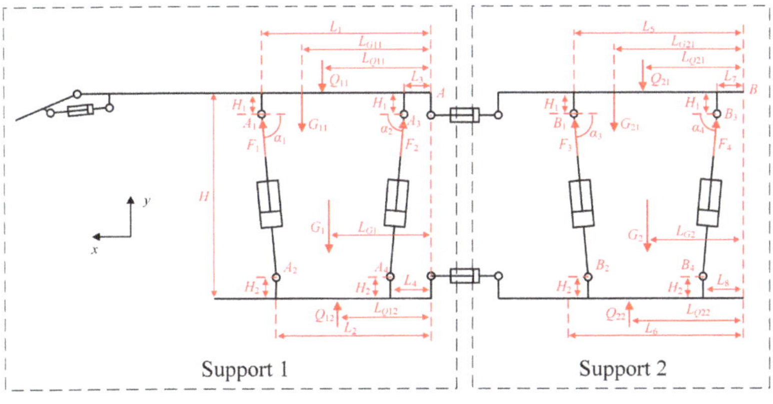

Figure 5. Force analysis of the temporary support robot in a stable support state.

The x-axis represents the direction of roadway excavation, and the y-axis represents the roadway height direction; the vertical distance from the roadway roof to the roadway floor is H; and the top beams and bases of support 1 and support 2 are aligned at the tail end. For ease of analysis, the distance from each hinge point on the top beams of support 1 and support 2 to the roof is H_1, and the distance from each hinge point on the bases of support 1 and support 2 to the base is H_2; the distances from points A_1, A_2, A_3, and A_4 to the tail end of support 1 are L_1, L_2, L_3, and L_4, respectively; and the distances from points B_1, B_2, B_3, and B_4 to the tail end of support 2 are L_5, L_6, L_7, and L_8, respectively. The external loading of the roof on the top beam of support 1 is Q_{11}, the supporting force of the floor on the base of support 1 is Q_{12}, and the distances from forces Q_{11} and Q_{12} to the tail end of support 1 are L_{Q11} and L_{Q12}, respectively. The external loading of the roof on the top beam of support 2 is Q_{21}, the supporting force of the floor on the base of support 2 is Q_{22}, and the distances from forces Q_{21} and Q_{22} to the tail end of support 2 are L_{Q21} and L_{Q22}, respectively. The weight of the top beam of support 1 is $G11$, and the distance from the center of gravity to the tail end of support 1 is L_{G11}. The overall weight of support 1 is G_1, and the distance from the center of gravity to the tail end of support 1 is L_{G1}. The weight of the top beam of support 2 is G_{21}, and the distance from the center of gravity to the tail end of support 2 is LG_{21}. The overall weight of support 2 is G_2, and the distance from the center of gravity to the tail end of support 2 is L_{G2}. The angles between the front and rear supporting cylinders of support 1 and the top beam are α_1 and α_2, respectively, and the working resistances are F_1 and F_2, respectively. The angles between the front and rear supporting cylinders of support 2 and the top beam are α_3 and α_4, respectively, and the working resistances are F_3 and F_4, respectively. The external loading Q_{11} and Q_{21} of the roof on the top beams of support 1 and support 2 are numerically equal to the supporting forces of support 1 and support 2 on the roof. The relative displacement of the top beams and bases of support 1 and support 2 of the TSR in the x-axis direction can be ignored.

When support 1 stably supports the roof, taking the top beam of support 1 as a separate body, the top beam of support 1 is in force equilibrium at this time, then the sum $\sum F_{y11}$ of the forces on the top beam of support 1 in the y-axis direction equal zero; the sum $\sum M_{A1}$ of all moments about point A_1 on the top beam of support 1 equal zero; and the sum $\sum M_{A3}$ of all moments about point A_3 on the top beam of support 1 equal zero. The force equilibrium equations are as follows:

$$\begin{cases} \sum F_{y11} = 0 \\ \sum M_{A1} = 0 \ , \\ \sum M_{A3} = 0 \end{cases} \tag{1}$$

According to the force equilibrium equations, the following can be obtained:

$$\begin{cases} F_1 \sin\alpha_1 + F_2 \sin\alpha_2 - Q_{11} - G_{11} = 0 \\ F_2 \sin\alpha_2 (L_1 - L_3) - Q_{11}(L_1 - L_{Q11}) - G_{11}(L_1 - L_{G11}) = 0 \\ G_{11}(L_{G11} - L_3) + Q_{11}(S_1 - L_3) - F_1 \sin\alpha_1 (L_1 - L_3) = 0 \end{cases} \tag{2}$$

Taking the overall support 1 as the research object, support 1 as a whole is in force equilibrium, then the sum $\sum F_{y1}$ of the forces on support 1 in the y-axis direction equals zero; the sum $\sum M_A$ of all moments about point A on support 1 equal zero; the force equilibrium equations are as follow:

$$\begin{cases} \sum F_y = 0 \\ \sum M_A = 0 \end{cases} \tag{3}$$

From the force equilibrium equations, the following can be obtained:

$$\begin{cases} Q_{12} - G_1 - Q_{11} = 0 \\ G_1 L_{G1} + S_1 Q_{11} - Q_{12} L_{Q12} = 0 \end{cases}, \tag{4}$$

Similarly, when support 2 of the TSR stably supports the roof, it can be seen that

$$\begin{cases} F_3 \sin\alpha_3 + F_4 \sin\alpha_4 - Q_{21} - G_{21} = 0 \\ F_4 \sin\alpha_4 (L_5 - L_7) - Q_{21}(L_5 - L_{Q21}) - G_{21}(L_5 - L_{G21}) = 0 \\ G_{21}(L_{G21} - L_7) + Q_{21}(L_{Q21} - L_7) - F_3 \sin\alpha_3 (L_5 - L_7) = 0 \\ Q_{22} - Q_{21} - G_2 = 0 \\ G_2 L_{G2} + Q_{21} S_3 - Q_{22} S_4 = 0 \end{cases}, \tag{5}$$

where

$$\begin{cases} \sin\alpha_1 = \frac{(H-H_1-H_2)^2}{(L_1-L_2)^2+(H-H_1-H_2)^2} \\ \sin\alpha_2 = \frac{(H-H_1-H_2)^2}{(L_4-L_3)^2+(H-H_1-H_2)^2} \\ \sin\alpha_3 = \frac{(H-H_1-H_2)^2}{(L_5-L_6)^2+(H-H_1-H_2)^2} \\ \sin\alpha_4 = \frac{(H-H_1-H_2)^2}{(L_8-L_7)^2+(H-H_1-H_2)^2} \end{cases}. \tag{6}$$

3.2. Construction of a Dynamic Model for Driving Under Pressure

According to the working principle of driving under pressure for the TSR, analyzing the force on the TSR during the driving under pressure process yields the principle model of driving under pressure for the TSR, as shown in Figure 6.

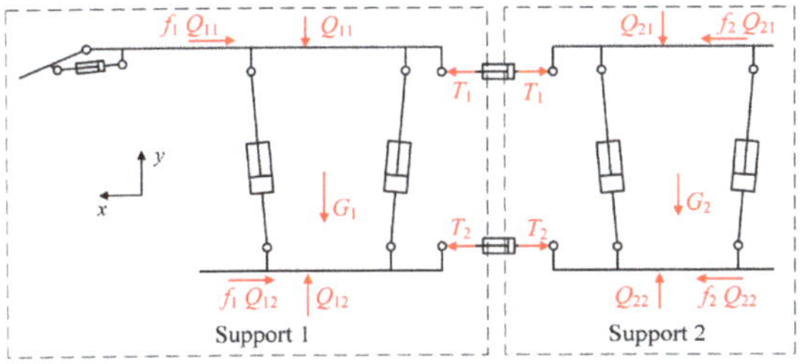

Figure 6. Force analysis of the temporary support robot in driving under pressure state.

The x-axis represents the direction of roadway excavation, and the y-axis represents the height direction of the roadway. The pushing forces of the upper and lower sets of moving cylinders connecting support 1 and support 2 are denoted as T_1 and T_2, respectively. Let f_1 and f_2 be the friction coefficients between support 1, support 2, and the surrounding rock. The pushing and friction forces experienced by the two parts, support 1 and support 2, during the driving under pressure process, are parallel to the x-axis. Therefore, the resultant external loading Q_{11} and Q_{21} of the roof on the top beam of support 1 and support 2, and the resultant supporting force Q_{12} and Q_{22} of the floor on the base of support 1 and support 2, can still be expressed by Equations (2), (4) and (6). Assuming that support 1 is in force equilibrium during the driving under pressure process, the pushing force of the moving cylinder on support 1 and support 2 is equal to its load, i.e., $T_1 = T_{1z}$ and $T_2 = T_{2z}$.

The process of driving under pressure for the TSR includes the driving under pressure of support 1 and the driving under pressure of support 2. When support 1 is driving under pressure, perform force analysis on the entire support 1. Assume that support 1 is in force equilibrium during the driving under pressure process. Then, the sum of forces $\sum F_{x1}$ on the entire support 1 in the x-axis direction equals zero, and the sum of forces $\sum F_{y1}$ on the entire support 1 in the y-axis direction equals zero. The force equilibrium equations are as follows:

$$\begin{cases} \sum F_{x1} = 0 \\ \sum F_{y1} = 0 \end{cases}. \tag{7}$$

From the force equilibrium equations, it can be obtained that

$$\begin{cases} T_{1z} + T_{2z} - f_1 Q_{a11} - f_1 Q_{12} = 0 \\ Q_{12} - G_1 - Q_{11} = 0 \end{cases}. \tag{8}$$

When support 1 is accelerating, according to Newton's second law, the dynamic model of the moving cylinder pushing support 1 is as follows:

$$T_1 + T_2 = f_1(Q_{11} + Q_{12}) + \frac{m_1 d^2 x_1}{dt^2}, \tag{9}$$

where m_1 is the mass of support 1, kg; t is the time, s; x_1 is the displacement of support 1, m; and f_1 is the friction coefficient between support 1 and the surrounding rock.

When support 2 is in the state of driving under pressure, assuming that it is in the state of force equilibrium, similarly, it can be known that the dynamic model of the moving cylinder pulling support 2 is as follows:

$$\begin{cases} T_1 + T_2 = f_2(Q_{21} + Q_{22}) + \frac{m_2 d^2 x_2}{dt^2} \\ Q_{22} - G_1 - Q_{21} = 0 \end{cases}, \tag{10}$$

where m_2 is the mass of support 2, (kg); x_2 is the displacement of support 2, (m); and f_2 is the friction coefficient between support 2 and the surrounding rock.

When the TSR is driving under pressure, there is a transition from static friction to dynamic friction between the TSR and the roof and floor. To accurately describe this friction process, this paper adopts the Stribeck friction theory [25,26] to analyze the friction coefficient between them. The model is as follows:

$$\begin{cases} f_1 = f_d + (f_s - f_d)e^{-(v_1/v_{st})^2} \\ f_2 = f_d + (f_s - f_d)e^{-(v_2/v_{st})^2} \end{cases}, \tag{11}$$

where f_d is the dynamic friction coefficient between the TSR and the surrounding rock; f_s is the static friction coefficient between the TSR and the surrounding rock; v_{st} is the critical Stribeck velocity, (m/s); v_1 is the moving speed of support 1, m/s; and v_2 is the moving speed of support 2, m/s.

3.3. Boundary Condition Analysis of the Dynamic Model for Driving Under Pressure

When studying the driving under pressure process of the TSR, it is necessary to consider the boundary conditions of its dynamic mode and analyze its criterion system. Since support 2 must maintain a stable support state and not move during the driving under the pressure process of support 1, the friction force generated by its contact with the surrounding rock must be able to overcome the pushing force of the moving cylinder. The same applies when support 2 is driving under pressure.

When support 1 is driving under pressure, it can be obtained from Equation (9) that

$$f_1(Q_{11} + Q_{12}) + \frac{m_1 d^2 x_1}{dt^2} < f_s(Q_{21} + Q_{22}), \tag{12}$$

When support 2 is driving under pressure, it can be obtained from Equation (10) that

$$f_2(Q_{21} + Q_{22}) + \frac{m_2 d^2 x_2}{dt^2} < f_s(Q_{11} + Q_{12}). \quad (13)$$

The base area of each support 1 and support 2 is smaller than the top beam area. Due to its weight's influence, the base's specific pressure against the floor is greater than the specific pressure of the top beam against the roof. To ensure that the TSR can stably support the roof and not damage the surrounding rock during the driving under pressure process, it is necessary to analyze the relationship between the top beam and the base area of support 1 and support 2, and the specific pressure of the surrounding rock.

Since $f_1 \leq f_s$ and $f_2 \leq f_s$, according to the pressure formula $F = PS$, it can be obtained that

$$\begin{cases} P_{11d}S_{11} = P_{12d}S_{12} - G_1 \\ P_{21d}S_{21} = P_{22d}S_{22} - G_2 \\ P_{22s}S_{22} - P_{12d}S_{12} > \frac{m_1 d^2 x_1}{2 f_s dt^2} + \frac{(G_2 - G_1)}{2} \\ P_{12s}S_{12} - P_{22d}S_{22} > \frac{m_2 d^2 x_2}{2 f_s dt^2} + \frac{(G_1 - G_2)}{2} \end{cases}, \quad (14)$$

where P_{11d} is the specific pressure of the top beam against the roof when support 1 is in the state of driving under pressure, Pa; P_{12d} is the particular pressure of the base against the floor when support 1 is in the state of driving under pressure, Pa; P_{12s} is the specific pressure of the base against the floor when support 1 is in stable support, Pa; P_{21d} is the particular pressure of the top beam against the roof when support 2 is in the state of driving under pressure, Pa; P_{22d} is the specific pressure of the base against the floor when support 2 is in the state of driving under pressure, Pa; P_{22s} is the specific pressure of the base against the floor when support 2 is in stable support, Pa; S_{11} is the area of the top beam of support 1, m^2; S_{12} is the area of the base of support 1, m^2; S_{21} is the area of the top beam of support 2, m^2; and S_{22} is the area of the base of support 2, m^2.

3.4. Analysis of Mechanical Properties of Roof and Floor

The mechanical properties of the roof and floor are analyzed to obtain the minimum support strength required for the TSR to support the roof stably and the maximum allowable value of the specific pressure between the base and the floor.

To ensure that the roof does not fracture, the support strength of the TSR must ensure that the deformation of the roof is maintained within a certain range, ensuring that the tensile stress of the roof does not exceed the tensile strength limit of the roof. The thin plate theory [27] is used to study the support strength. Assume that the roof is a continuous layered elastic medium, the roof rock mass is an isotropic homogeneous body, and there is no tie force between the roof layers. The roof model of the section coal pillar excavation and mining working face is shown in Figure 7. The TSR is responsible for supporting the empty top area; the two sides of the empty top area are sidewalls with a length of a (m), the area to be excavated is located in front of the direct roof with a width of b (m), the thickness of the roof is δ (m), and the plane of the coordinate axis $z = 0$ is located at $\delta/2$ (m) of the roof thickness. The anchoring area comprises anchor bolts and bolt nets behind the roof. Therefore, the boundary conditions of the roof can be regarded as three sides with a clamped edge and one side with a simply supported edge.

The boundary conditions of the clamped edge OC, OD, and DE are as follows [28]:

$$\begin{cases} (w)_{y=0} = (w)_{x=0} = (w)_{y=b} = 0 \\ \left(\frac{\partial w}{\partial y}\right)_{y=0} = \left(\frac{\partial w}{\partial y}\right)_{x=0} = \left(\frac{\partial w}{\partial y}\right)_{y=b} = 0 \end{cases}, \quad (15)$$

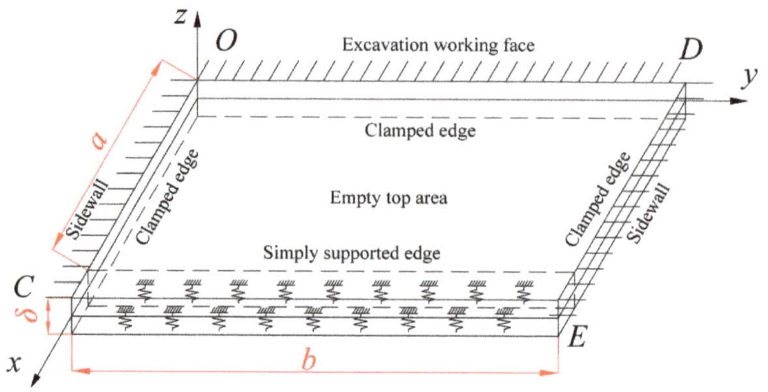

Figure 7. Mechanical model of roof.

where w is the deflection equation of the roof.

The boundary conditions of the simply supported edge CE are as follows:

$$\begin{cases} (w)_{x=a} = 0 \\ \left(\frac{\partial^2 w}{\partial^2 y}\right)_{x=a} = 0 \end{cases}. \tag{16}$$

Based on the assumption, after the thin plate is deformed, the straight line originally perpendicular to the middle plane remains straight, and the length remains unchanged and is always perpendicular to the deformed middle plane. The strain in the thickness direction can be neglected, and the deflection w is only related to the plane coordinates (x, y) and has nothing to do with the thickness direction coordinate z. The stress state of the thin plate can be approximately regarded as a plane stress state; that is, the normal stress and shear stress perpendicular to the middle plane are much smaller than the normal stress and shear stress in the middle plane and can be ignored. The deformation of the middle plane of the thin plate is very small, and it can be considered that there is no tensile or compressive deformation of the middle plane. The external loading on the roof is q. According to the thin plate theory, the differential equation representing the deflection w of the roof can be obtained as follows:

$$\begin{cases} \frac{\partial^4 w}{\partial x^4} + 2\frac{\partial^4 w}{\partial x^2 \partial y^2} + \frac{\partial^4 w}{\partial y^4} = \frac{q}{D} \\ D = \frac{E\delta^3}{12(1-\mu^2)} \end{cases}, \tag{17}$$

where D is the bending stiffness of the roof, N/m; E is the elastic modulus of the roof, MPa; and μ is the Poisson's ratio.

Then, the tensile stresses σ_x and σ_y in the x and y directions of the roof are as follows:

$$\begin{cases} \sigma_x = -\frac{8\pi^2 AEz}{a^2(1-\mu^2)}\left[\sin^2\frac{\pi y}{b}\cos\frac{2\pi x}{a} + \mu\left(\frac{a}{b}\right)^2\sin^2\frac{\pi x}{a}\cos\frac{\pi y}{b}\right] \\ \sigma_y = -\frac{8\pi^2 AEz}{b^2(1-\mu^2)}\left[\sin^2\frac{\pi x}{a}\cos\frac{2\pi y}{b} + \mu\left(\frac{a}{b}\right)^2\sin^2\frac{\pi y}{b}\cos\frac{\pi x}{a}\right] \\ A = \frac{qa^2}{4\pi^4 D\left[3+3\left(\frac{a}{b}\right)^4+2\left(\frac{a}{b}\right)^2\right]} \end{cases}, \tag{18}$$

Taking the tensile stress on the bottom surface of the roof, that is the $z = -\delta/2$ plane, as the research object, the maximum tensile stress values in the x and y directions of the roof can be obtained as follows:

$$\begin{cases} \sigma_{\text{xmax}} = \frac{4\pi^2 AE\delta}{a^2(1-\mu^2)} \\ \sigma_{\text{ymin}} = \frac{4\pi^2 AE\delta}{b^2(1-\mu^2)} \end{cases}. \tag{19}$$

For the roof supported by the TSR in actual work, its length a must be less than width b, then the stress on the roof in the y direction must be greater than the stress on the roof in the x direction. From Equation (19), it can be obtained that

$$\frac{12qa^2}{\pi^2 b^2 \delta^2 \left[3 + 3\left(\frac{a}{b}\right)^4 + 2\left(\frac{a}{b}\right)^2\right]} < \sigma_\mu, \tag{20}$$

where σ_μ is the tensile strength limit of the roof material, Mpa. Considering the support strength $p_{\min}$ of the TSR to the roof and the rock load q_o of the roof, Equation (20) can be rewritten as follows:

$$p > q_o - \frac{\pi^2 b^2 \delta^2 \sigma_\mu \left[3 + 3\left(\frac{a}{b}\right)^4 + 2\left(\frac{a}{b}\right)^2\right]}{12a^2}, \tag{21}$$

Equation (21) provides the minimum allowable value of the TSR's support strength to the roof.

To prevent the support force of the TSR from being too large and causing the floor to break, it is necessary to calculate the maximum specific pressure $p_{\max}$ that the floor can withstand according to the maximum compressive strength of the floor [29]. Since the actual contact area between the base of the TSR and the floor is smaller than the area of the base, the cutting, pushing, and other behaviors during the excavation process will directly damage the integrity of the floor and generate defects such as cracks and micro-cracks, these defects will reduce the bearing capacity of the floor. Therefore, the coefficient C represents the influence on the maximum specific pressure the floor can withstand.

$$p_{\max} = C\sigma_b. \tag{22}$$

where σ_b is the uniaxial compressive strength limit of the floor material.

4. Simulation Experiment and Mathematical Model Validation

4.1. Determination of Simulation Parameters for the Temporary Support Robot

According to the working environment of the TSR, we set the relevant parameters for the surrounding rock of the working face, as shown in Table 1. The minimum allowable value of the support strength of the TSR to the roof, $p_{\min} = 0.02$ MPa, is calculated by Equation (21). The uniaxial compressive strength of the floor material is taken as $\sigma_b = 4.1$ MPa; the coefficient is C = 0.05; and the minimum allowable value of the support strength of the TSR to the roof, $p_{\max} \approx 0.2$ MPa, is calculated by Equation (22).

Table 1. The relevant parameters for the surrounding rock of the working face.

Parameter	Value
the tensile strength limit of the roof σ_μ/MPa	1.2
the roof rock load is q_o/MPa	233
length of the empty top area a/m	15
width of the empty top area b/m	30
the thickness of the roof δ/m	4

To analyze the boundary conditions of the driving under pressure dynamic model of the TSR under given conditions and to obtain the relationship between the specific pressure of the top beam and base of support 1 and support 2 on surrounding rock, the boundary conditions of the driving under pressure dynamic model of the TSR are simulated. Relevant parameters are shown in Table 2. It is assumed that the support strength of the TSR to the roof cannot be less than 0.02 MPa, and the specific pressure in contact with the surrounding rock cannot be greater than 0.2 MPa. To ensure the stability of the driving under pressure motion process of the TSR, the acceleration of support 1 and support 2 during movement is taken not to exceed 0.2 m/s^2. According to the cooperation mode between the TSR and the cutting robot, the TSR's width is 2 m. The space length required for the cutting robot and scraper conveyor located below the top beam of support 1 is at least 3 m, and the length of the top beam and floor of support 2 are the same. Then, the area relationship between the top beam and base of support 1 is $S_{11} - S_{12} = 6$ m^2, and the area relationship between the top beam and base of support 2 is $S_{21} = S_{22}$. The supporting force of support 1 and support 2 is the largest during stable support. Therefore, the specific pressure of the base of support 1 and support 2 against the floor during stable support 1s is taken as $P_{12s} = P_{22s} = 0.2$ MPa. From Equation (13), the value range of the specific pressure P_{12d} of the base of support 1 against the floor during the state of driving under pressure and the value range of the specific pressure P_{22d} of the base of support 2 against the floor during in the state of driving under pressure can be obtained, as shown in Figures 8 and 9, which vary with the area S_{12} of the base of support 1 and the support area S_{22} of support 2.

Analyzing Figures 8 and 9, it can be seen that when the ratio of the base area of support 1 to support 2 is smaller, the value range of P_{12d} is larger, and the value range of P_{22d} is smaller. When the ratio of the base area of support 1 to support 2 is larger, the value range of P_{12d} is smaller, and the value range of P_{22d} is larger. The upper limit of P_{12d} and P_{22d} determines the critical value at which support 1 and support 2 can drive under pressure, and the lower limit determines the critical value for ensuring that the roof does not collapse during the driving under pressure process of support 1 and support 2.

Table 2. Simulation parameter table of boundary conditions for driving under pressure dynamic model.

Parameter	Value
overall mass of support 1 m_1/kg	18,000
overall mass of support 2 m_2/kg	16,000
mass of top beam of support 1 m_a/kg	8000
mass of top beam of support 2 m_b/kg	5000
dynamic friction coefficient f_d	0.28
static friction coefficient f_s	0.3

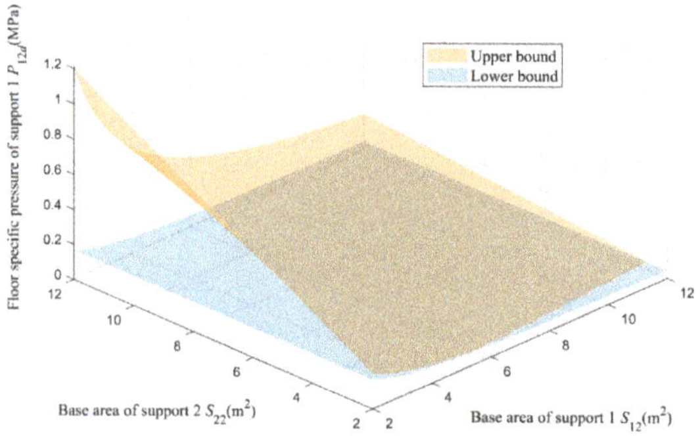

Figure 8. Value range of specific pressure P_{12d}.

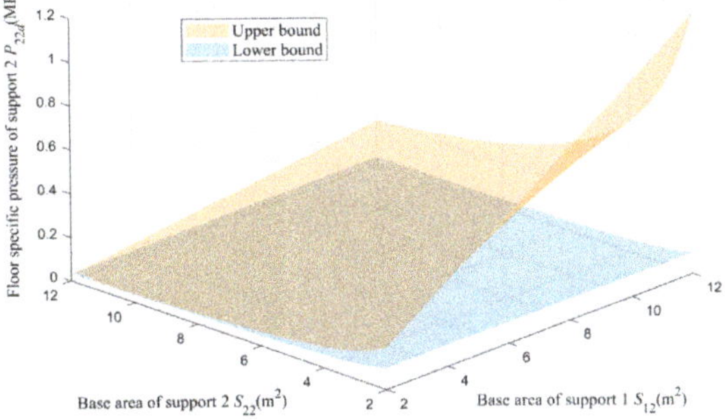

Figure 9. Value range of specific pressure P_{22d}.

Taking the area of support 1's top beam as S_{11} = 8 m^2; the area of support 1's base as S_{12} = 9 m^2; the area of support 2's top beam as S_{21} = 8 m^2; and the area of support 2's base as S_{21} = 8 m^2, the value range of the specific pressure of the base of support 1 and support 2 against the floor can be calculated by Equation (14) as 0.056 MPa < P_{12d} < 0.22 MPa and 0.038 MPa < P_{22d} < 0.17 MPa. For ease of analysis, the angles of the supporting cylinders for both support 1 and support 2 are set to 90 degrees. The other parameters of the TSR are listed in Table 3.

Table 3. Other parameters for the virtual prototype model.

Parameter	Value
the distance from each hinge point on the top beams of support 1 and support 2 to the roof H_1/mm	0.3
the distance from each hinge point on the bases of support 1 and support 2 to the base H_2/mm	0.3
the distances from point A_1 to the tail end of support 1 L_1/mm	2.8
the distances from point A_2 to the tail end of support 1 L_2/mm	2.8
the distances from point A_3 to the tail end of support 1 L_3/mm	1.2
the distances from point A_4 to the tail end of support 1 L_4/mm	1.2
the distances from point B_1 to the tail end of support 2 L_5/mm	2.9
the distances from point B_2 to the tail end of support 2 L_6/mm	2.9
the distances from point B_3 to the tail end of support 2 L_7/mm	1.2
the distances from point B_4 to the tail end of support 2 L_8/mm	1.2
the vertical distance from the roof to the floor H/m	3

4.2. Finite Element Simulation of the Temporary Support Robot and the Floor

To analyze whether the stresses on the TSR itself and the floor under stable support conditions meet the strength requirements, the stress characteristics of the floor and the TSR were simulated and analyzed using finite element analysis. In the finite element analysis process, the model constructed in Section 2.3 of the TSR was imported into the ANSYS Workbench 2023 R1 software, omitting non-load-bearing components such as support columns; small structures like lifting rings and mounting holes were ignored; the effects of rounded corners and welding on the load-bearing characteristics of the support were not considered; and equivalent loads were used to replace the column structure. The relevant parameters of the simulation model are consistent with those described in Section 4.1.

According to the actual working environment of the TSR, appropriate parameters are selected, and the relevant parameters are shown in Table 4. Based on this, the automatic mesh generation function in the software was used to mesh the simulation models of the

TSR and its corresponding floor, resulting in a finite element model with 29,282 elements and 13,631 nodes for support 1, and a model with 25,762 elements and 11,204 nodes for support 2. When the TSR achieves a bottom pressure of 0.2 MPa, it can be calculated using the pressure formula and Equation (2) that the bottom pressure of support 1 on the roof is approximately 0.1 MPa. Similarly, when the TSR reaches a bottom pressure of 0.2 MPa, it can be calculated using the pressure formula and Equation (5) that the bottom pressure of support 2 on the roof is approximately 0.18 MPa. Based on the model shown in Figure 4, a simulation analysis of the load on the top beam was conducted, as illustrated in Figures 4 and 10. Figure 10 shows the simulation results under a uniform load of 0.1 MPa applied to the top beam of support 1, where Figure 10a represents the stress cloud diagram of support 1 and Figure 10b represents the stress cloud diagram of the floor under support 1. Figure 11 shows the simulation results under a uniform load of 0.18 MPa applied to the top beam of support 2, with Figure 11a representing the stress cloud diagram of support 2 and Figure 11b representing the stress cloud diagram of the floor under support 2.

Table 4. Relevant material parameters for the finite element simulation.

Parameter	Value
elastic modulus of Q690 Steel/GPa	206
density of Q690 Steel kg/m^3	7850
Poisson's ratio of Q690 Steel	0.26
yield strength of Q690 Steel/MPa	690
bulk modulus of sandstone/GPa	21.3
Young's modulus of sandstone/GPa	34
Poisson's Ratio of sandstone	0.233
shear modulus of sandstone/GPa	13.78

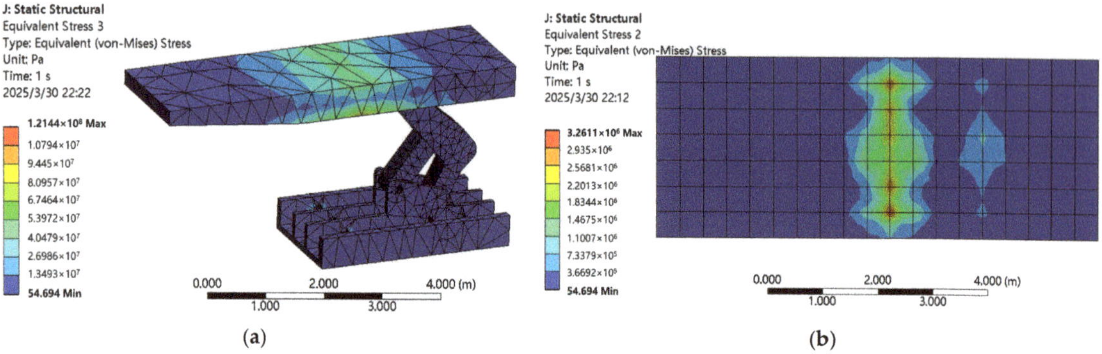

Figure 10. Finite element simulation results of support 1 under a load of 0.1 MPa applied to the top beam: (**a**) stress cloud of support 1; (**b**) stress cloud of the floor under support 1.

From Figure 10a, it can be seen that under a uniform load of 0.1 MPa applied to the top beam of support 1, the overall stress on support 1 is within the range of 121 MPa, which is below the yield strength of Q690. The peak stress is concentrated on the rib plate at the hinge between the top beam and the support cylinder, indicating that this part of the structure is more prone to damage under these conditions. The displacement of support 1 is within the range of 11 mm. From Figure 10b, it can be seen that regarding the stress conditions of the floor, the stress on the surface of the floor is within the range of 3.26 MPa, which is below the uniaxial compressive strength limit of the floor material. The peak stress is concentrated at the front end of the base of support 1. Therefore, under the 0.1 MPa loading condition on the top beam, the stress on the structure of support 1 is less than the yield strength of its material, meeting the strength requirements of the support, and the stress value on the floor is less than its uniaxial compressive strength, ensuring that the floor will not be damaged.

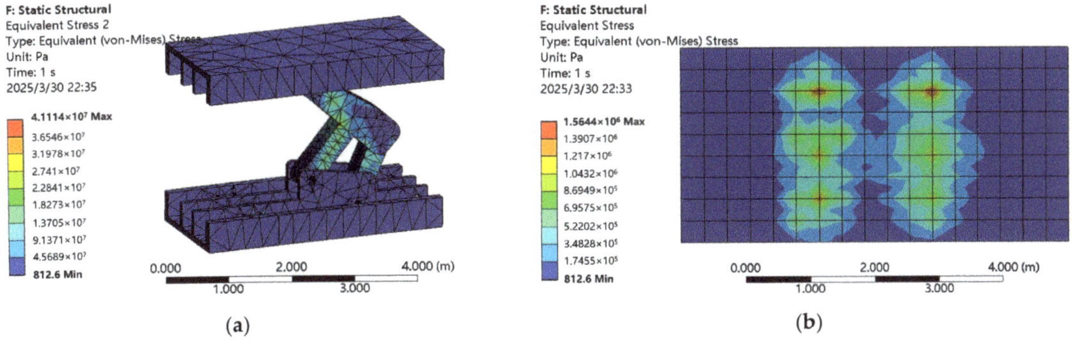

Figure 11. Finite element simulation results of support 2 under a load of 0.18 MPa applied to the top beam: (**a**) stress cloud of support 1; (**b**) stress cloud of the floor under support 1.

From Figure 11a, it can be seen that under a uniform load of 0.18 MPa applied to the top beam of support 2, the overall stress on support 2 is within the range of 41 MPa, with a peak value below the yield strength of Q690, concentrated on the four-bar mechanism, indicating that this part of the structure is more prone to damage under these conditions. From Figure 11b, it can be noted that regarding the stress conditions of the floor, the stress on the surface of the floor is within the range of 1.56 MPa, which is below the uniaxial compressive strength limit of the floor material, with peaks mainly concentrated at the installation position of the support cylinder on the base of support 2. Therefore, under a loading condition of 0.18 MPa, the stress on the structure of support 2 is less than the yield strength of its material, satisfying the strength requirements of the support, and the stress value on the floor is less than its uniaxial compressive strength, ensuring that the floor will not be damaged.

4.3. Critical Value Simulation of Boundary Conditions for Driving Under Pressure Dynamic Model

Import the model constructed in Section 2.3 of the TSR into the Adams View 2018 software. The driving under pressure process of support 1 and support 2 is simulated and analyzed using the Adams software to obtain the pushing force of the moving cylinder and the critical values of the movement of support 1 and support 2 to verify the accuracy of the boundary conditions of the driving under pressure dynamic model. The relevant parameters of the simulation model are consistent with those described in Section 4.1. The contact stiffness between the surrounding rock and the TSR is 1 × 108 N/m, the damping coefficient is 1×10^5 Ns/m, and the penetration depth is 0.1 mm.

When support 1 is in the state of driving under pressure, it is known from the value range of the specific pressure of the base of support 1 against the floor, 0.056 MPa $< P_{12d} <$ 0.22 MPa, that the specific pressure P_{12d} of the base of support 1 against the floor falls within the range of the maximum allowable specific pressure of 0.2 MPa for the contact between the TSR and the surrounding rock, enabling driving under pressure action. Therefore, two cases, P_{12d} = 0.1 MPa and P_{12d} = 0.2 MPa, are used for the simulation analysis. When support 2 is stably supporting, its base is under the specific pressure P_{22s} = 0.2 MPa. Assuming $F_1 = F_2$ and $F_3 = F_4$, it can be calculated from Equations (2) and (5) that the working resistance of each supporting cylinder of support 2 is approximately 423 kN, and the maximum friction force generated by contact with the surrounding rock is approximately 1033 kN. When P_{12d} = 0.1 MPa, the specific pressure of the top beam of support 1 against the roof, P_{11d}, is approximately 0.045 MPa, satisfying the support conditions. Currently, each supporting cylinder of support 1 has a working resistance of approximately 175.5 kN, and the maximum friction force generated by contact with the surrounding rock is 427 kN. When P_{12d} = 0.2 MPa, the specific pressure of the top beam of support 1 against the roof, P_{11d}, is approximately 0.1 MPa, satisfying the support conditions. Currently, each supporting cylinder of support 1 has a working resistance of approximately 376 kN, and the maximum friction force generated by contact with the surrounding rock is 907 kN. A gradually increasing pushing force is applied synchronously to the four moving cylinders for simulation, and the variation in the displacement of support 1 and support 2, as well as the friction between them and the surrounding rock with the resultant pushing force, are shown in Figures 12 and 13.

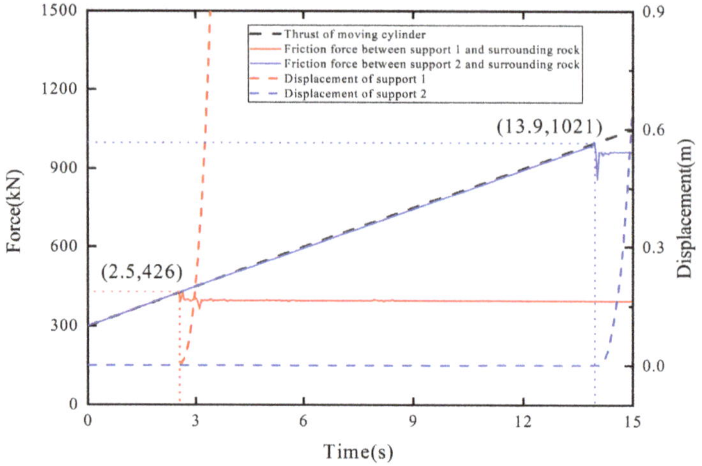

Figure 12. Critical values of motion for support 1 and support 2 at P_{12d} = 0.1 MPa.

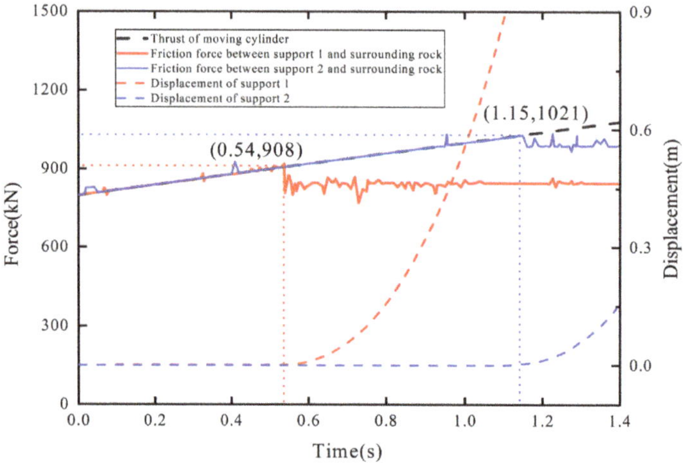

Figure 13. Critical values of motion for support 1 and support 2 at P_{12d} = 0.2 MPa.

Analyzing Figure 12, it can be seen that under the condition that the specific pressure of the base of support 1 against the floor is P_{12d} = 0.1 MPa, when the pushing force of the moving cylinder exceeds 426 kN, the friction force between support 1 and the surrounding rock reaches its maximum value, and support 1 begins to move. The friction force between support 2 and the surrounding rock continues to increase with the pushing force of the moving cylinder, and support 2 remains stationary. At this time, support 1 can normally drive under pressure. When the pushing force of the moving cylinder exceeds 1021 kN, the friction force between support 2 and the surrounding rock reaches its maximum value, and support 2 begins to move. At this time, support 1 cannot drive under pressure. Analyzing Figure 13, it can be seen that under the condition that the specific pressure of the base of support 1 against the floor is P_{12d} = 0.2 MPa when the pushing force of the moving cylinder exceeds 908 kN, the friction force between support 1 and the surrounding rock reaches its maximum value, and support 1 begins to move. The friction force between support 2 and the surrounding rock continues to increase with the pushing force of the moving cylinder, and support 2 remains stationary. At this time, support 1 can normally drive under pressure. When the pushing force of the moving cylinder exceeds 1031 kN, the friction force between support 2 and the surrounding rock reaches its maximum value, and support 2 begins to move. At this time, support 1 cannot drive under pressure. Compared with the theoretical values, the maximum error of the maximum friction force between support 1 and support 2 and the surrounding rock obtained by simulation is 1.2%, less than 5%.

When support 2 is in the state of driving under pressure, it is known from the value range of the specific pressure of the base of support 2 against the floor, 0.038 MPa < P_{22d} < 0.17 MPa, that support 2 is in the state of driving under pressure when the specific pressure P_{22d} of the base of support 2 against the floor is taken in the range of 0.038 MPa to 0.17 MPa; support 2 cannot drive under pressure when the specific pressure P_{22d} of the base of support 2 against the floor is taken in the range of 0.17 MPa to 0.2 MPa. Therefore, two cases, P_{22d} = 0.1 MPa and P_{22d} = 0.19 MPa, are used for the simulation analysis. When support 1 is stably supporting, its base is under the specific pressure P_{12s} = 0.2 MPa. Assuming $F_1 = F_2$ and $F_3 = F_4$, it can be calculated from Equations (2) and (5) that each supporting cylinder of support 1 has a working resistance of approximately 376 kN, and the maximum friction force generated by contact with the surrounding rock is approximately 908 kN. When P_{22d} = 0.1 MPa, the specific pressure of the top beam of support 2 against the roof, P_{21d}, is approximately 0.082 MPa, satisfying the support conditions. Each supporting cylinder of support 2 has a working resistance of approximately 198 kN, and the maximum friction force generated by contact with the surrounding rock is 492 kN. When P_{22d} = 0.19 MPa, the specific pressure of the top beam of support 2 against the roof, P_{21d}, is approximately 0.17 MPa, satisfying the support conditions. Currently, each supporting cylinder of support 1 has a working resistance of approximately 401 kN, and the maximum friction force generated by contact with the surrounding rock is 979 kN. A gradually increasing pushing force is applied synchronously to the four moving cylinders for simulation, and the variation in the displacement of support 1 and support 2, as well as the friction between them and the surrounding rock with the resultant pushing force, are shown in Figures 14 and 15.

Analyzing Figure 14, it can be seen that under the condition that the specific pressure of the base of support 2 against the floor is P_{12d} = 0.1 MPa, when the pulling force exceeds 496 kN, the friction force between support 2 and the surrounding rock reaches its maximum value, and support 2 begins to move. The friction force between support 1 and the surrounding rock continues to increase with the pulling force of the moving cylinder, and support 1 remains stationary. At this time, support 2 can normally drive under pressure. When the pulling force exceeds 908 kN, the friction force between support 1 and the surrounding rock reaches its maximum value, and support 1 begins to move. At this time, support 2 cannot drive under pressure.

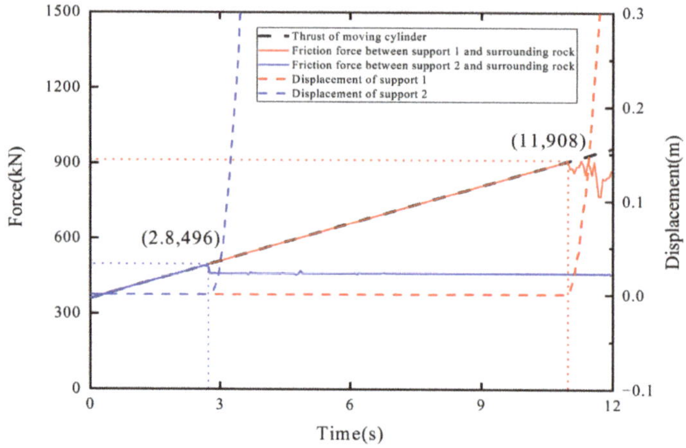

Figure 14. Critical values of motion for support 1 and support 2 at P_{22d} = 0.1 MPa.

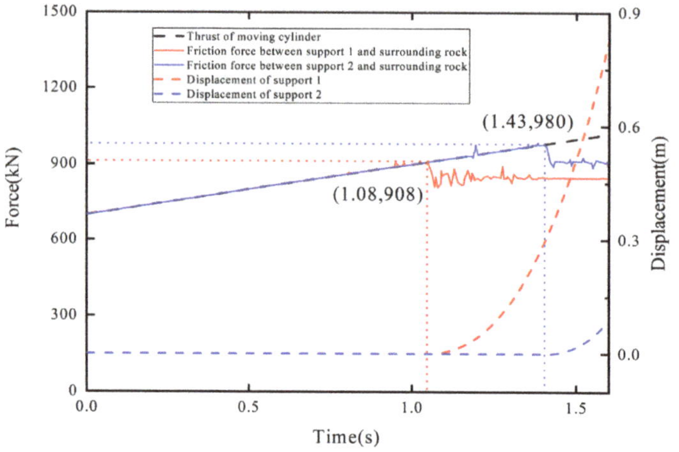

Figure 15. Critical values of motion for support 1 and support 2 at P_{22d} = 0.19 MPa.

Analyzing Figure 15, it can be seen that under the condition that the specific pressure of the base of support 2 against the floor is P_{12d} = 0.19 MPa when the pulling force exceeds 908 kN, the friction force between support 1 and the surrounding rock reaches its maximum value, and support 1 begins to move. The friction force between support 2 and the surrounding rock continues to increase with the pulling force of the moving cylinder, and support 2 remains stationary. When the pulling force exceeds 980 kN, the friction force between support 2 and the surrounding rock reaches its maximum value, and support 2 begins to move. Therefore, support 2 cannot be driven under pressure under this condition. Compared with the theoretical values, the maximum error of the maximum friction force between support 1 and support 2 and the surrounding rock is 1%, which is less than 5%.

4.4. Simulation of Driving Under Pressure Dynamic Model

To analyze the variation in the pushing and pulling forces of the moving cylinder, as well as the supporting force of the top beam of support 1 and support 2 on the roof, and to verify the accuracy of the dynamic model during the driving under pressure motion of support 1 and support 2, the driving under pressure process and its dynamic model of the TSR are simulated through the Adams software based on the simulation model of the boundary condition simulation experiment of the driving under pressure dynamic model taking $P_{12s} = P_{22s} = 0.2$ MPa. The effective area of the piston rod in the piston chamber of the push hydraulic cylinder compared to the effective area of the piston rod in the rod chamber typically ranges from 1.2 to 2. Therefore, the ratio of the thrust to the pull force provided by the push hydraulic cylinder is also between 1.2 and 2. Taking the effective area ratio of the piston chamber piston rod to the rod chamber piston rod as 1.3, during pressurized operation of the temporary support robot, in order to achieve a more rational distribution of thrust and pull force of the push hydraulic cylinder, P_{12d} is set to 0.1 (MPa). Based on the parameters of the virtual prototype model of the TSR, and assuming that support 1 and support 2 are in uniform motion, the maximum thrust required for support 1 is calculated to be approximately 427 (KN) using the pressure formula, Equations (2) and (9). Consequently, the maximum pull force for support II during pressurized operation is about $427/1.3 \approx 328$ (KN). Further calculations using the pressure formula, Equations (5) and (10), indicate that P_{22d} is approximately 0.07 (MPa), with both P_{12d} and P_{22d} remaining within their respective value ranges. And, the critical Stribeck velocity $v_{st} = 0.01$ m/s, a step function of the displacement of the moving cylinder piston rod relative to the cylinder, is constructed in the Adams software as a driver for simulation. The displacement increases from 0 m to 0.8 m within 0 to 60 s and decreases from 0.8 m to 0 m within 70 s to 130 s. The simulation time is 140 s. The displacement curve of the moving cylinder piston rod relative to the cylinder and the displacement variation in support 1 and support 2 obtained by simulation are shown in Figure 16. Using the MATLAB R2023a software, the displacement data of support 1 and support 2 are substituted into their respective dynamic models to simulate two cases: considering the Stribeck friction theory and not considering the Stribeck friction theory (when the Stribeck friction theory is not considered, take $f_1 = f_2 = 0.28$). The theoretical values of the pushing and pulling forces of the moving cylinder are obtained. The force value pushing support 1 is positive, and the force value pulling support 2 is negative. The pushing and pulling forces of the moving cylinder obtained by the Adams simulation are compared with them, and the results are shown in Figure 17.

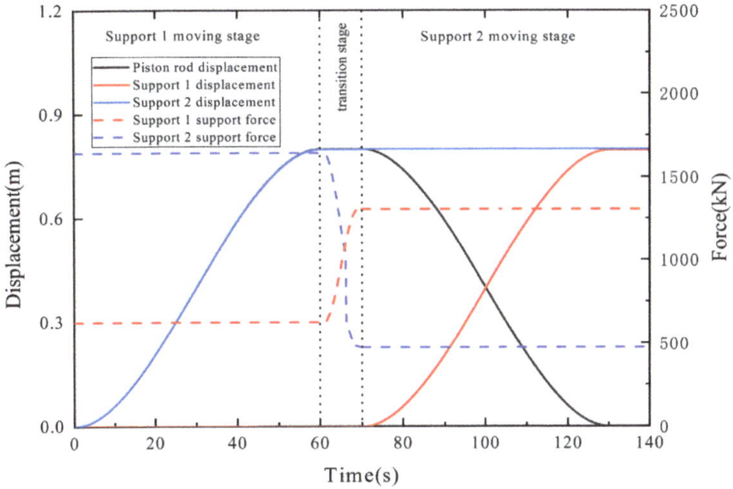

Figure 16. Displacement and supporting force curves of support 1 and support 2.

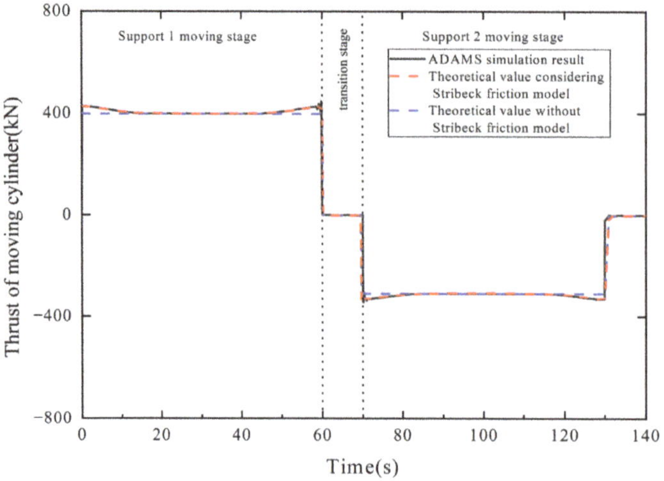

Figure 17. Simulation results of the pushing force for the moving cylinder.

As shown in Figure 16, the stage from 0 s to 60 s is the driving under pressure stage of support 1. In this stage, driven by the moving cylinder, the speed of support 1 gradually increases from zero within 0 s to 16 s, remains constant within 16 s to 44 s, and gradually decreases to zero within 44 s to 60 s, with a displacement of 0.8 m during the whole process. The stage from 60 s to 70 s is the transition stage. The stage from 70 s to 130 s is the driving under pressure stage of support 2. In this stage, pulled by the moving cylinder, the speed of support 2 gradually increases from zero between 70 s and 86 s, remains constant between 86 s and 114 s, and gradually decreases to zero between 114 s and 130 s, with a displacement of 0.8 m during the whole process. The supporting force of the top beam of support 1 on the roof is 623 kN within 0 s to 60 s, gradually increases to 1303 kN within 60 s to 70 s, and remains stable. The supporting force of the top beam of support 2 on the roof is 1643 kN within 0 s to 60 s, gradually decreases to 473 kN within 60 s to 70 s, and remains stable.

As shown in Figure 17, the pushing force value of the moving cylinder obtained by simulation gradually decreases from 426 kN to 398 kN within 0 s to 16 s, remains stable within 16 s to 44 s, and gradually increases from 399 kN to 426 kN within 44 s to 60 s. The force value decreases to 0 N at 60 s. At 70 s, the pushing force of the moving cylinder changes to pulling force, and the force value is 333 kN, which decreases from 333 kN to 305 kN within 70 s to 86 s, remains stable within 86 s to 114 s, and increases from 305 kN to 330 kN within 114 s to 130 s, and remains constant at 0 N after 130 s. The theoretical values of the pushing and pulling force of the moving cylinder in the dynamic model of driving under pressure considering the Stribeck friction theory gradually decrease from 427 kN to 399 kN within 0 s to 16 s, remain stable within 16 s to 44 s, gradually increase from 399 kN to 427 kN within 44 s to 60 s, and remain constant at 0 N within 60 s to 70 s. At 70 s, the pushing force of the moving cylinder changes to pulling force, and the force value is 331 kN, which decreases from 331 kN to 309 kN within 70 s to 86 s, remains stable within 86 s to 114 s, increases from 309 kN to 331 kN within 114 s to 130 s, and remains constant at 0 N after 130 s. The theoretical value of the pushing and pulling force of the moving cylinder in the driving under pressure dynamic model without considering the Stribeck friction theory is 398 kN within 0 s to 60 s and 0 N within 60 s to 70 s. From 70 s to 130 s, the pushing force of the moving cylinder changes to the pulling force with a force of 309 kN and remains constant at 0 N after 130 s.

The simulation results show that the theoretical value of the dynamic model of driving under pressure, considering the Stribeck friction theory, has the same trend as the pushing force value of the moving cylinder obtained by the simulation, and its maximum error is 1.3%, which does not exceed 5%. The maximum error between the theoretical value of the driving under pressure dynamic model without considering the Stribeck friction theory and the pushing force value of the moving cylinder obtained by the simulation is 7.8%. Therefore, considering the Stribeck friction theory can make the driving under pressure dynamic model reflect the real values of pushing and pulling force required by support 1 and support 2 during the driving under pressure process of TSR more accurately.

5. Conclusions

Facing the support challenges of short-wall working face (15–40 m) roadways in the 'excavation–backfill–retention' tunneling method for section coal pillars, traditional equipment struggled to achieve stable, reliable, and efficient support. This paper proposed a temporary support robot for the excavation and mining system of section coal pillars to ensure the safety of equipment and personnel in short-wall working faces. The support requirements of the section coal pillar excavation and mining system were analyzed, and the overall scheme of the temporary support system was proposed. The working principle of the temporary support robot was introduced. The temporary support robot consisted of two parts, support 1 and support 2, which advanced by pushing and pulling each other.

A mechanical model for the stable support of the temporary support robot was established. The mechanical properties of the surrounding rock were analyzed, and the allowable range of the temporary support robot's supporting force under stable support conditions was determined while ensuring the stability of the surrounding rock. Based on the Stribeck friction theory, a dynamic model of the temporary support robot in the driving under pressure state was constructed. The boundary conditions of the dynamic model were set, and the corresponding relationship between the temporary support robot's supporting force and its maximum static friction force was determined. Precise dynamic modeling of heavy equipment under complex contact conditions was completed, accurately describing the influence of the supporting force and pushing (pulling) force on the movement during the temporary support robot's driving under pressure, and limiting the allowable range of the supporting force in the driving under pressure state.

Through finite element simulation, the stress on the temporary support robot and the floor under the given load was analyzed, verifying that this load condition would not cause damage to the temporary support robot or the surrounding rock. Through multi-body dynamics simulation, the pushing (pulling) forces required for the temporary support robot's movement under different supporting force conditions were obtained. Compared with the theoretical values, the error was less than 1.2%, verifying the feasibility of the driving under pressure action under different supporting force conditions. In addition, through multi-body dynamics simulation, the driving under pressure process of the temporary support robot was analyzed. The changes in supporting force and displacement of support I and support II in the TSR were obtained. The model-predicted values and simulated values of the required pushing (pulling) forces were compared. The simulation results showed that the model's prediction accuracy was significantly better than that of the traditional simplified model, with an error of only 1.3%, validating the accuracy of the dynamic model.

This research provided a safe and reliable support scheme for the excavation of short-wall working faces in section coal pillar mining, offering a new theoretical framework for the design and dynamic analysis of temporary support equipment in mining engineering. It holds significant academic value and broad application prospects, driving the development of support equipment towards higher precision, efficiency, and safety, and providing strong technical support for achieving the goals of mine safety production and green mining.

Author Contributions: Conceptualization, H.M. and J.C.; methodology, J.C., C.W. and X.X.; software, J.C.; validation, J.C., H.Z. and Q.M.; formal analysis, P.L.; investigation, Z.Y.; resources, J.C.; data curation, W.C.; writing—original draft preparation, J.C.; writing—review and editing, Y.G. and P.W.; visualization, H.T.; supervision, H.S.; project administration, H.M.; funding acquisition, H.M. and C.W. All authors have read and agreed to the published version of the manuscript.

Funding: This research was funded by the Key Technologies Research and Development Program of China under grant 2023YFC2907600, the Key Research and Development Projects of Shaanxi Province under grant 2023-LL-QY-03, the National Natural Science Foundation of China project under grant 52374161, the Shaanxi Provincial Department of Education to Serve Local Special under grant 22JC051, and the Shaanxi Science and Technology Association under grant 2023-JC-YB-331.

Institutional Review Board Statement: Not applicable.

Informed Consent Statement: Not applicable.

Data Availability Statement: The original contributions presented in the study are included in the article, and further inquiries can be directed to the corresponding author.

Conflicts of Interest: The authors declare no conflicts of interest.

Abbreviations

The following abbreviations are used in this manuscript:

TSR	temporary support robot

References

1. Wang, S.M.; Liu, L.; Zhu, M.B.; Wei, B.N.; Zhuang, D.D.; Qu, H.S.; He, W.; Shao, C.C.; Xia, L.; Zhou, J. Scientific Problems and Technology of The Integration of 'Excavation-Backfill-Retention' of Section Coal Pillar and Mining Roadway. *J. China Coal Soc.* **2024**, *49*, 3291–3315. [CrossRef]
2. Xu, Z.; Li, C.; Cao, Y.; Tai, L.; Han, J. A Case Study on New High-Strength Temporary Support Technology of Extremely Soft Coal Seam Roadway. *J. Sci. Rep.* **2023**, *13*, 21333. [CrossRef]
3. Choi, S.O.; Shin, H.S. Stability Analysis of a Tunnel Excavated in a Weak Rock Mass and the Optimal Supporting System Design. *Int. J. Rock Mech. Min. Sci.* **2004**, *41*, 876–881. [CrossRef]
4. Guo, W.X. Application of Temporary Support Device in Coal Mine Tunneling Face. *Coal Eng.* **2018**, *50*, 39–42.
5. Liu, J.; Cheng, F.; Guo, X.; Lu, Z.; Li, Z. Hydraulic System Design of Temporary Support for Fast Excavation of Top Coal. *J. IOP Conf. Ser. Earth Environ. Sci.* **2021**, *772*, 012053. [CrossRef]
6. Wang, Y.; Liu, K.J. Design of Self-Moving Non-Mounted Tunneling Advanced Support Device. *J. Coal Mine Mach. Ery.* **2021**, *42*, 113–114. [CrossRef]
7. Ding, S.; Bai, J.; Han, J.; Wang, H.; Ma, F. Mechanical characteristics analysis and structural optimization of key component of self-moving temporary support. *Appl. Sci.* **2022**, *12*, 10745. [CrossRef]
8. Zuo, G. Design of Crawler Walking Hydraulic System for Coal Mine Equipment. *Mach. Tool Hydraul.* **2019**, *47*, 96–98. [CrossRef]
9. Zhao, H.B.; Yan, J.; Zhang, H.F.; Yang, J.; Chen, Q.Q. Application and Technical Optimization of Push-Type Roadway Advance Support Device in Coal Mine Mining. *Mach. China* **2024**, *29*, 61–65.
10. Yang, X.S.; Yang, Z.G. Design of Roadway Advanced Support and Study on Its Mechanical Characteristics. *J. Mine Autom.* **2019**, *45*, 35–40. [CrossRef]
11. Mao, J.; Guo, G.L.; Xie, M. Finite Element Analysis and Optimization of Top beam Structure for Advance Supporting Equipment of Arch. *J. Mech. Strength* **2019**, *41*, 1400–1407.
12. Wang, D.; Cheng, J.; Li, R.; Qu, Y.; Jiang, H.; Shen, Y.; Yang, S.; Zhao, S.; Wu, M. Research on the Twin-Link Stepping Temporary Support Mechanism and the Repeatable Supportability of the Roof in the Underground Excavation Roadway of Coal Mine. *Appl. Sci.* **2024**, *14*, 6659. [CrossRef]
13. Xu, Y.J.; Zhang, D.S.; Li, D.Y. Study on Advanced Powered Support with Omni-Directional Walking Function. *Coal Sci. Technol.* **2019**, *47*, 161–166. [CrossRef]
14. Ma, H.W.; Li, L.; Xue, X.S.; Wang, C.; Wang, S.S.; Zhao, Y.J.; Zhang, H. Research on Hydraulic Control System for Shield Type Temporary Support Robot Driving Under Pressure. *J. Mine Autom.* **2024**, *50*, 21–31. [CrossRef]

15. Gong, X.R.; Zhang, L.X.; Fan, X.Q. Analysis about Cutting Mechanism Motion of Transverse Road header. *Coal Mine Mach.* **2013**, *34*, 115–117. [CrossRef]
16. Yue, Z.W.; Wang, D.L.; Wang, G.D.; Hao, X.D.; Li, Y.L.; Li, A.K.; Dong, H.R. Research Progress and Development Path of Temporary Support Technology and Equipment for Coal Mine Roadway Excavation. *J. Min. Strat. Control Eng.* **2023**, *5*, 5–20. [CrossRef]
17. Zhang, J.; Li, W.Y.; Guo, J.H.; Li, J.K.; He, X.Y.; Wu, Z.B. Research on trajectory planning method of anchor drilling robot manipulator. *J. Min. Sci. Technol.* **2024**, *9*, 807–816. [CrossRef]
18. Lei, M.Y.; Zhang. X.H.; Yang, W.J.; Dong, Z.; Wan, J.C.; Zhang, C.; Du, Y.Y. Manipulator trajectory planning method of anchor drilling robot. *Coal Geol. Explor.* **2023**, *51*, 180–190. [CrossRef]
19. Yang, Y. Research and Application of temporary support technology in the excavation face of Wangpo coal mine. *J. Coal Eng.* **2019**, *51*, 42–46.
20. Wang, S.B.; Zhang, H. Dynamic Model and Simulation Analysis of Advancement of Fully Mechanized Mining Face. *J. Mech. Eng.* **2022**, *58*, 117–130.
21. Wang, C.L.; Gao, Y.H.; He, T.; Ye, F. Bearing Characteristics Analysis of Hydraulic Chock Column Using External control constant pressure speed regulating valve. *Coal Eng.* **2024**, *56*, 158–164.
22. Li, T.J.; Jin, F.T. Design and Optimization on Analytic Method of Support Four-Bar Linkage. *Min. Process. Equip.* **2015**, *43*, 25–27. [CrossRef]
23. Wen, Y.C.; Ding, L.H.; Bai, Y.B. Development of Shield Type Hydraulic Support ZY12000/18/33D. *Colliery Mech. Electr. Technol.* **2019**, *40*, 109–111. [CrossRef]
24. Wang, Q. Study on Bearing Characteristics and Applicability Analysis of Hydraulic Support for Large Mining Height. *Mech. Manag. Dev.* **2019**, *34*, 83–85. [CrossRef]
25. Wang, Y.Z.; Guo, C.; Jia, S.; Ning, K.; Lan, H. Stability Analysis of Disc Friction Pairs Based on Stribeck Model. *J. China Mech. Eng.* **2017**, *28*, 2521–2525.
26. Qi, Z.B.; Guo, L.L.; Lan, S.H.; Sang, Y. Research on Friction Compensation of Servo System Based on Modified Stribeck Model. *Micromotors* **2024**, *57*, 20–25+42. [CrossRef]
27. Lin, H.L. Stability of Goaf with Shallow Buried and Large area Based on Thin Plate Theory. *J. Coal Min. Technol.* **2016**, *21*, 28–30+105. [CrossRef]
28. Hu, D.J.; Yang, Y.P.; Yan, J.S.; Cheng, G.S.; Yang, C.S. Analysis of Mechanical Model and Creep Damage Fracture of Metal Mines Stope Roof for Shrinkage Mining Method. *World Sci-Tech. R D* **2016**, *38*, 763–767. [CrossRef]
29. Meng, E.C.; Yang, J.Z.; Chen, X.M.; Wang, B.M. Analysis of The Underframe Sinking of Hydraulic Support 1n Fully Mechanized Mining Face. *Coal Min. Technol.* **2003**, *8*, 35–37. [CrossRef]

applied sciences

MDPI

Article

Evaluation of Leakage Currents of Semiconductor Packages Due to High-Voltage Stress Under an Immersion Cooling Environment

Kyuhae Min [1,†], Taejun Kang [2,†], Tae Yeob Kang [3,*] and Jae-Bum Pyo [1,4,*]

1 Department of Mechanical and Automotive Engineering, Kongju National University, Cheonan-daero 1223-24, Seobuk-gu, Cheonan-si 31080, Chungnam, Republic of Korea; polamgh@naver.com
2 Department of Mechanical Engineering, Kongju National University, Cheonan-daero 1223-24, Seobuk-gu, Cheonan-si 31080, Chungnam, Republic of Korea; rkdxowns0531@smail.kongju.ac.kr
3 Department of Mechanical Engineering, The University of Suwon, Hwaseong 18323, Gyeonggi, Republic of Korea
4 Research Institute of Global Manufacturing Technology, Kongju National University, Cheonan-daero 1223-24, Seobuk-gu, Cheonan-si 31080, Chungnam, Republic of Korea
* Correspondence: tykang@suwon.ac.kr (T.Y.K.); jbpyo@kongju.ac.kr (J.-B.P.)
† These authors contributed equally to this work.

Abstract: As data centers expand, immersion cooling systems are gaining attention for thermal management of memory devices. To enable widespread adoption, it is essential to evaluate the impact of coolants on the reliability of memory packages. In this study, high-voltage direct current (DC) stress tests were conducted on commercial dynamic random access memory (DRAM) packages in both single-phase coolant and air environments to analyze heat generation and electrical characteristics. A DC voltage ranging from 2.5 to 3.1 V, which is higher than the regular operating voltage of 1.2 V, was applied. Temperature changes were measured using an infrared camera in the air, and a contact-based thermometer in the coolant. The leakage current was also evaluated through I-V curve analysis. Heat generation and changes in leakage currents were not significant in either environment until the applied voltage stress exceeded approximately twice the standard voltage (2.5–2.8 V). However, the package's degradation accelerated when the applied voltages exceeded 3.0 V, demonstrating a nonlinear increase in temperature and leakage current.

Keywords: semiconductor package; high voltage stress test; immersion cooling; mechanical behavior; leakage current; reliability; oxide film damage

1. Introduction

In recent years, with the development of cloud systems and AI technology, the demand for computing in data centers has been constantly increasing, and the importance of energy consumption and cooling issues has also been growing [1]. As advances in semiconductor technology increase the power density of processors, traditional air-cooling methods are reaching their limits, and cooling systems account for a significant portion of a data center's power consumption. Therefore, the introduction of more efficient cooling solutions is imperative [2]. To address this issue, memory device cooling technology utilizing an immersion cooling system is gaining attention. In high-power-density environments, it provides greater cooling efficiency than traditional air-cooling methods, making it a promising alternative for energy savings and operational efficiency [3]. It also offers several advantages, including compact size, easy maintenance, and eco-friendliness [4]. Therefore, memory devices should maintain their integrity even under this cooling environment in order to guarantee the stability of data storage.

Evaluating the impact of the dielectric coolant used in immersion cooling on the reliability of memory packages is essential. However, previous research has primarily focused on thermal management and heat transfer performance. A study on the heat distribution and heat transfer characteristics of a CPU in a single-phase immersion cooling system revealed that increasing the coolant flow rate reduced the temperature stabilization time, while the heat sink material had no effect on cooling performance [5]. In water-cooled immersion cooling experiments involving individual GaN transistors and PCB substrates, water and water ethylene glycol mixtures exhibited higher heat flux than dielectric fluids. However, the devices failed before reaching the critical heat flux (CHF), whereas dielectric fluids successfully reached the CHF and demonstrated greater thermal stability [6]. Meanwhile, there was research on the reliability of package substrate under immersion cooling environments, but it primarily focused on the impact of coolant absorption on mechanical behavior. The absorption of dielectric fluid EC 100 reduced the stiffness of PCBs and mitigated the warpage phenomenon [7], while mineral oil increased the stiffness of PCBs and passive components but had no significant impact on the reliability [8].

I-V curve analysis has been employed to assess internal degradation mechanisms. Typically, semiconductor packages are tested under high-temperature and high-humidity conditions, as well as under voltage stress condition exceeding standard operating levels, to detect defects and ensure their reliability [9,10]. DRAM, a volatile memory, is composed of capacitors and metal–oxide–semiconductor field-effect transistors (MOSFETs). Applying DC voltage stress to MOSFETs accelerates degradation due to electrical and thermal stress, leading to increased leakage current and additional heat generation [11]. If this phenomenon persists, it can cause permanent damage to the semiconductor chip [12]. Therefore, it is necessary to investigate the effects of voltage stress on the reliability of semiconductor packages, even under immersion cooling environment.

This study evaluated the effects of DC voltage stress on heat generation and electrical degradation in air and single-phase immersion cooling environments for commercial DRAM packages, analyzing the acceleration mechanisms of the degradation. Heat generation characteristics were measured using an infrared camera in an air environment and a contact-based thermometer in an immersion environment. The experimental results showed that the immersion cooling environment allowed a stable temperature of the packages via its cooling performance. In contrast, heat generation continued to increase in the air environment, resulting in more rapid degradation at relatively high voltages (3.0 V and 3.1 V). The electrical characteristics were measured using a probe station and a current–voltage analyzer to evaluate the package's I-V curves. The analysis confirmed that heat generation is a critical factor in accelerating electrical degradation. In air, accumulated heat accelerated degradation, leading to a substantial increase in leakage current. In contrast, under immersion cooling, heat generation was significantly suppressed, minimizing the increase in leakage current.

These findings are expected to define the reliable voltage range that DRAM packages can withstand, verify the effectiveness of immersion cooling technology at the package level, and contribute to the establishment of design standards for stable data center operation.

2. Materials and Methods

2.1. Semiconductor Package

The DRAM used in this experiment was a fine-pitch ball grid array (FBGA) type 4 GB DDR4 synchronous dynamic random access memory (SDRAM) (H5AN4G6NBJR-UHC, SK hynix, Icheon, Republic of Korea). The package dimensions were 13 mm × 7.5 mm × 1.1 mm, with 96 balls, a ball pitch of 0.8 mm, and a ball diameter of 0.45 mm, as shown in Figure 1a,b. The regular operating voltage was 1.2 V, the absolute maximum DC ratings ranged from −0.3 V to 1.5 V, and the normal operating temperature range was 0 °C to 85 °C. This memory package consisted of a die that performed calculation and storage functions, an epoxy molding compound (EMC) that provided protection, and solder balls that electrically connected it to a printed circuit board (PCB); see Figure 1c. When voltage stress is applied to DRAM, leakage current occurs due to high-energy carriers colliding with gate oxide film, leading to the formation of trap states through hot carrier injection (HCI) [13,14]. This process induces oxide film damage and, over time, results in gate oxide breakdown due to trap-assisted degradation, also known as time-dependent dielectric breakdown (TDDB) [11]. The increase in leakage current leads to greater heat generation, further accelerating the degradation of the semiconductor chip. If this phenomenon persists, heat generation and leakage current will increase exponentially, ultimately causing a significant reduction in DRAM reliability [15]. The leakage current characteristics under voltage stress are depicted in Figure 1d.

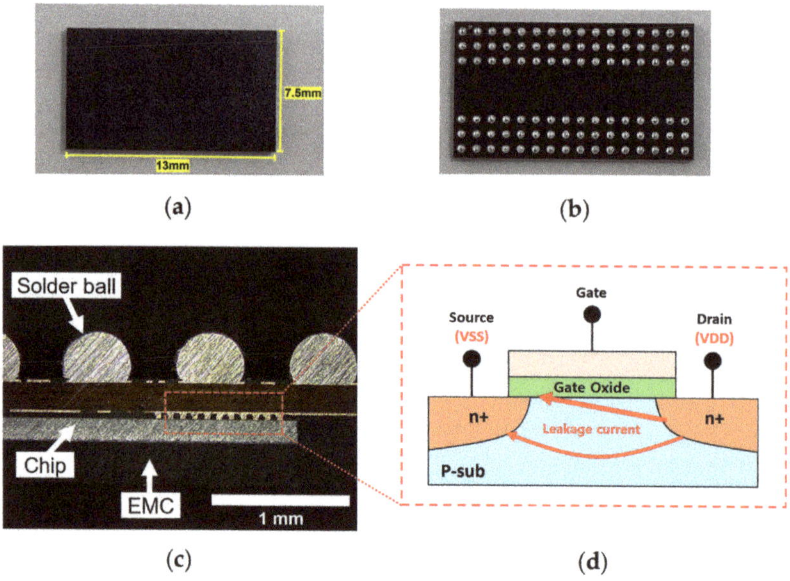

Figure 1. Memory package: (**a**) top view and (**b**) bottom view; (**c**) cross-sectional image showing the chip, solder balls, and EMC; (**d**) schematic of leakage current in the MOSFET structure.

2.2. *Accelerated Stress Test*

Reliability tests for memory packages are typically conducted under harsh environments, including high temperature, high humidity, and voltage stress. However, since direct heat application to the package is not feasible in an immersion environment, this study focused on the high-voltage stress test (HVST). It is an accelerated life evaluation method that applies a voltage exceeding the standard operating voltage to assess device stability under overvoltage conditions [16].

To proceed with the HVST, a high DC voltage was applied to the power supply pins (VDD/VSS) of the semiconductor package for an extended duration using a DC power supply (UTP3305-II, UNI-T, China). Subsequently, electrical characteristics were measured using a probe station (mst4000A, MSTECH, Hwaseong, Republic of Korea) and a precision I-V analyzer (E5270B, KEYSIGHT, Santa Rosa, CA, USA) as shown in Figure 2a.

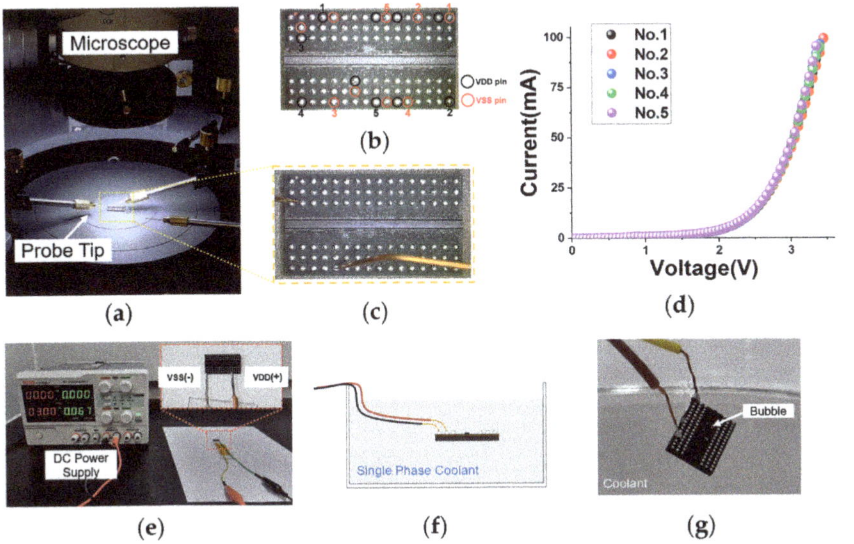

Figure 2. (**a**) Probe station setup for electrical measurement. (**b**) Identification of VDD (black) and VSS (red) pins. (**c**) Close-up view of the measuring process with probe tips. (**d**) I-V characteristics of VDD/VSS pairs. (**e**) DC power supply setup for HVST. (**f**) Schematic of the immersion cooling environment with a single-phase coolant. (**g**) Bubble generation in an immersion cooling environment under voltage stress.

Because of the small size of the solder balls, jumper wires could be applied only to a single VDD/VSS pair (No. 1) [Figure 2b]. To ensure that the selected pair effectively delivered voltage across the package, I-V curves of four different VDD/VSS pairs were measured using a probe station [Figure 2c]. The measurement results demonstrated that all pairs exhibited identical electrical characteristics in fresh state [Figure 2d]. Based on this, it was concluded that the selected pair could reliably represent the entire set of VDD/VSS pairs, as all pairs exhibited consistent electrical behavior.

To investigate the thermal and electrical characteristics of DRAM under voltage stress in air and immersion cooling environments, DC voltages of 2.5 V, 2.8 V, 3.0 V, and 3.1 V were applied to the semiconductor chip for up to 1 h [Figure 2e]. However, when 3.1 V was applied, excessive heat generation caused detachment at the junction between the jumper wire and the solder ball, limiting the test duration to a maximum of 30 min. An I-V sweep was performed using a probe station in order to analyze electrical changes after voltage stress application. The sweep voltage started from 0 V and went up to 5 V, and the maximum measurable current was 100 mA.

2.3. Dielectric Coolant

The immersion cooling environment was formed by submerging a single memory package in a polystyrene container filled with a nonconductive single-phase coolant (FC-3283, 3M, St. Paul, MN, USA). Although single-phase coolants have lower cooling performance than two-phase coolants [17], they offer relatively high stability and boiling points. Given these properties, a single-phase coolant was selected as the most suitable option for the experimental setup [Figure 2f]. This coolant had a boiling point of 128 °C. Typical single-phase immersion cooling systems require an additional coolant cooling device. However, in this experiment, no additional cooling device was used, as the heat generated by a single chip had a negligible impact on coolant temperature variation. When a high DC voltage was applied to the package, nucleate boiling occurred near the wafer within the package [Figure 2g].

2.4. Temperature Measurement

To assess the heat generation characteristics under voltage stress, temperature variations in the package were measured. In the air environment, the maximum package temperature was recorded at 5, 10, and 30 min intervals for each applied voltage using an infrared camera (RSE300, FLUKE, Everett, WA, USA) [Figure 3a]. The measurement range was set from 25 °C to 190 °C, with an emissivity of 0.90 and a frame rate of 30 Hz. In the immersion cooling environment, since infrared radiation could not pass through the dielectric coolant, it was challenging to evaluate the heat generation of the memory package. Instead, a contact-based thermometer (54-2 B, FLUKE, USA) was attached to the semiconductor package using adhesive tape, and temperature readings were taken every minute for 30 min depending on the applied voltage.

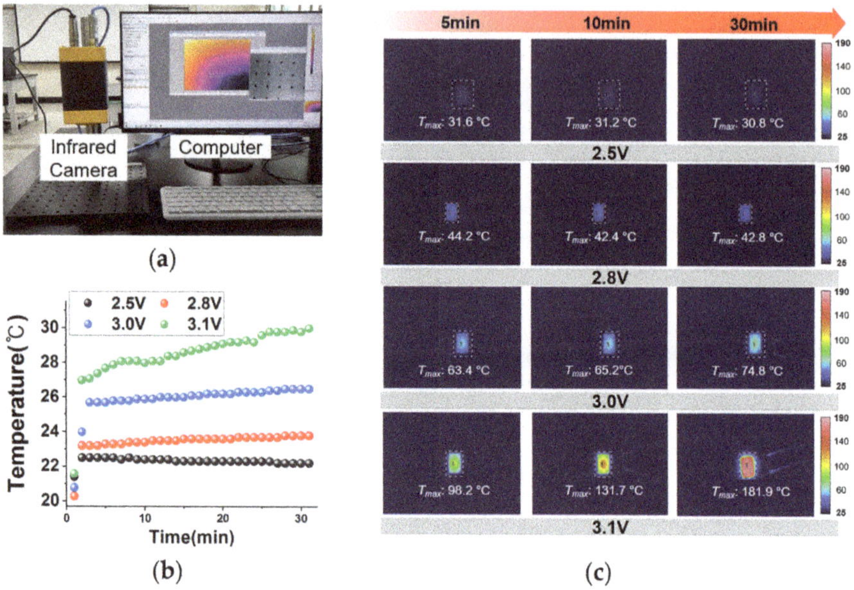

Figure 3. (**a**) Experimental setup with an infrared camera for temperature measurement. (**b**) Temperature variation over time in an immersion environment measured using a contact-based thermometer under different voltage conditions. (**c**) Infrared thermal images captured by an IR camera, showing the heat generation and temperature distribution changes over time under different voltage conditions.

3. Results and Discussion

3.1. Thermal Characteristics of Packages Under Voltage Stress

In this work, temperature variations by heat generation due to voltage stress were investigated in both air and immersion cooling environments. The maximum temperature was measured for 30 min as described in the section above. In the immersion cooling environment, thermally accelerated degradation seemed to minimize because of the higher cooling performance of immersion cooling than air, and no sudden temperature changes were observed [Figure 3c]. However, a relatively rapid initial increase in package temperature was observed. At 2.5 V, the temperature initially increased by 1.1 °C, then began to decrease after 7 min. At 2.8 V, the temperature initially increased by 2.9 °C, followed by an additional rise of 0.1 °C at 10 min and 0.5 °C at 30 min, based on the 5 min measurement interval. At 3.0 V, the temperature initially increased by 4.9 °C, with further increases of 0.2 °C at 10 min and 0.8 °C at 30 min. At 3.1 V, the temperature initially increased by 5.4 °C, then rose by 0.3 °C at 10 min and 2.2 °C at 30 min [Figure 3b]. As described above, the immersion cooling ensured that the package temperature increase remained below ~10 °C, even at voltages 2.5 times higher than the regular operating voltage.

In the air environment, natural cooling was observed; however, when the package experienced relatively high voltages, heat accumulation accelerated, leading to a rapid increase in the package's maximum temperature compared with the initial state [Figure 3c]. At 2.5 V, the temperature increased by 8.6 °C at 5 min but gradually decreased as time passed because of air cooling, preventing further thermal acceleration. At 2.8 V, the initial temperature rise was 21.2 °C, which was higher than that at 2.5 V. However, temperature variation was not accelerated because of the natural cooling effect. At 3.0 V, the increase in initial temperature was 40.4 °C, leading to additional temperature rises of 1.8 °C at 10 min and 9.6 °C at 30 min. At 3.1 V, thermal degradation progressed rapidly as soon as the voltage was applied. The temperature increased by 75.2 °C at 5 min, followed by additional rises of 33.5 °C at 10 min and 50.2 °C at 30 min. At relatively low voltage stress (2.5 V, 2.8 V) in both air and immersion cooling environments, thermal accelerations were not critical because of lower heat generation. However, as the stress voltage exceeded 3.0 V and 3.1 V, a nonlinear increase in maximum temperature was observed because the generated heat effectively dissipated. At 25 °C, air has a thermal conductivity of 0.026 W/m·K [18], while FC-3283 exhibits a higher value of about 0.066 W/m·K [19], which is approximately 2.5 times greater than that of air. The improved cooling performance in immersion environments can be attributed not only to the higher thermal conductivity of the liquid coolant but to the generally higher heat transfer coefficient at the solid–liquid interface, which enhances heat dissipation efficiency compared with solid–air systems.

This difference explains why thermal accelerations were minimized in the immersion cooling environment, confirming that this advanced cooling method provides greater thermal stability than air cooling even under elevated voltage conditions. Based on the above results, the changes in electrical characteristics due to voltage stress are expected to demonstrate a similar trend with thermal performance characterization. This would imply that the immersion cooling environment is more effective at suppressing the thermally induced performance degradation of semiconductor devices under elevated voltage stress conditions.

To ensure consistency between measurement methods, additional temperature measurements were conducted under air conditions using a contact-based thermometer (Figure S1A). The results showed good agreement with infrared measurements at 2.5 V and 2.8 V, with differences within approximately 10% (Figure S2A,B). At higher voltages, stable contact could not be maintained because of thermal degradation of the attachment tape (Figure S1B).

3.2. *I-V Curve*

The I-V curve was measured using a probe station to evaluate leakage current caused by the electrical stress. Although thermal resistance is commonly used as an indicator of packaging failure [20,21], this study employed the I-V curve to characterize internal electrical degradation. At 2.5 V and 2.8 V, the electrical characteristics of the package remained identical to those of the undamaged (fresh) package up to 1 h. In the previous heat generation measurements shown in Figures 4a–d and S3, only slight thermal accelerations were observed under these voltage conditions. It was interesting to note that the packages exhibited a maximum temperature difference of approximately 13 °C among the cooling environments. However, the measurement results demonstrated no significant differences in electrical behavior.

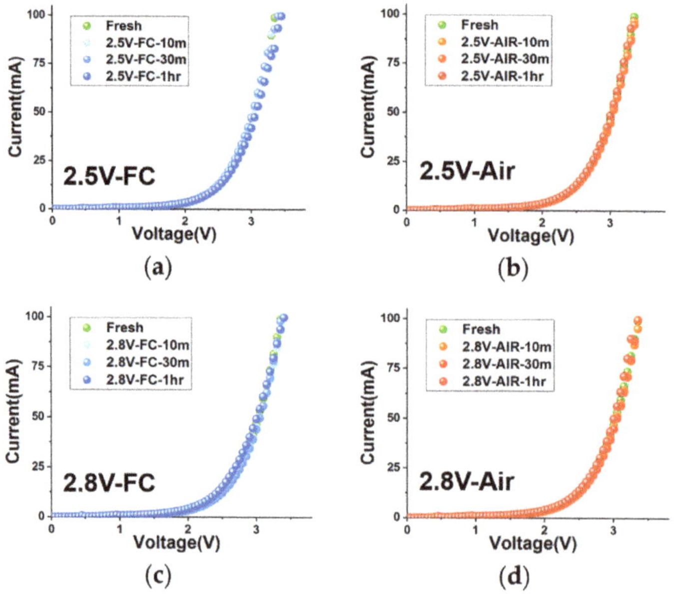

Figure 4. I-V characteristics under different environmental conditions and voltage: (**a**) 2.5 V applied over time in coolant, (**b**) 2.5 V applied over time in air, (**c**) 2.8 V applied over time in coolant, and (**d**) 2.8 V applied over time in air. Measurements were taken for fresh samples and after exposure to voltage stress conditions for 10 min, 30 min, and 1 h.

On the other hand, distinct electrical behaviors were observed under 3.0 V and 3.1 V conditions, as shown in Figures 5a–d and S4. As previously anticipated, the greatest difference in electrical behavior occurred when 3.1 V was applied for 30 min in the air environment. Variations in the I-V curve exhibited a time-dependent trend in both the immersion and air cooling environments. Based on the regular operating voltage of 1.2 V, the package currents were compared under 3.0 V and 3.1 V conditions in both two environments. At 3.0 V, the current of the package stressed in the immersion cooling environment was 0.905 mA at 10 min, 1.105 mA at 30 min, and 1.127 mA at 60 min, while the current of the package in the air was 0.921 mA at 10 min, 1.558 mA at 30 min, and 1.705 mA at 60 min. At 3.1 V, the package stressed in the coolant showed a current of 1.033 mA at 10 min and 1.704 mA at 30 min, whereas that cooled in the air environment showed increases in current to 1.545 mA at 10 min and 3.282 mA at 30 min.

These electrical behaviors were consistent with the thermal performance characterizations. Interestingly, no significant degradation of electrical performance was observed at relatively low voltage stress, whereas a nonlinear increase in leakage currents occurred at higher voltages, accompanied by accumulated heat within the package. This indicates that heat accumulation is a primary factor influencing package leakage current and suggests that immersion cooling is an effective method for maintaining device reliability under elevated voltage stress conditions.

These time-dependent I-V characteristics indicate that electrical degradation accelerated notably beyond 3.0 V, as reflected in the increasing slope of the I-V curve. This nonlinearity suggests the onset of stress-induced leakage current mechanisms, which may stem from charge trapping and oxide weakening in the MOSFET structure. The substantial current increase at 3.0 V, particularly in the air-cooled environment, implies that this voltage exceeds the safe operational margin and could act as a practical failure threshold for long-term reliability. These observations further support the need to define conservative voltage limits in package design, especially when operated under limited cooling conditions.

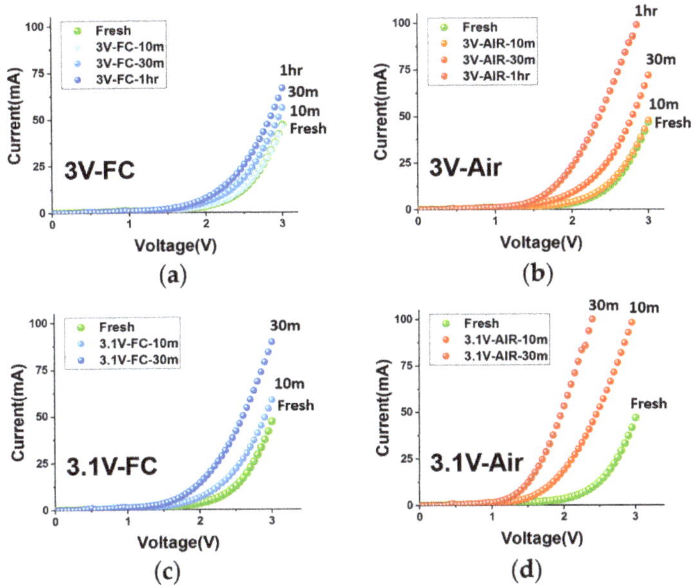

Figure 5. I–V curve characteristics with (**a**) 3 V applied over time in coolant, (**b**) 3 V applied over time in air, (**c**) 3.1 V applied over time in coolant, and (**d**) 3.1 V applied over time in air. Measurements were taken for fresh samples and after exposure to voltage stress for 10 min, 30 min, and 1 h (except for 3.1 V, which was measured up to 30 min).

3.3. Leakage Current Increase Rate and Degradation Mechanism

To assess the electrical performance of two different cooling methods, we compared the leakage current of an undamaged package (fresh) at the operating voltage of 1.2 V with that of packages that were exposed to stress at 3.0 V and 3.1 V over time [Figure 6a]. At 3.0 V, the leakage current of the immersion cooling package increased by approximately 13% after 30 min and 15% after 1 h relative to fresh. In contrast, the leakage current of the air cooling package increased by ~59% after 30 min and 74% after 1 h. At 3.1 V, the leakage current of the package under immersion cooling increased by 74% after 30 min, while that of the package in the air environment increased by 234%. The leakage current caused by voltage stress was approximately three times lower in the immersion cooling environment than in the air.

Based on these results, it is noteworthy that the immersion cooling environment provided superior cooling performance to that of air, effectively reduced electrical and thermal stress caused by elevated voltage and enhanced the electrical stability of the package. Furthermore, the following mechanism explains this effect. When elevated voltage was applied to DRAM, heat generated by electrical stress and thermal acceleration was not effectively dissipated in the air environment, resulting in a significant increase in leakage current. As a result, the package leakage current increased rapidly, leading to oxide degradation and instability of the semiconductor device, which in turn caused an additional increase in leakage current [Figure 6b]. In contrast, in the immersion cooling environment, the heat generated by electrical stress was dissipated more effectively, minimizing further increases in leakage current and enhancing the reliability of the semiconductor package [Figure 6c].

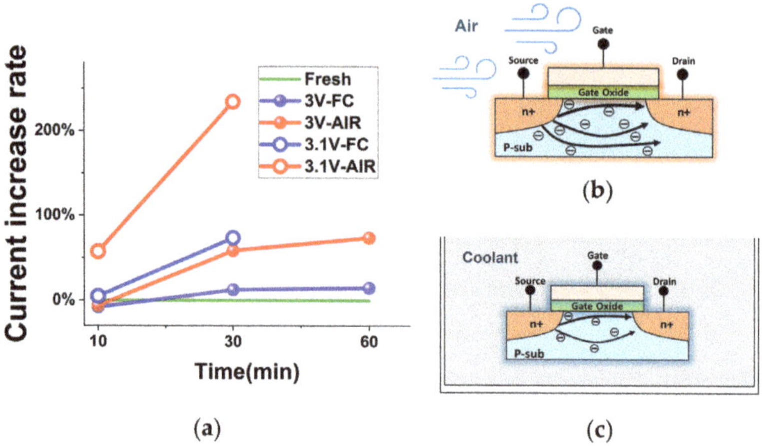

Figure 6. (**a**) Rate of leakage current increase at 1.2 V compared with a fresh package under different voltage and environmental conditions. Schematics describing of leakage current reduction mechanisms due to cooling performance (**b**) in air and (**c**) in an immersion environment.

These results indicate a nonlinear correlation between stress voltage and leakage current growth rate, which is consistent with degradation mechanisms such as hot carrier injection and time-dependent dielectric breakdown. The observed current increase under air environment, particularly at 3.0 V, suggests that this condition surpasses the critical stress limit for DRAM packages. As such, it is recommended that operating voltages be maintained below 2.8 V to prevent accelerated degradation in air-cooled systems.

4. Conclusions

In this study, we evaluated heat generation and electrical degradation in DRAM packages under DC voltage stress (2.5–3.1 V) in air and single-phase immersion cooling environments. The results demonstrated that immersion cooling significantly reduced heat accumulation and suppressed the leakage current approximately 59% compared to air cooling. At 3.0 V and 3.1 V, the leakage current in air increased up to three times more than that in immersion cooling, confirming the electrical stability of immersion cooling. These findings provide essential data for assessing DRAM reliability and establish design criteria for stable data center operations. Based on the observed leakage current behavior and thermal trends, it is analytically evident that DRAM packages experience accelerated degradation when stressed above 3.0 V. While the recommended operating voltage remains at 1.2 V, our findings highlight 2.8 V as a critical stress threshold beyond which reliability rapidly declines. These results offer valuable insights for determining safe stress margins and reliability limits in package-level design and accelerated testing frameworks, particularly for systems evaluated under overvoltage conditions.

Supplementary Materials: The following supporting information can be downloaded at: https://www.mdpi.com/article/10.3390/app15094668/s1, Figure S1: Tape detachment under thermal conditions during contact-based temperature measurements; Figure S2: Comparison of temperature measurements using an infrared camera and a contact thermometer under different voltage conditions; Figure S3: IV curve characteristics with 2.5 V, 2.8 V applied over time in coolant and air; Figure S4: IV curve characteristics with 3.0 V, 3.1 V applied over time in coolant and air.

Author Contributions: Conceptualization, K.M. and J.-B.P.; methodology, K.M.; validation, K.M.; formal analysis, K.M., T.K. and J.-B.P.; investigation, K.M. and T.K.; resources, J.-B.P.; writing—original draft preparation, K.M., T.Y.K. and J.-B.P.; writing—review and editing, T.K., T.Y.K. and J.-B.P.; supervision, T.Y.K. and J.-B.P.; project administration, J.-B.P.; funding acquisition, J.-B.P. All authors have read and agreed to the published version of the manuscript.

Funding: This work was supported by the research grant of Kongju National University in 2022, "Regional Innovation Strategy (RIS)", through the National Research Foundation of Korea (NRF), funded by the Ministry of Education (MOE) (No. 2021RIS-004), the Korea Institute of Energy Technology Evaluation and Planning (KETEP), and the Ministry of Trade, Industry, and Energy (MOTIE) of the Republic of Korea (No. RS-2024-00394769).

Institutional Review Board Statement: Not applicable.

Informed Consent Statement: Not applicable.

Data Availability Statement: The original contributions presented in the study are included in the article. Further inquiries can be directed to the corresponding authors.

Conflicts of Interest: The authors declare no conflicts of interest.

References

1. Zhang, C.; Wang, H.; Huang, Y.; Zhang, L.; Chen, Y. Immersion liquid cooling for electronics: Materials, systems, applications and prospects. *Renew. Sustain. Energy Rev.* **2025**, *208*, 114989. [CrossRef]
2. Azarifar, M.; Arik, M.; Chang, J.-Y. Liquid cooling of data centers: A necessity facing challenges. *Appl. Therm. Eng.* **2024**, *247*, 123112. [CrossRef]
3. Haghshenas, K.; Setz, B.; Blosch, Y.; Aiello, M. Enough hot air: The role of immersion cooling. *Energy Inform.* **2023**, *6*, 14. [CrossRef]
4. Pambudi, N.A.; Sarifudin, A.; Firdaus, R.A.; Ulfa, D.K.; Gandidi, I.M.; Romadhon, R. The immersion cooling technology: Current and future development in energy saving. *Alex. Eng. J.* **2022**, *61*, 9509–9527. [CrossRef]
5. Cheng, C.-C.; Chang, P.-C.; Li, H.-C.; Hsu, F.-I. Design of a single-phase immersion cooling system through experimental and numerical analysis. *Int. J. Heat Mass Transf.* **2020**, *160*, 120203. [CrossRef]
6. Birbarah, P.; Gebrael, T.; Foulkes, T.; Stillwell, A.; Moore, A.; Pilawa-Podgurski, R.; Miljkovic, N. Water immersion cooling of high power density electronics. *Int. J. Heat Mass Transf.* **2020**, *147*, 118918. [CrossRef]
7. Ramdas, S.; Rajmane, P.; Chauhan, T.; Misrak, A.; Agonafer, D. Impact of immersion cooling on thermo-mechanical properties of PCB's and reliability of electronic packages. In Proceedings of the ASME 2019 International Technical Conference and Exhibition on Packaging and Integration of Electronic and Photonic Microsystems, Anaheim, CA, USA, 7–9 October 2019; American Society of Mechanical Engineers: New York, NY, USA, 2019; p. V001T02A011. [CrossRef]
8. Shah, J.M.; Padmanaban, K.; Singh, H.; Asokan, S.D.; Saini, S.; Agonafer, D. Evaluating the reliability of passive server components for single-phase immersion cooling. *J. Electron. Packag.* **2022**, *144*, 021109. [CrossRef]
9. Forster, J.C. Single chip test and burn-in. In Proceedings of the 50th Electronic Components and Technology Conference, Las Vegas, NV, USA, 21–24 May 2000; IEEE: Piscataway, NJ, USA, 2000; pp. 810–814. [CrossRef]
10. Suhir, E. To burn-in, or not to burn-in: That's the question. *Aerospace* **2019**, *6*, 29. [CrossRef]
11. Bepary, M.K.; Talukder, B.M.S.B.; Rahman, M.T. DRAM retention behavior with accelerated aging in commercial chips. *Appl. Sci.* **2022**, *12*, 4332. [CrossRef]
12. White, M.; Qin, J.; Bernstein, J.B. A study of scaling effects on DRAM reliability. In Proceedings of the Annual Reliability and Maintainability Symposium (RAMS), Lake Buena Vista, FL, USA, 24–27 January 2011; IEEE: Piscataway, NJ, USA, 2011; pp. 1–6. [CrossRef]
13. Baeg, S.; Chia, P.C.F.; Wen, S.J.; Wong, R. DRAM failure cases under hot-carrier injection. In Proceedings of the 18th IEEE International Symposium on the Physical and Failure Analysis of Integrated Circuits (IPFA), Incheon, Republic of Korea, 4–8 July 2011; IEEE: Piscataway, NJ, USA, 2011; pp. 1–3. [CrossRef]
14. Wang, T.; Chiang, L.-P.; Zous, N.-K.; Hsu, C.-F.; Huang, L.-Y.; Chao, T.-S. A comprehensive study of hot carrier stress-induced drain leakage current degradation in thin-oxide n-MOSFETs. IEEE Trans. *Electron. Devices* **1999**, *46*, 1877–1882. [CrossRef]
15. Kim, J.-H.; Jeong, Y.-H.; Kim, C.-H.; Kim, J.-H.; Kim, J.-H. DRAM reliability. *Microelectron. Reliab.* **2002**, *42*, 543–553. [CrossRef]
16. Ooi, M.P.-L.; Kassim, Z.A.; Demidenko, S.N. Shortening burn-in test: Application of HVST and Weibull statistical analysis. *IEEE Trans. Instrum. Meas.* **2007**, *56*, 990–999. [CrossRef]

17. Roe, C.; Feng, X.; White, G.; Li, R.; Wang, H.; Rui, X.; Li, C.; Zhang, F.; Null, V.; Parkes, M.; et al. Immersion cooling for lithium-ion batteries—A review. *J. Power Sources* **2022**, *525*, 231094. [CrossRef]
18. Stephan, K.; Laesecke, A. The thermal conductivity of fluid air. *J. Phys. Chem. Ref. Data* **1985**, *14*, 227–234. [CrossRef]
19. Jouhara, H.; Robinson, A.J. Experimental investigation of small diameter two-phase closed thermosyphons charged with water, FC-84, FC-77 and FC-3283. *Appl. Therm. Eng.* **2010**, *30*, 201–211. [CrossRef]
20. Xin, Y.; Ke, H.; Xingyu, D.; Xinlong, W.; Guoyou, L. A Temperature-Dependent Cauer Model Simulation of IGBT Module With Analytical Thermal Impedance Characterization. *IEEE J. Emerg. Sel. Top. Power Electron.* **2021**, *10*, 3055–3065. [CrossRef]
21. Mingyao, M.; Weisheng, G.; Xuesong, Y.; Shuying, Y.; Xing, Z.; Wenjie, C. A Three-Dimensional Boundary-Dependent Compact Thermal Network Model for IGBT Modules in New Energy Vehicles. *IEEE Trans. Ind. Electron.* **2020**, *68*, 5248–5258. [CrossRef]

applied sciences

MDPI

Article

Design of Man-Machine Synergic Lunar Coring Device and Its Coring Dynamic Analysis

Xu Zhang [1], Guoqing Zhang [1,*], Mingzhong Gao [2], Yufeng Wen [1] and Yaohui Wang [1]

1 College of Mechatronics and Control Engineering, Shenzhen University, Shenzhen 518060, China
2 Guangdong Provincial Key Laboratory of Deep Earth Sciences and Geothermal Energy Exploitation and Utilization, Institute of Deep Earth Sciences and Green Energy, College of Civil and Transportation Engineering, Shenzhen University, Shenzhen 518060, China
* Correspondence: zhanggq@szu.edu.cn; Tel.: +86-755-26536306; Fax: +86-755-26557471

Abstract: The Moon is the closest extraterrestrial celestial body to the Earth. Sampling and analysis of lunar regolith or rocks can pave the way for the development and utilization of lunar resources. The acquisition of lunar regolith samples with original stratigraphic information by astronauts on the lunar surface is one of the essential missions in the manned lunar landing project. Therefore, to maintain the original stratigraphic information of the lunar samples during the sampling process while further improving the coring rate and sampling depth, a handheld dual-mode lunar regolith coring device is proposed in this paper. The device innovatively combines impact penetration and rotary drilling sampling, which allows the selection of a suitable sampling method according to the environment. In addition, this study designs a synergic coring device that can be operated by the astronaut and carried on the lander or rover based on the handheld coring device, which can ensure safe and stable coring mission. The mechanical analysis is carried out for the key properties in the coring device, the corresponding mechanical model is established, the structural parameters are optimally designed, and the performance analysis is carried out accordingly. Finally, the impact and drilling process of the coring device is simulated in explicit dynamics, and the results show that the optimized impact module can effectively penetrate the lunar rocks. The research work will provide technical reference and theoretical support for the design of human–machine synergic coring devices in manned lunar exploration missions.

Keywords: manned lunar landing; high-frequency impact; man-machine synergic; coring device

1. Introduction

The moon is the closest extraterrestrial celestial body to the Earth, with abundant mineral resources, and has been the first stop for human deep space exploration. The study of lunar geology can provide insight into the formation and evolution of the moon and thus infer the geological history of other planets in the solar system [1]. At the same time, ice exists at the poles of the moon, and the study of the geological structure of the moon's poles can also provide valuable geological information for the subsequent development of lunar resources and the construction of lunar bases [2–5]. Headed by the United States and the former Soviet Union, countries worldwide have launched more than 100 lunar probes to the moon [6,7]. The United States, the former Soviet Union, and China have realized the sampling work on the lunar surface and obtained information on the lunar regolith structure and mineral elements, laying a solid foundation for the subsequent mining project of lunar resources [8]. There are still many unknown areas on the moon worthy of human exploration, and future lunar exploration will involve deeper drilling, as well as the realization of manned lunar landings and the establishment of lunar research bases [9,10].

The first manned lunar landing was achieved as early as July 1969 with the United States Apollo 11, followed by five other successful manned missions to the moon, sending

12 astronauts to the moon. These manned lunar landings have achieved various results and greatly enriched humanity's knowledge of the moon [11]. Half a century after the first mission to the moon, humanity plans to return to the moon, and several countries have announced the timing of implementing a manned lunar landing. For example, The United States' Artemis lunar landing program, which plans to return to the moon in 2025; China and Russia plan to achieve the first manned mission to the moon in 2030; and countries such as Japan, Italy, and Canada have also joined in the craze to land on the moon [12–14]. The human return to the moon is a comprehensive exploration under new technological conditions and a springboard for the subsequent establishment of a lunar base and manned exploration of more distant planets (including Mars) [15,16]. Coring on the Moon or Mars to maintain the stratigraphic information can provide a good understanding of its geological structure and pave the way for later coring at greater depths [17,18].

One of the essential missions of manned lunar landings is the acquisition of lunar regolith samples with original lamination information by astronauts on the lunar surface. For handheld coring devices, the United States used coring tubes for impact penetration sampling of lunar regolith by astronauts on the Apollo 11, Apollo 12, and Apollo 14 missions. In Apollo15, Apollo16, and Apollo17 missions, the Apollo Lunar Surface Drill (ALSD) was used for sampling. The drilling depth reached 3.05 m in the Apollo 17 mission, which is the deepest depth ever drilled for lunar sampling [19,20]. Chen Huazhi et al. developed a high-frequency impact coring device based on the unidirectional flow effect of particles, which can realize the unidirectional transport effect of particles under vibration conditions and better maintain the stratification of lunar regolith [21,22]. Sun Feng et al. proposed a double-body vibrating through sampling magnetically driven lunar regolith collection method, which has high digging efficiency for loose lunar regolith and a certain crushing effect for hard lunar rocks [23]. Although handheld coring devices play a crucial role in the lunar surface coring process, astronauts have significant limitations in working on the lunar surface [24,25]. For example, the limited working time on the lunar surface; the harsh lunar environment will limit astronauts' travel capability; with increasing sampling depth, the lunar soil density will enlarge, the astronauts' work intensity will increase dramatically, the drill bit may be stuck and overheat damage, etc. [26–28]. A single sampling method may increase the risk of the sampling mission and more likely lead to mission failure. Therefore, to guarantee the safe and effective extraction of lunar surface samples during the manned lunar landing project, a synergic coring device that can be operated handheld by astronauts and installed on the lander or rover is needed.

The coring device in this paper is based on the lunar surface manual impact penetration coring method of Apollo's previous sampling exploration missions. It introduces high-frequency impact penetration and rotary drilling. Moreover, a dual-mode lunar coring device, which is convenient for astronauts to operate, has been developed to meet the performance requirements of the lunar surface handheld sampling device, such as a high coring rate and excellent stratification information retention. In addition, this study further develops the man-machine synergic coring device to reduce the work intensity of astronauts and ensure a safe and stable sampling mission, which will provide support for selecting the lunar surface man-machine synergic coring scheme and the design of the coring device. Some of the coring capabilities of this coring device, including impact energy and coring rate, were analyzed theoretically, and the simulation analysis of the coring performance was conducted to provide theoretical support for the optimization of the coring device.

2. Process Analysis of Coring

Currently, there are two methods to obtain lunar regolith samples with stratigraphic information (information on the layering of soil or rock along the vertical direction): impact penetration and rotary drilling sampling. These two sampling methods have advantages and limitations in the lunar surface sampling process. Rotary drilling methods can be roughly divided into single-blade/double-blade spiral drill rod drilling, hollow drill tube drilling, and no-slippage double-tube soft bag drilling [7]. The single-blade/double-blade spiral drilling method (Figure 1a) has a solid rock-breaking ability and high drilling efficiency. However, this coring method completely loses the stratification of lunar regolith samples. The hollow drill tube drilling method (Figure 1b) has a solid rock-breaking ability and high sampling efficiency and can maintain a certain sample of stratigraphic information. However, the rotary motion of the drilling tube causes the sample particles near the inner wall of the drilling tube to mix up and cannot keep the in situ stratigraphic information well [29]. The no-slippage double-tube soft bag drilling method (Figure 1c) has a hollow drill tube with an embedded holding coring tube and an inward-flip soft bag. A soft bag can collect the sample without slippage during sampling, keeping the sample's stratification [30]. Nevertheless, the mechanism is more complex, and flexible soft bag winding on the small diameter cylinder is bound to squash the force, thus affecting the laminarity of the sample. In addition, during the common drilling and sampling process, the friction between the drilling tool and the lunar regolith and rock generates a large amount of heat, which affects the life of the drilling tool and the quality of the sample [27,31,32]. An in-depth study on the optimal design of drilling tools is needed.

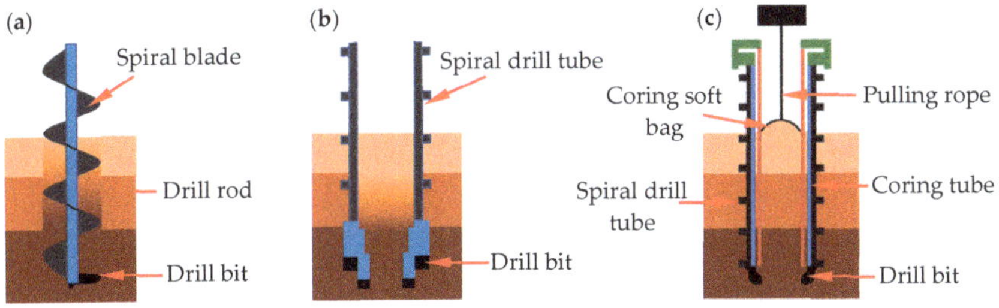

Figure 1. Rotary drilling method diagrams. (**a**) Single-blade/ double-blade spiral drill rod drilling; (**b**) Hollow drill tube drilling; (**c**) No-slippage double-tube soft bag drilling.

Compared with the rotary drilling sampling method, impact penetration coring has better retention of sample stratigraphic information. The impact penetration method is generally used to obtain lunar regolith samples by manually striking the thin-walled coring tube and making the tube penetrate downward continuously [33]. However, the frequency of manual striking is low, and the squeezing of lunar soil particles near the coring tube generates enormous contact stress. This leads to increased friction between the lunar soil particles and the surface of the coring tube, which increases energy consumption and hinders sample collection, as shown in Figure 2a. It is found that high-frequency dynamic impact can reduce the contact stress between the coring tube and lunar soil particles and drive the lunar soil particles on the surface of the coring tube to move toward the lunar surface. The use of coring tubes with an anisotropic frictional surface profile can further enhance the transport effect of lunar soil particles and thus improve the coring rate [34,35]. The coring tube has wedge-shaped "barbs" on the inner and outer surfaces so that the lunar soil particles near the outer wall of the coring tube are discharged from the lunar surface. In contrast, those near the inner wall of the coring tube are transported upward, keeping the length of the sample consistent with the penetration length of the coring tube, as shown in Figure 2b.

These two sampling methods have their respective advantages and limitations in the process of lunar surface sampling. This study combines impact penetration and rotary drilling to ensure a stable sampling process. When working on the lunar surface, the astronaut or lander provides the feed force for the coring device. Impact penetration sampling is used to maximize the original lunar soil stratigraphy information for sampling the lunar regolith layers. When sampling deeper layers or encountering hard lunar rocks, the astronaut can start the impact penetration module and the rotary module at the same time. The coring tube can be replaced by an auger drilling tube to realize the cutting and drilling action of lunar regolith or lunar rocks to achieve the purpose of deep coring, as shown in Figure 2c.

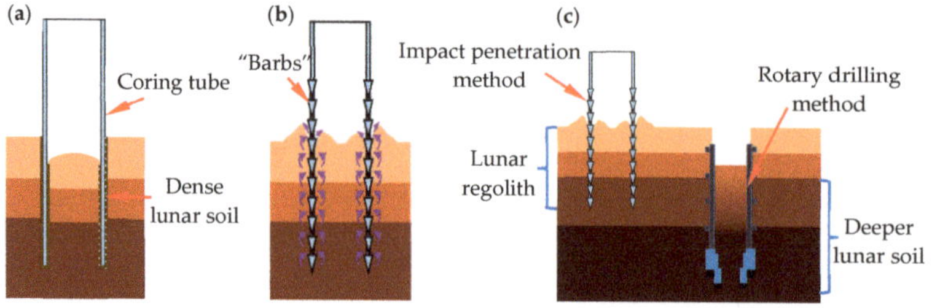

Figure 2. Impact penetration method diagrams. (**a**) Impact penetration coring; (**b**) Impact penetration coring after morphologic treatment; (**c**) Schematic diagram of the dual-mode coring method.

3. Man-Machine Synergic Lunar Coring Device Scheme Design

3.1. Design Requirements for Coring Devices

Coring devices working on the lunar surface are subject to many limitations of the lunar surface environment. For example, overly complex devices are prone to malfunction during work, so coring devices, especially handheld coring devices, should be simple in structure and easy to operate. In the sampling process, the energy required for sampling the lunar regolith at different depths differs, so the coring device should adjust the impact frequency in real time to improve the sampling efficiency. The sampling methods applicable to lunar soil and lunar rockare different, and suitable sampling methods need to be selected for the sampling environment to improve the sampling success rate. When collecting deep samples, the length of the coring tubes needs to be increased. However, too-long coring tubes are not easily transported and operated by astronauts, which requires multiple sections of coring tubes to be interconnected. In particular, it should be noted that the lunar surface environment is very harsh and unsuitable for astronauts to work outside the landing module for long periods. Therefore, the coring device can be hand-held by the astronaut and quickly installed on the lander or rover for the autonomous operation of the coring.

The man-machine synergic coring device should have the following characteristics:

(1) Astronauts' handheld coring device structure should be simple, easy to operate, and low power consumption.
(2) The coring device should have extremely high stability to ensure that the coring missions are carried out safely and stably.
(3) The coring device's impact frequency and energy can be adjusted according to the sampling depth.
(4) The sampling method of the coring device (impact penetration and rotary drilling) can be changed according to the sampling environment.
(5) The coring or drilling tube can be assembled freely to achieve depth sampling.
(6) The handheld coring device is easy to assemble and disassemble and can be mounted on the lander or rover for autonomous operation.

The design parameters of the man-machine synergic coring device were determined by considering the above design requirements and referring to the design parameters of ALSD, as shown in Table 1.

Table 1. Design parameters of the coring device.

Items	Impact Frequency	Impact Energy	Rotational Speed	Single Tube Length	Inner Diameter of Coring Tube	Coring Rate
Parameters	0~20 Hz	5–15 J	0~300 rpm	350 mm	40 mm	≥85%

3.2. Structure Design of the Coring Device

3.2.1. Handheld Dual-Mode Coring Device

The dual-mode coring device mainly includes two methods of coring: impact penetration method and rotary drilling method, and its structural composition is shown in Figure 3a,b.

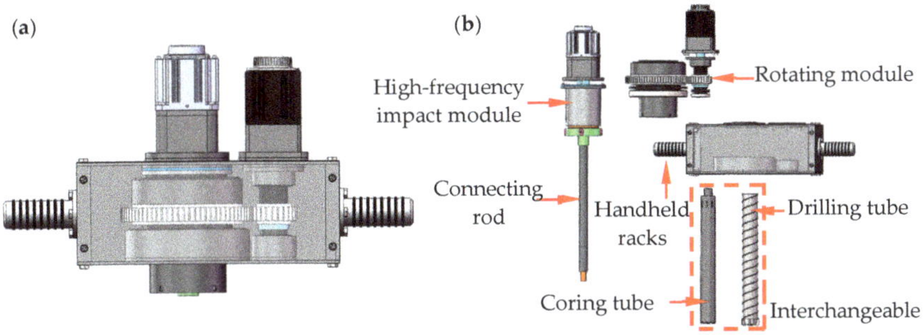

Figure 3. (**a**) Schematic diagram of the handheld dual-mode lunar coring device; (**b**) Handheld coring device module composition diagram.

In the process of sampling the loose lunar regolith layer, to ensure the stratification of the lunar regolith sample to the maximum extent, the impact penetration method sampling is selected, which mainly relies on the high-frequency impact mechanism to realize the coring function. The high-frequency impact mechanism consists of a drive motor, drive shaft, cylindrical cam, energy storage spring, cam roller, impact hammer, and stop-rotation slider, as shown in Figure 4a. The cylindrical cam and the impact hammer are connected, and the impact hammer can only move axially along the limit groove under the restriction of the stop-rotation slider. The rotation of the drive shaft drives the impact hammer to continuously apply high-frequency impact energy on the coring connection body to realize the downward impact penetration action of the coring tube. Adjusting the speed of the drive shaft can change the impact frequency of the impact hammer.

When encountering dense layers of lunar soil or hard lunar rocks that cannot be penetrated, the astronauts can activate the rotating mechanism, relying mainly on gearing. The rotation of the gear drives the movement of the rotating barrel, and the coring connector cooperates with the rotating barrel through the slide key, which does not affect its axial movement along the limit slot while rotating with the rotating barrel. The coring connector further drives the coring tube to cut and drill into the denser lunar soil layer, as shown in Figure 4b. If hard lunar rocks are encountered, and the impact penetration method cannot penetrate, the drive motors of the impact mechanism and rotary mechanism are started at the same time. The coring device is converted into rotary-impact drilling and can achieve excellent drilling results by replacing the bottom penetration coring tube with a spiral drilling tube. The working schematic of the astronaut using the handheld dual-mode coring device is shown in Figure 4c.

The coring tube mainly comprises the sample storage chamber and the debris storage chamber. The sample storage chamber keeps the acquired lunar soil samples in the chamber with stratification. In contrast, the debris storage chamber collects the debris generated during sampling to prevent debris from accumulating in the upper part of the coring tube, which affects the downward penetration of the coring tube and recovery of samples. Therefore, it can effectively reduce the power consumption during the sampling process and improve the sampling efficiency. The inner and outer surfaces of the coring tube are treated to produce a serrated shape, and the rotating cutting teeth set at the bottom can realize the rotating penetration action of the dense lunar soil layer. When a single coring operation is completed and the coring tube is lifted out of the borehole, the debris in the chamber will be discharged out of the tube through the debris removal hole. A schematic diagram of the internal structure of the coring tube is shown in Figure 5a. Unlike the traditional equal-diameter coring tube and connecting tube, the diameter of the connecting rod in this design is smaller than that of the coring tube. The coring structure is similar to the Luoyang shovel (a coring tool, the shovel body is semi-cylindrical and can penetrate more than ten meters of stratum, commonly used in archaeology and prospecting and other fields), as shown in Figure 5b. During the coring process, only the coring tube of the whole coring device is subjected to the frictional force of the lunar soil, which reduces the frictional power consumption and improves the sampling efficiency.

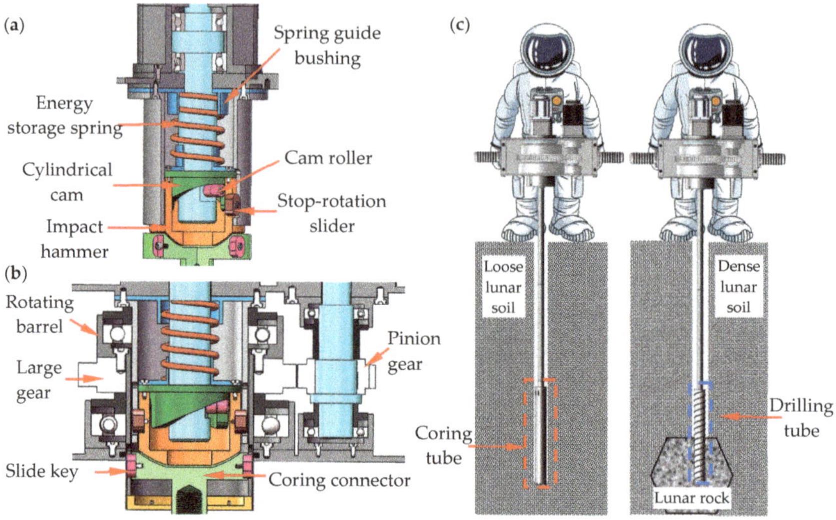

Figure 4. (**a**) Schematic diagram of the structure of the high-frequency impact module; (**b**) Schematic diagram of the structure of the rotating module; (**c**) Schematic diagram of the coring process of the handheld coring device.

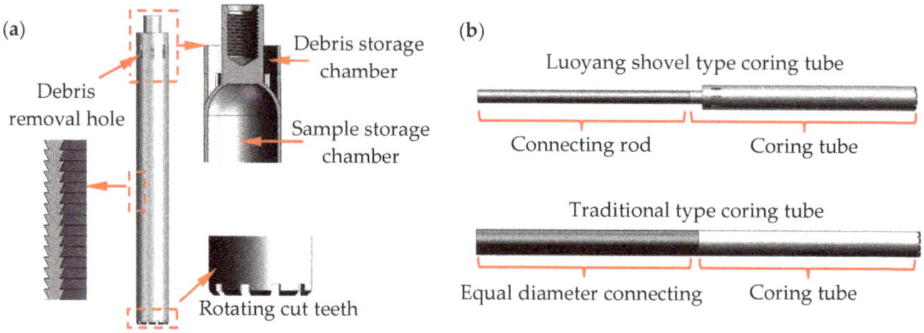

Figure 5. (**a**) Schematic diagram of the structure of the coring tube; (**b**) Comparison of Luoyang shovel-type coring tube and traditional coring tube.

3.2.2. Man-Machine Synergic Coring Device

During a manned lunar mission, astronauts face many limitations and hazards [25]. Therefore, to improve the mobility of the sampling mission, this design is based on the handheld coring device, and the man-machine synergic coring device is designed, as shown in Figure 6a. The astronaut attaches the handheld coring device to the lifting device via a quick interface, and the lifting device provides the feed force for the coring process instead of the astronaut. The drive motor controls the rotation of the chassis rotation device where the coring tube and connecting rod are placed and turns the coring tube and connecting rod to the fixed clamping port, as shown in Figure 6b. The movable clamping device transfers the coring tube or connecting rod to the coring port, and the fixed clamping device assists, and the two work together to realize the assembling and disassembling of the coring tube and connecting rod, as shown in Figure 6c.

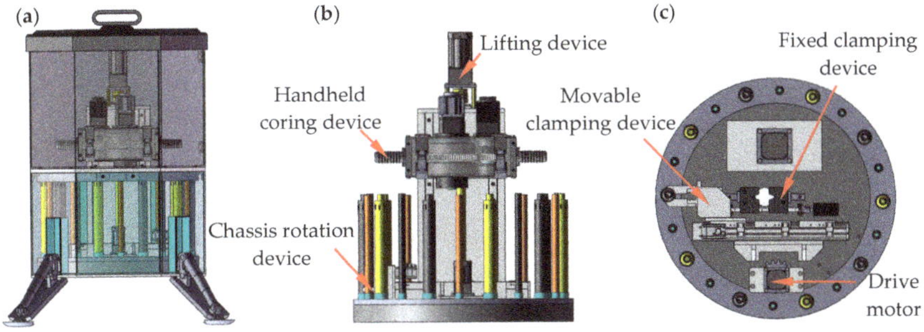

Figure 6. (**a**) Overall structure of the man-machine synergic coring device; (**b**) Internal diagram of the man-machine synergic coring device; (**c**) Clamping device of the man-machine synergic coring device.

A comparison of the dimensions and performance of the handheld and man-machine synergic coring devices is shown in Table 2. The man-machine synergic coring device can be used as a landing module for independent coring on the lunar surface. It can also be installed on the lander or rover for remotely operated coring, as shown in Figure 7.

Table 2. Performance comparison of the handheld coring device and man-machine synergic coring device.

	Outline Dimension/mm (L × W × H)	Weight/kg	Maximum Input Power/kw	Effective Sampling Depth/m
Handheld coring device	400 × 210 × 380	≤25	≤1.5	≥2
Synergic coring device	820 × 800 × 1400	≤150	≤4	≥3

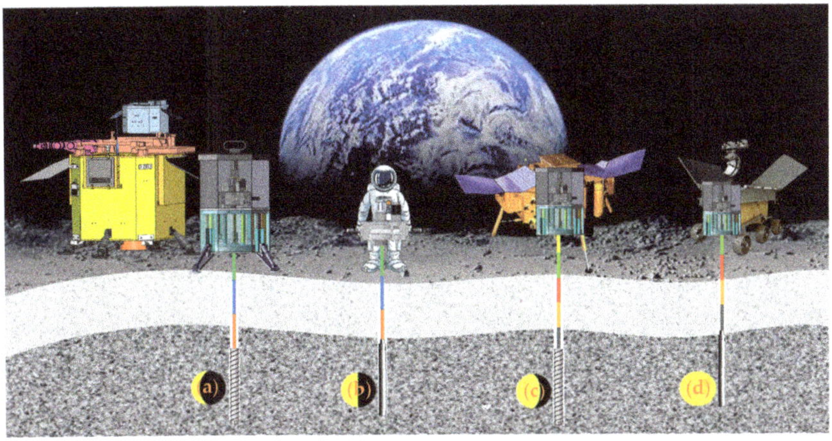

Figure 7. Schematic diagram of the sampling pattern of the coring device. (**a**) Man-machine synergic coring; (**b**) Astronaut handheld coring; (**c**) Coring device mounted on the lander; (**d**) Coring device mounted on rover.

4. Dynamic Analysis and Verification of the Coring Device

The schematic diagram of the impact mechanism is shown in Figure 8a. The cam roller compresses the spring under the action of the contour line of the cylindrical cam and accumulates elastic potential energy. When the cam roller moves to the position of the crest of the cylindrical convex contour line, the elastic potential energy of the spring is released, as shown in Figure 9a. It pushes the follower (cylindrical cam and impact hammer) toward the coring tube at high speed. In turn, the impact sampling of lunar soil or rock is realized.

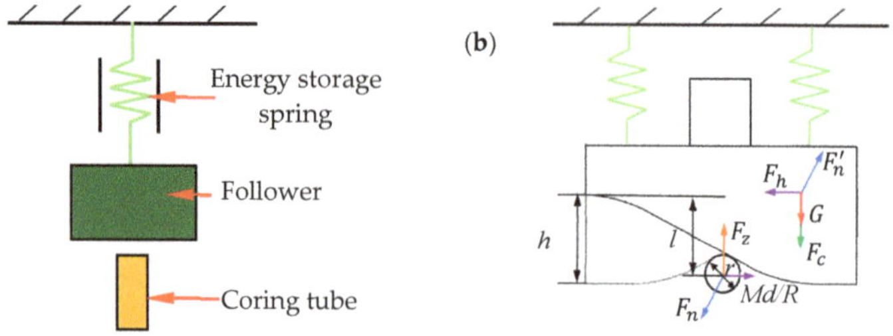

Figure 8. (**a**) Schematic diagram of the impact mechanism; (**b**) Force analysis diagram of the cylindrical cam.

Since the cylindrical cam moves at high speed, the design should pay special attention to the impact of the cam roller when cutting into and out of the convex profile line. Therefore, the convex profile line is selected as a modified sine curve, which means that the profile equation before and after the cam is a sine acceleration motion curve, and the curve in the middle part is an isokinetic motion curve, as shown in Figure 9b. This ensures that the follower maintains a uniform motion for most of its travel and avoids shocks in the start and end phases of the cam.

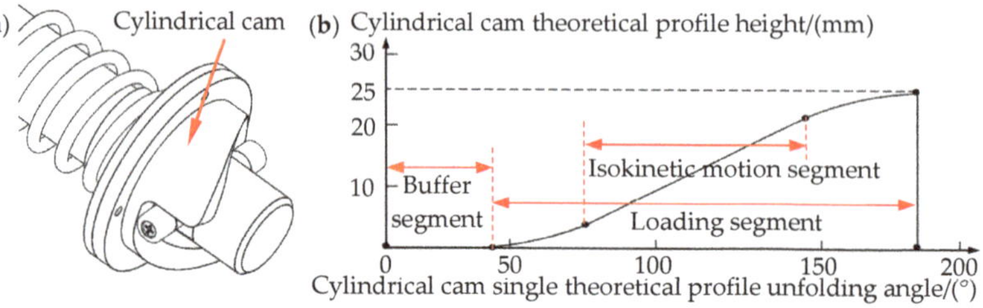

Figure 9. (**a**) Schematic diagram of cylindrical cam; (**b**) Cylindrical cam curve expansion diagram.

To analyze the dynamic and further optimize the structure, a mechanical model between the motor, the cylindrical cam, and the impact hammer was established, and the boundaries of the structural parameters were determined accordingly. Since the impact module achieves energy storage and releases through the cam mechanism, the simplified cam curve is expanded along a straight line for dynamic analysis. The cylindrical cam radius R, spring preload length l_0, cam stroke height h, energy storage spring stiffness k_c, cam loading section ratio α, and cam roller radius r are all impact module structural parameters in Figure 8b. These partial structural parameters need to be optimized and designed before the prototype is made, resulting in the maximum single-impact work under limited conditions.

The relationship between motor torque and cam shape during energy storage of the cylindrical cam can be obtained from Figure 8b:

$$M_d \geq [G + k_c(l_0 + l)]\frac{h}{\pi\alpha} \tag{1}$$

where: M_d is the rated torque of the motor; l is the current axial displacement of the roller; G is the gravity of the impact hammer.

For the impact hammer drop process, if the friction between the impact hammer and the guide wall is neglected, the equation of state of the impact hammer during release is:

$$l = \iint -\left(g_{lunar} + \frac{k(l_0 + l)}{m}\right) \tag{2}$$

Since the equation of the profile line before and after the cylindrical cam is a sinusoidal acceleration motion curve, the initial velocity of the impact hammer in the initial motion condition is 0.

$$\begin{cases} l(0) = l_{max} \\ \dot{l}(0) = 0 \\ \ddot{l}(0) = -\left(g_{lunar} + \frac{k(l_0+l_{max})}{m}\right) \end{cases} \tag{3}$$

The differential equation of the state of motion of the impact hammer is obtained from Equations (2) and (3):

$$l = \left(l_{max} + \frac{mg_{lunar}}{k} + l_0\right)\cos\left(\sqrt{\frac{k}{m}}t\right) - \frac{mg_{lunar}}{k} - l_0 \tag{4}$$

When the cylindrical cam reaches the bottom, i.e., $l = 0$, the time from release to contact of the impact hammer is obtained as:

$$t = \sqrt{\frac{m}{k}}\arccos\left(1 - \frac{l_{max}}{\frac{mg_{lunar}}{k} + l_0 + l_{max}}\right) \tag{5}$$

To ensure that the impact energy of the impact hammer is effectively released to the coring tube, a certain length of the gentle section is set on the cylindrical cam for the release of the impact energy. If the impact energy is fully released at time t_2, the required length of the gentle section of the cam to ensure that the impact energy is fully released before loading is:

$$l_\alpha = \pi R(1 - \alpha) \geq \pi R\lambda(t_1 + t_2) + 2r \tag{6}$$

At present, the rated torque of the impact module motor is 10 Nm, and the speed is 0~1000 rpm, while the estimated mass is 0.9 kg based on the 3D model of the impact hammer and the cylindrical cam. If 5 ms is reserved for the impact hammer impact energy release process, the boundary conditions for the cam height, spring stiffness, and spring preload length can be obtained from Equations (1) and (4), as shown in Figure 10a,b.

By limiting the size of the structural dimensions under the boundary conditions, the structural design parameters that can achieve the maximum impact energy under the boundary conditions can be found, as shown in Figure 10b. The optimized structural parameters of the impact mechanism are shown in Table 3. After optimization, the theoretical maximum single impact energy can reach 14.9 J, which can realize the impact coring effect well.

Table 3. Relevant parameters of the optimized impact structure.

Motor Torque M_d (Nm)	Impact Frequency λ (Hz)	Cam Height h (mm)	Preload Height l_0 (mm)	Spring Elastic Stiffness k (N/m)	Impact Mass m (kg)
10	20	25	10	30,000	0.9

Simulation of the impact process of the simulated lunar rock was carried out in ANSYS Workbench according to the optimized in-structure parameters. The coring and drilling tube materials are chosen as steel material, and the simulated lunar rock is taken as sandstone material. The lunar regolith will not be an entirely loose lunar soil, which can be intermixed with fragmented lunar rocks. If coring tools cannot penetrate the lunar rocks, the coring mission will fail. Therefore, the coring device should perform experiments on the coring performance of simulated lunar rocks to ensure the feasibility of the schemes. According to the lunar rock samples obtained at present, the structure and genesis of lunar rocks can be divided into three categories, namely crystalline igneous rocks, breccias, and lunar soils or moon dust. The simulated lunar rocks have similar mineral composition and chemical composition, similar density, shear modulus, mechanical strength, and Poisson's ratio as the replica of the experimental properties of the lunar samples. The parameter settings of the simulated lunar rock part are shown in Table 4.

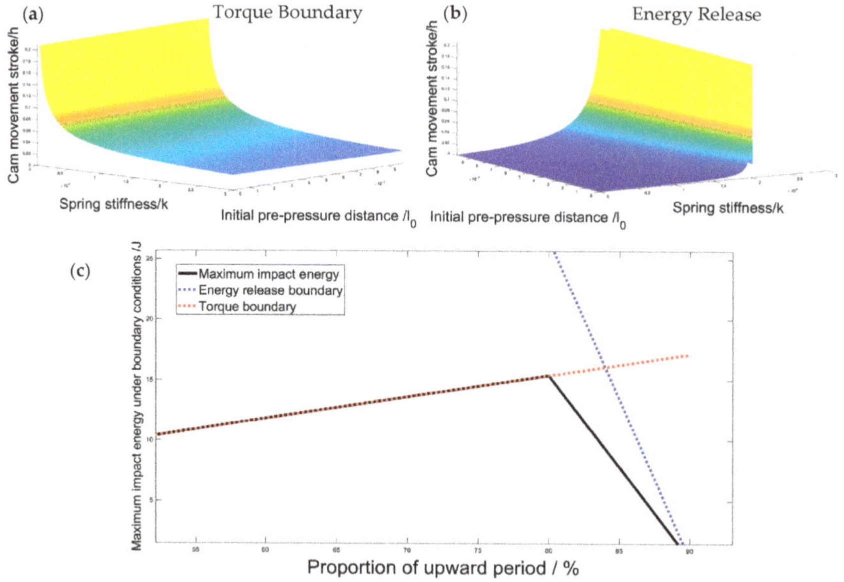

Figure 10. (**a**) Torque boundary conditions for structural parameters of the impact module; (**b**) Energy release boundary conditions for structural parameters of the impact module; (**c**) Maximum impact energy under boundary constraints.

Table 4. Basic physical and mechanical parameters of simulated lunar rock.

Density ρ (kg/m^3)	Shear Modulus G (GPa)	Tensile Strength T (MPa)	Compressive Strength f_c (MPa)	Modulus of Elasticity E (GPa)	Poisson's Ratio ν
2164	4.437	1.107	70.27	12.27	0.38

According to the current international research on lunar coring devices, it is found that the coring process for lunar surface regolith is relatively simple, requiring only 2~4 J of impact energy, and both the coring tube and the drilling tube can achieve the coring work well. However, in the case of hard lunar rocks, the choice of the coring method is significant for the success of the coring process. Therefore, the focus was on coring simulation experiments for simulated lunar rocks. After setting the material parameters of the model, the coring/drilling tube and the simulated lunar rock have meshed, as shown in Figure 11. For the simulated lunar rocks with fixed constraints around the perimeter, the coring and drilling tubes are subjected to the pressure exerted by the coring device regardless of the coring method used (about 200 N, not considering the pressure exerted by the astronauts). When using the coring tube impact penetration method, a certain amount of impact energy (about 14.9 J) is applied to the coring tube. If the coring tube impact rotary penetration method is used, a certain additional rotational speed (300 rpm) is applied to the coring tube, as shown in Figure 11a. When using rotary drilling for coring, only a certain amount of rotational speed is applied to the drilling tube. The sampling method is converted to impact-drilling, as shown in Figure 11b, where additional impact energy is applied to the drill tube to achieve a more significant impact-crushing effect. After setting various parameters, the simulation analysis was performed for different coring methods.

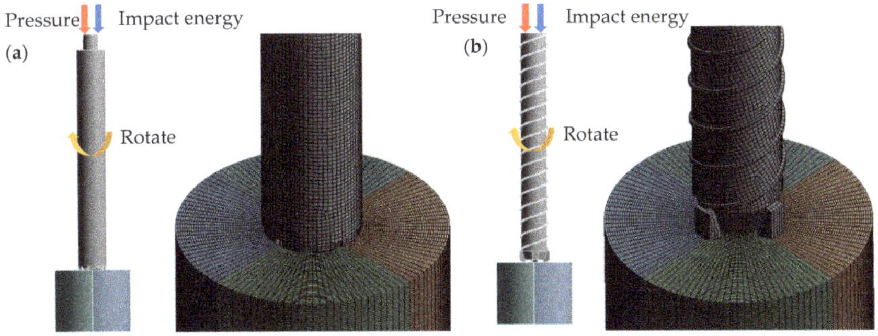

Figure 11. Parameter setting and meshing of the coring model (**a**) Impact penetration method; (**b**) Rotary drilling method.

In the simulation, the impact energy (14.9 J) released by the impact hammer was applied to the coring tube with a loading time assumed to be 5 ms. During the process of impact energy loading, the coring tube has a certain impact effect on the simulated lunar rocks. However, the impact energy alone could not induce significant deformation of the simulated lunar rocks, with a maximum plastic deformation of only 0.029 mm and without the desired impact-crushing effect (Figure 12a). Even if a certain rotation speed is applied based on impact penetration, the crushing effect of the coring tube on the simulated lunar rocks is not very obvious, and the maximum plastic deformation is only 0.042 mm (Figure 12b). The actual geology of the moon is very complex, and the impact penetration method simply cannot penetrate the rock for sampling. Therefore, the coring device must replace the coring tube with an auger tube when facing hard lunar rocks. Compared with the coring tube, the drilling tube has a significant crushing effect on the simulated lunar rocks during rotational drilling, and the maximum plastic deformation of the rocks can reach 0.35 mm within a loading time of 5 ms (Figure 12c). When a certain amount of impact energy (14.9 J) is added to the rotation drilling process, the sampling method will be converted to impact drilling type, and the crushing effect on the simulated lunar rocks will be significantly increased. The maximum plastic deformation of the simulated lunar rocks can be increased to 0.47 mm during the loading period (Figure 12d). Therefore, according to the sampling environment, choosing the appropriate sampling method can improve sampling efficiency, ensuring the work is safe and stable.

In summary, the magnitude of the impact energy (5~15 J) is closely related to the structural parameters of the impact module and the impact frequency. In addition, the impact frequency also affects the response speed of the impact energy. The impact frequency can be adjusted within 0~20 Hz, and the increase in the impact frequency can effectively destroy the formation of internal stress in the coring tube and improve the coring rate. Although the coring tube under the action of impact energy can achieve the sampling of lunar regolith, the simulation results show that the coring tube cannot penetrate the rock. Therefore, only with the combined effect of impact energy and rotation speed can the drilling tube achieve a significant crushing effect on the lunar rock. In addition, the impact frequency and rotation speed are adjustable to suit different sampling environments.

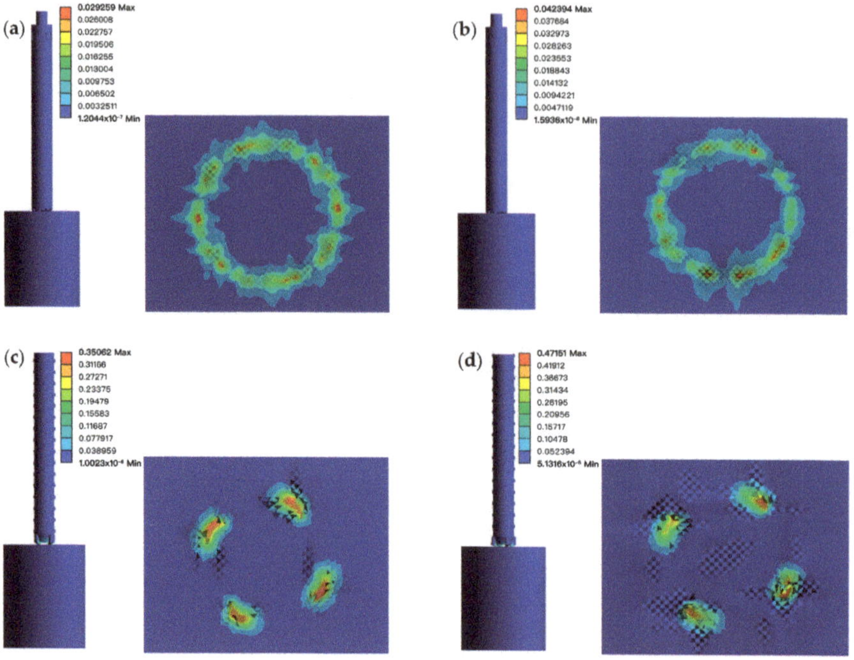

Figure 12. Crushing effects on simulated lunar rocks under different conditions (Strain, mm) (**a**) Coring tube under impact; (**b**) Coring tube under impact and rotation; (**c**) Drilling tube under rotation; (**d**) Drilling tube under impact and rotation.

5. Conclusions

In this paper, a scheme is designed for a synergic coring device in a manned lunar landing sampling mission. It can be handheld by astronauts and mounted on a lander or rover to collect deeper lunar soil samples in their original state. The main work and conclusions are as follows:

(1) In response to the problem of the low coring rate of the static impact penetration method, a composite coring method of high-frequency impact penetration and rotary drilling coring is proposed. According to the simulation analysis, the impact-rotary drilling method is the more effective way to achieve rock crushing and coring in the lunar regolith.

(2) The coring device for astronauts' handheld operation was designed according to the requirements of coring exploration for the manned lunar landing. The coring device can change the impact frequency (0~20 Hz), impact energy (5~15 J), and rotation speed (0~300 rpm) to adapt to different working environments during the operation. The coring tube and connecting rod can be interconnected to obtain deep lunar soil samples.

(3) The impact module of the coring device was simulated and analyzed for its ability to crush rocks in the lunar regolith, and the optimal impact structure based on the spring energy storage scheme was determined. Additionally, the impact process is simulated by ANSYS explicit dynamics to determine the impact-crushing effect of the coring device on the lunar rocks. Under the action of the maximum impact energy (14.9 J), it can produce a plastic deformation effect of 0.47 mm on the lunar rocks within a time period of 5 ms.

(4) Based on the handheld coring device, a man-machine synergic coring device was designed that can be carried on the lander or rover to address the many constraints of

astronauts sampling on the lunar surface. This coring device provides more significant drilling pressure and counter torque, significantly reducing the work effort of the astronauts and increasing the sampling depth.

The man-machine synergic coring device has a broad application prospect in the manned lunar landing sampling mission. In future research, the optimized design of a coring device will be carried out to further improve the synergy between the astronaut and man-machine synergic coring devices and achieve the goals of low power consumption, lightweight, and high coring rate.

Author Contributions: X.Z. and G.Z. completed the main research tasks and wrote the manuscript. G.Z. revised the whole manuscript. M.G. proposed the initial ideas and finished deriving the theory related to soil mechanics. Y.W. (Yufeng Wen) and Y.W. (Yaohui Wang) assisted in the design of the mechanical structure. All authors have read and agreed to the published version of the manuscript.

Funding: The work described in this paper was supported by the National Natural Science Foundation of China (Grant Nos. U2013603, 51827901) and the Shenzhen Natural Science Foundation (Grant Nos. JCYJ20220531103614032, 20200826160002001, JCYJ20220818102409021).

Institutional Review Board Statement: Not applicable.

Informed Consent Statement: Not applicable.

Data Availability Statement: Not applicable.

Conflicts of Interest: The authors declare no conflict of interest.

References

1. Halliday, A.N. Terrestrial accretion rates and the origin of the Moon. *Earth Planet. Sci. Lett.* **2000**, *176*, 17–30. [CrossRef]
2. Kenyo, U.; Hasumi, H.; Ogawa, M. Effects of magma-generation and migration on the expansion and contraction history of the Moon. *Earth Planets Space* **2022**, *74*, 78. [CrossRef]
3. Kereszturi, A. Polar Ice on the Moon. In *Encyclopedia of Lunar Science*; Cudnik, B., Ed.; Springer International Publishing: Cham, Switzerland, 2020; pp. 1–9.
4. Spudis, P.D.; Bussey, D.B.J.; Baloga, S.M.; Cahill, J.T.S.; Glaze, L.S.; Patterson, G.W.; Raney, R.K.; Thompson, T.W.; Thomson, B.J.; Ustinov, E.A. Evidence for water ice on the Moon: Results for anomalous polar craters from the LRO Mini-RF imaging radar. *J. Geophys. Res. Planets* **2013**, *118*, 2016–2029. [CrossRef]
5. Boazman, S.; Kereszturi, A.; Heather, D.; Sefton-Nash, E.; Orgel, C.; Tomka, R.; Houdou, B.; Lefort, X. *Analysis of the Lunar South Polar Region for PROSPECT, NASA/CLPS*; Copernicus Meetings: Palacio de Congresos de Granada, Spain, 2022.
6. Slyuta, E. The Luna program. In *Sample Return Missions*; Elsevier: Amsterdam, The Netherlands, 2021; pp. 37–78.
7. Zhang, T.; Xu, K.; Yao, Z.; Ding, X.; Zhao, Z.; Hou, X.; Pang, Y.; Lai, X.; Zhang, W.; Liu, S.; et al. The progress of extraterrestrial regolith-sampling robots. *Nat. Astron.* **2019**, *3*, 487–497. [CrossRef]
8. Wen, Y.; Zhang, G.; Xie, H.; Gao, M.; Zhang, X.; Wang, Y.; Li, C. Design and Dynamic Analysis of the Wire-Line Coring Robot for Deep Lunar Rocks. *Appl. Sci.* **2023**, *13*, 1722. [CrossRef]
9. Sun, W.; Wang, Z.; Zhao, Q. Lunar Exploration and Development Vision. *Aerosp. China* **2020**, *21*, 28–34.
10. Guardabasso, P.; Paternostro, S.; Bedialauneta, P.; Fonteyne, R. Lunar landing necessary building blocks and good practices for a sustainable development of human lunar activities. *Acta Astronaut.* **2023**, *202*, 782–790. [CrossRef]
11. Scherer, L. The Apollo Missions. *Highlights Astron.* **1971**, *2*, 125–141. [CrossRef]
12. MacIsaac, D. NASA Returns to the Moon: The Artemis Missions. *Phys. Teach.* **2023**, *61*, 239. [CrossRef]
13. Crane, L. A Different Kind of Space Race. *New Sci.* **2022**, *255*, 39–41. [CrossRef]
14. Gross, J. From Apollo to Artemis and beyond: How the Apollo Next Generation Sample Analyses (ANGSA) program helps to prepare for future sample missions to the Moon and beyond. In Proceedings of the AAS/Division for Planetary Sciences Meeting Abstracts, London, ON, Canada, 2–7 October 2022; p. 110.103.
15. Xu, L.; Li, H.; Pei, Z.; Zou, Y.; Wang, C. A Brief Introduction to the International Lunar Research Station Program and the Interstellar Express Mission. *Chin. J. Space Sci.* **2022**, *42*, 511–513. [CrossRef]
16. Biswal, M.; Malaya, K.; Gomez-Fernandez, D.; Das, N.B.; Kumar V, R. Design Study and Validation of Mars Underground Habitat for Human Settlement on Mars. In Proceedings of the AIAA Propulsion and Energy 2021 Forum, Virtual Event, 9–11 August 2021; p. 3725.
17. Kereszturi, A.; Bradak, B.; Chatzitheodoridis, E.; Ujvari, G. Indicators and Methods to Understand Past Environments from ExoMars Rover Drills. *Orig. Life Evol. Biosph.* **2016**, *46*, 435–454. [CrossRef]
18. Yang, H.; Yang, R.; Wang, Q. Laboratory construction and curation scheme for returned samples of the chang'e-5 mission. *Geosci. Lett.* **2022**, *9*, 19. [CrossRef]

19. Zhang, T.; Wang, B.; Wei, H.; Zhang, Y.; Chao, C.; Xu, K.; Ding, X.; Hou, X.; Zhao, Z. Review on planetary regolith-sampling technology. *Prog. Aerosp. Sci.* **2021**, *127*, 100760. [CrossRef]
20. Zhang, X.; Zhang, G.; Xie, H.; Gao, M.; Wen, Y. A Review of Sampling Exploration and Devices for Extraterrestrial Celestial Bodies. *Space Sci. Rev.* **2022**, *218*, 59. [CrossRef]
21. Chen, H.; Li, L.; Cui, Y.; Jiang, S. A novel lunar soil coring approach based on particle unidirectional flow effect to reduce drag and increase efficiency. *Adv. Space Res.* **2021**, *68*, 117–133. [CrossRef]
22. Chen, H.; Liu, R.; Ma, C.; Jiang, S. Design of handheld corer for lunar regolith based on particle directional flow method. *J. Deep Space Explor.* **2020**, *7*, 164–170. [CrossRef]
23. Sun, F.; Huo, X.; Mao, M.; Zhao, H.; Xu, F.; Zhang, W.; Chen, H.; Tang, J.; Zhang, X.; Liu, Y. Design of Double-Body Vibration Penetration Lunar Soil Sampler by Magnetic Driven. *J. Deep Space Explor.* **2022**, *9*, 157–164. [CrossRef]
24. Delp, M.D.; Charvat, J.M.; Limoli, C.L.; Globus, R.K.; Ghosh, P. Apollo Lunar Astronauts Show Higher Cardiovascular Disease Mortality: Possible Deep Space Radiation Effects on the Vascular Endothelium. *Sci. Rep.* **2016**, *6*, 29901. [CrossRef]
25. Braddock, M. Hazards of Lunar Regolith for Respiratory, Central Nervous System, Cardiovascular and Ocular Function. *Hum. Factor Settl. Moon Interdiscip. Approach* **2021**, *9*, 141–157. [CrossRef]
26. Zacny, K.; Bar-Cohen, Y.; Brennan, M.; Briggs, G.; Cooper, G.; Davis, K.; Dolgin, B.; Glaser, D.; Glass, B.; Gorevan, S.; et al. Drilling systems for extraterrestrial subsurface exploration. *Astrobiology* **2008**, *8*, 665–706. [CrossRef] [PubMed]
27. Zhao, D.; Cheng, Z.; Zhang, W.; Cui, J.; Wang, H. Numerical Modeling of Thermal Behavior during Lunar Soil Drilling. *Aerospace* **2023**, *10*, 472. [CrossRef]
28. Korotev, R.L.; Haskin, L.A. Some lessons from Apollo for a sampling strategy on Mars for understanding the origin of the ancient igneous crust and the composition of the mantle. In Proceedings of the Lunar and Planetary Institute, Workshop on Mars Sample Return Science, Houston, TX, USA, 16–18 November 1987.
29. Kereszturi, Á.; Duvet, L.; Gróf, G.; Gyenis, Á.; Gyenis, T.; Kapui, Z.; Kovács, B.; Maros, G. Characterization and first results of the planetary borehole-wall imager—Methods to develop for in-situ exploration. *Open Astron.* **2019**, *28*, 13–31. [CrossRef]
30. Liang, J.; Tao, L.; Zhang, W.; Tang, J.; Pang, Y.; Jiang, S. Analysis of the lunar regolith sample obstruction in the Chang'E-5 drill and its improvement. *Adv. Space Res.* **2022**, *69*, 2248–2258. [CrossRef]
31. Tian, Y.; Zhang, J.; Zhang, W.; Xu, B.; Duan, Z. Drill-soil penetration model and its application to lunar exploration. *Adv. Space Res.* **2022**, *70*, 3436–3449. [CrossRef]
32. Xu, J.; Yuan, X.; Zhang, Y.; Yu, S.; Pang, Y.; Zhang, T.; Xu, K.; Ding, X. Real-time prediction of drilling forces inside lunar regolith based on recurrent neural networks. *Acta Astronaut.* **2022**, *201*, 259–273. [CrossRef]
33. Zhao, D.; Cheng, Z.; Zeng, K.; Hu, M.; Gao, X. Optimized design of high-efficiency lunar soil sampling tube structure based on stress–strain law. *Adv. Space Res.* **2023**, *71*, 2128–2139. [CrossRef]
34. Gao, Y.; Ellery, A.; Jaddou, M.; Vincent, J. Deployable wood wasp drill for planetary subsurface sampling. In Proceedings of the 2006 IEEE Aerospace Conference, Big Sky, MT, USA, 4–11 March 2006; p. 8.
35. Gao, Y.; Ellery, A.; Jaddou, M.; Vincent, J.; Eckersley, S. Planetary micro-penetrator concept study with biomimetic drill and sampler design. *IEEE Trans. Aerosp. Electron. Syst.* **2007**, *43*, 875–885. [CrossRef]

applied sciences

MDPI

Article

An Innovative System of Deep In Situ Environment Reconstruction and Core Transfer

Xiaobo Peng [1,*], Xiongjun Li [2,*], Shigang Yang [1], Jinjie Wu [2], Mingwei Wu [2], Langhui Wan [2], Huaiyu Zhang [2] and Heping Xie [3]

1. Guangdong Key Laboratory of Electromagnetic Control and Intelligent Robot, College of Mechatronics and Control Engineering, Shenzhen University, Shenzhen 518060, China
2. College of Physics and Optoelectronic Engineering, Shenzhen University, Shenzhen 518060, China
3. Guangdong Provincial Key Laboratory of Deep Earth Sciences and Geothermal Energy Exploitation and Utilization, Institute of Deep Earth Sciences and Green Energy, College of Civil and Transportation Engineering, Shenzhen University, Shenzhen 518060, China

* Correspondence: pengxb@szu.edu.cn (X.P.); lixj@szu.edu.cn (X.L.)

Featured Application: Only when deep in situ rock samples are tested in the same environments as their occurrences can their true physical and mechanical properties be obtained. Therefore, a fidelity test system that can simulate the deep in situ geological conditions has become an urgent need to promote the deep in situ rock mechanics. This work is the key component of the fidelity test system, being used to accurately reconstruct a deep in situ high-temperature and high-pressure environment in the system.

Abstract: The reconstruction of deep in situ environment up to 95 °C and 70 MPa using water is critical for the fidelity testing of deep Earth rocks. The temperature and pressure of the water have strong coupling in such an environment, which makes the control of temperature and pressure very difficult. The paper firstly presents the design of the system of deep in situ environment reconstruction and core transfer (SERCT); secondly, for the problem of high temperature and pressure control, a pressure-temperature (P-T) interpolation control algorithm based on the iso–density P-T curves of water is proposed. A P-T coupling control path is decomposed into two independent interpolation paths: an iso–thermal pressure control and an iso–mass temperature control, which realizes the decoupling control of temperature and pressure. Then, a fuzzy-PID dual mode method is adopted for the pressure control after decoupling, which reduces the overshoot and the dynamic response time of the system. For temperature control, a segmented and grouped electric heating mode is designed to improve the uniformity of the temperature field. A fuzzy PID temperature control algorithm based on grey prediction is proposed to achieve high precision temperature control with small overshoot. Finally, the effectiveness of the proposed methods is verified by experiments.

Keywords: deep in situ environment; deep Earth rock; pressure-temperature decoupling control; fuzzy PID control; grey prediction

1. Introduction

As the shallow resources are gradually exhausted, human beings began to collect resources from the deep Earth [1]. Rocks at different depths may have different physical and mechanical properties. However, currently the basic physical and mechanical properties of rocks, such as porosity, Poisson's ratio, elastic modulus, etc., are obtained by empirical rock mechanics theory and experimental methods based on standard cores, in which the effects of deep in situ environment, such as temperature and pressure, are not considered, and the obtained parameters, mathematical models and theories are independent of the occurrence depth of rocks [2,3].

Therefore, it is necessary to analyze the physical and mechanical behaviors of rocks in the deep in situ environment, and develop a rock mechanics theory that considers the influence of the deep in situ environment [4]. To achieve this goal, a platform that can reconstruct and simulate the deep in situ environment of high temperature and high pressure—and complete the transfer, preparation and testing of the core in this environment—is essential. One key difficulty in the development of this platform is the control of temperature and pressure, because under high temperature and pressure, the temperature and the pressure affect each other, and the movement of core may cause great fluctuations in pressure and temperature.

In this study, the SERCT is designed to reconstruct a deep in situ environment of 2500 m underground. At this depth, the temperature is approximately 95 °C and the pressure is highly likely to be less than 70 MPa. A P-T decoupling control method is then proposed to achieve the in situ environment reconstruction with high temperature (up to 95 °C) and high pressure (up to 70 MPa). For the independent controls of pressure and temperature after decoupling, a fuzzy-PID dual mode pressure control and a fuzzy PID temperature control based on grey prediction are presented.

2. Related Works

Deep in situ environment reconstruction is mainly used in the field of deep Earth and deep sea science research to build the deep in situ environment with specific temperature and pressure [5]. Researchers in the United States, Japan, Russia, South Korea, etc., began their study early in this field and have achieved significant results [6].

As early as 1951, a U.S. naval shipyard built a deep sea pressure simulation device, achieving a cyclic pressurization of 0.1–4 MPa with a maximum pressure of 4.2 MPa [7]. After that, a device with a maximum pressure of 82.75 MPa was developed [8]. A periodic pressure test device with a maximum pressure of 156 MPa was developed in Japan [9]. Furthermore, a medium-sized chamber was subsequently developed to simulate the dynamic pressure environment up to 154.9 MPa, and its maximum working pressure in the circulation mode could reach 113.7 MPa [10]. Researchers in Russia developed a series of deep sea environment simulation platforms, which could realize the test pressure up to 150 MPa [11]. The above equipment only focused on the pressure loading, and the influence of temperature was not considered.

In the fields of P-T control and core test under the in situ fidelity environment, researchers in the U.K., E.U., U.S. and China have achieved impressive results [12]. The MSCL system developed by Geotek in 2003 could be used for parametric analysis of cores or seafloor sediments. Although this system was not strictly a fidelity system, it helped to accumulate rich experience in core transfer under in situ fidelity environment [13,14]. In 2009, Geotek developed the PCATS system on the basis of MSCL, which could achieve a maximum pressure of 35 MPa and a temperature control of 4–20 °C. The HYACINTH system developed in Europe could cut, transfer and test samples in an in situ pressure environment with a maximum pressure of 25 MPa [15]. The pressure-holding transfer device for natural gas hydrate developed by Zhejiang University in China could achieve fidelity testing at a temperature of 2–4 °C and a pressure of up to 30 MPa [16].

In temperature and pressure control, many control methods have been produced. The earlier temperature control methods such as fuzzy logic controller [17], intelligent control [18] and cascade controller [19] all have good performance, but their computational efficiency and stability need to be further improved. Recently, temperature control methods based on prediction began to attract attention. The prediction-based methods have a good performance in improving response speed and reducing overshoot. Shakeri et al. proposed an intelligent random model prediction method, which used path integration method and particle swarm optimization algorithm to achieve optimal control of temperature [20]. Shi et al. proposed a delay-range-dependent robust constrained model predictive control method, which had better track and anti-interference performance for temperature control [21]. Aguilar et al. proposed a dual input and dual output predictive control strategy, which improved the production efficiency of temperature control [22]. In terms of pressure control, on the basis of the early standard PID control method, a lot of improved methods, such as fuzzy PID control, BP neural network control, and PID control based on ant colony algorithm, have been developed [23,24]. These methods generally have better performance than the conventional PID method. In the decoupling control of pressure and temperature, researchers in the chemical industry adopted the pressure-compensated temperature control method for the temperature and pressure control of mixed gas [25,26]. Zheng et al. proposed a dynamic pressure control method based on LPID, which created a scheduling table by pre calculated PID parameters, performed PID compensation under different temperature and pressure conditions, and realized stable pressure control [27].

In general, the existing research on in situ environmental reconstruction and core transfer systems needs further improvement in two aspects. On the one hand, a deep in situ simulation environment with higher temperature and higher pressure at the same time is necessary to obtain a wider range of the system applications; on the other hand, dynamic pressure and temperature control during the course of building the deep in situ environment and moving the cores, especially the P-T decoupling control under high pressure and high temperature, needs to be further explored.

3. Design of the SERCT

3.1. System Functions and Composition

The SERCT simulates the pressure and temperature of the environment where the cores stay in the deep Earth; additionally, it is the platform where the cores are moved and prepared for the fidelity physics test. The system composition is shown in Figure 1.

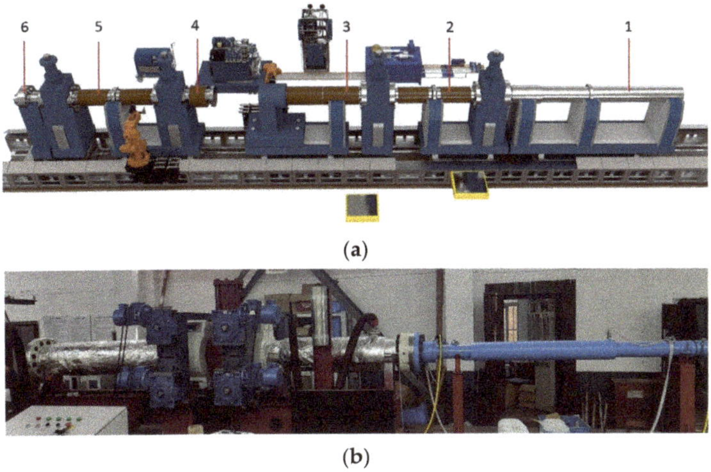

Figure 1. The SERCT; (**a**) The composition of the SERCT; (**b**) The actual picture of the SERCT.

As shown in Figure 1a, 1 is the push rod chamber. The push rod opens the docking chamber 3 which is the device for transporting the core from the deep Earth, grabs the core, pulls it out of the docking chamber, and transfers it between chambers. Moreover, 2 is the storage chamber used for temporary storage of the core; 4 is the non-contact test chamber for acoustic and electromagnetic tests of the core; 5 is the preparation chamber for core sample preparation; 6 is the pressure test chamber for core samples. The chambers are connected through high pressure flat gate valves.

During the core preparation and test, all the chambers are full of water whose pressure and temperature are kept the same as those inside the docking chamber. When the push rod moves or the valves open or close, the fluctuation of temperature and pressure should be less than ±3% F.S.

3.2. The Temperature and Pressure Decoupling Control System

The temperature and pressure control of SERCT is divided into two types: (1) Initial environment reconstruction and (2) P-T preservation. The initial environment reconstruction establishes the target deep in situ temperature and pressure in the chamber from the normal temperature and pressure, which is a heating and pressurizing process. The P-T preservation means that after the initial environment reconstruction finishes, the system needs to reduce the fluctuations of the temperature and pressure caused by the movements of the push rod and the valves.

The structure of the temperature and pressure control system is shown in Figure 2a. The loop of water includes: the working chamber, the pressure relief valve, the water tank, the preheating chamber, and the booster valve. We use a two-layer control structure for temperature and pressure control: in the inner layer, the central controller obtains the data of the temperature sensors and the pressure sensor located in the working chamber, plans the decoupling control targets of temperature and pressure based on the sensor data and transmits the targets to the temperature controller and the pressure controller, respectively. In the outer layer, the temperature and pressure are independently controlled. The decoupling control flow of temperature and pressure is shown in Figure 2b. The pressure control is accomplished through the pressure valves. The temperature control is much more complicated because SERCT is a complex nonlinear large time-delay system. In order to increase the speed of temperature regulation, a preheating chamber is designed to preheat the water to be as close to the target temperature as possible before it is replenished into the working chambers. In this way, when the target temperature is below 100 °C, the preheated water replenished into the working chambers causes little temperature change or fluctuations. When the target temperature is higher than 100 °C, by preheating the water, the temperature difference between the replenished water and the water in the working chambers is reduced, and thus, the time for temperature adjustment can be greatly shortened.

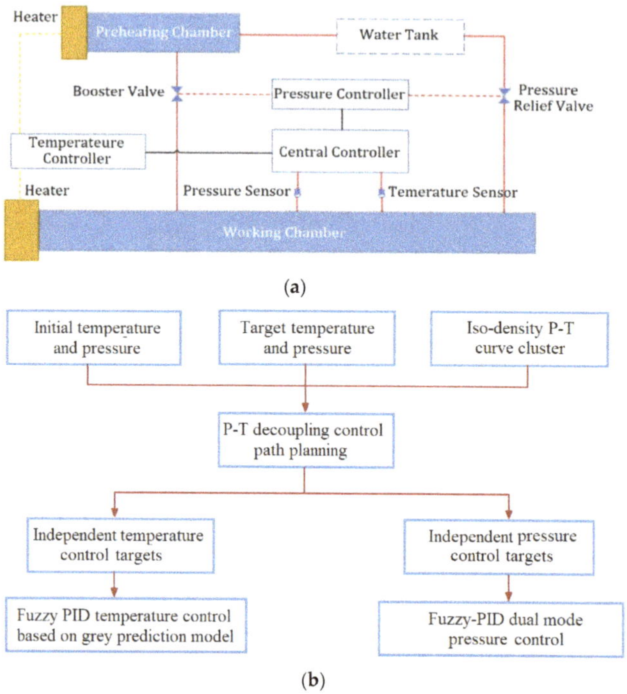

Figure 2. The temperature and pressure decoupling control system; (**a**) the structure of the temperature and pressure decoupling control system; (**b**) the decoupling control flow of temperature and pressure.

4. Temperature and Pressure Decoupling Control Based on the Iso–Density Curves of Water

4.1. State Surface of Water

According to IAPWS R6-95 (2018) [28], the state equation of liquid water within the range of 0~1000 MPa and 0~1000 °C is as follows:

$$p = \rho RT(1 + \delta\phi_\delta^r) \quad (1)$$

where p, ρ and T are, respectively, the pressure, density and temperature of water; the gas constant of water $R = 0.4651805$ Kj·kg^{-1}·K^{-1}; the critical density of water $\rho_c = 322$ kg·m^{-3}; $\delta = \rho/\rho_c$; the meaning of ϕ_δ^r was presented in [28].

We created the surface decided by Equation (1), as shown in Figure 3. It can be seen that if the density of water is constant, when its temperature rises, its pressure will increase accordingly.

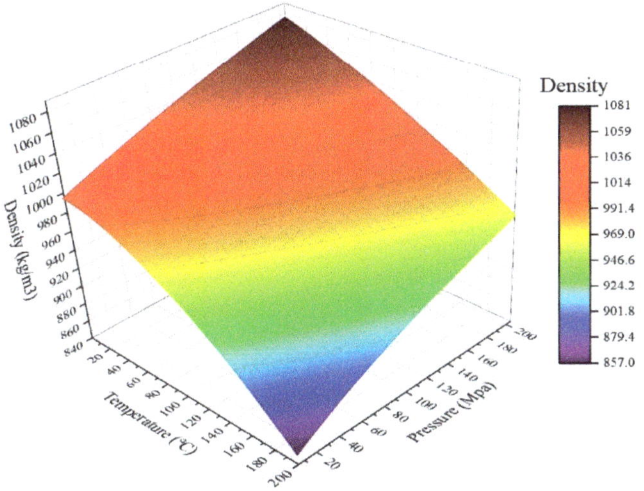

Figure 3. State surface of water.

4.2. Digitization of the Iso–Density Curves of Water

Equation (1) is too complicated to use in the temperature and pressure control. Alternatively, we create a set of iso–density P-T curves on the surface in Figure 3, and project these curves to the P-T plane; then, we get the iso–density P-T curve cluster of water as shown in Figure 4. Under the condition of constant density, the P-T relationship of water varies along a certain curve in the cluster. When the temperature changes, the pressure will change accordingly. When filling or draining water, the P-T relationship will jump to another curve due to the change of the water density. The mutual influence between temperature and pressure of water in the chambers makes it difficult to control the temperature and pressure precisely. To this end, we propose a P-T interpolation control method based on the iso–density P-T curves of water, which decomposes a P-T coupling path into two kinds of independent interpolation paths: iso–thermal pressure control and iso–density temperature control. The former only needs pressure control, and the latter only needs temperature control. As shown in Figure 4, the straight line $\overline{AF}$ is a P-T coupling path, and it can be decomposed into two iso–density temperature paths (solid curves) $\widehat{AB}$ and $\widehat{DE}$, and two iso–thermal pressure paths $\overline{BD}$ and $\overline{EF}$.

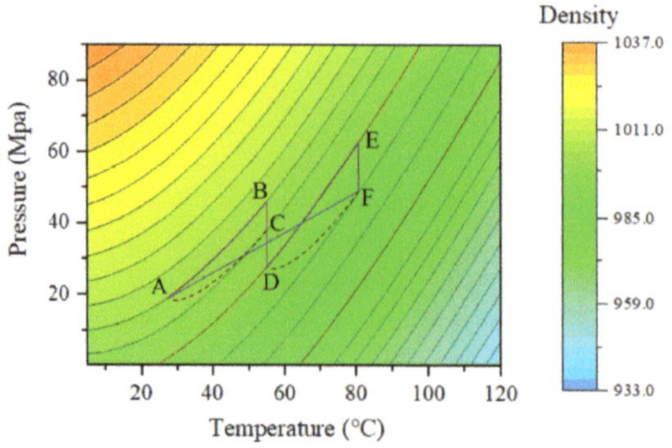

Figure 4. The iso–density P-T curve cluster of water and the interpolation control paths.

Sample each iso–density curve to generate its fitting equation, and the iso–density P-T curve cluster $S(C)$ can be expressed as:

$$S(C) = \{Curve_i \mid i = 1, \ldots, n\} \tag{2}$$

where

$$Curve_i\text{: } P_i = \{f_{ij}(T) \mid T \in [T_j, T_{j+1}]\} \tag{3}$$

Is the ith iso–density curve equation, and P_i is a piecewise fitting function, with the T axis being divided into n_i segments by $n_i + 1$ points $T_s = \{T_1, \ldots, T_{ni+1}\}$. It can be seen in Figure 4 that the shapes of the curves are regular, with no large curvature change or inflection point. Therefore, we use cubic polynomials to perform piecewise curve fitting, with the fitting errors less than 0.1 bar. In this way, each curve $Curve_i$ can be expressed as:

$$P_i = \sum_{j=1}^{n_i} \sum_{k=0}^{3} a_{jk} T^k \tag{4}$$

In which if $T \notin (T_j, T_{j+1}]$, $a_{jk} = 0 \,\Big|\, k = 0, 1, 2, 3$.

If a state point $S(P_s, T_s)$ satisfies Equation (5), then it is on the curve $Curve_s$.

$$|P_s - P_i| \leq \delta_c \tag{5}$$

where δ_c is the error threshold.

4.3. Initial Environment Reconstruction

As shown in Figure 4, let the initial state of a reconstruction process be A(ρ_a, P_a, T_a), and the reconstruction goal be F(ρ_f, P_f, T_f). The straight line $\overline{AF}$ is the ideal P-T control curve which is a P-T coupling control.

The proposed decoupling control method decouples $\overline{AF}$ by interpolation. First, heat the water from A to B along the iso–density curve $Curve_a$ where point A is located; then, conduct iso–thermal pressure relief from B to D. $\overline{BD}$ is a vertical line. $\hat{AB}$ and $\overline{BD}$ are decoupled independent temperature and pressure controls, respectively. They constitute an interpolation step. Repeat the interpolation step until point F is reached.

However, a real heating process does not run along an iso–density curve because, with the increase of temperature, the internal volume of the working chamber becomes larger, resulting in the reduction of the density of water. Therefore, the real heating process is a process of migration between iso–density curves. For example, in Figure 4, to reach point C, the real process is not to heat from A to B along the iso–density curve $Curve_a$ first and then iso–thermal depressurize to C, but to heat directly from A to C along the dotted curve between them, which is called an iso–mass heating process. Under the condition that the temperature difference between A and C is determined, the density difference between them can also be specified.

Suppose that the temperature difference between A and C is: $\Delta T_{ac} = T_c - T_a$, the change of the inner diameter of the chamber is $\Delta d = d \cdot \alpha_c \cdot \Delta T_{ac}$, and the change of the length of the chamber is $\Delta L = L \cdot \alpha_c \cdot \Delta T_{ac}$, where α_c is the coefficient of linear expansion of the chamber at the temperature of T_c; d and L are the inner diameter and the length of the chamber, respectively, at the temperature of T_a.

The water density difference between A and C is:

$$\Delta\rho_{ac} = \rho_c - \rho_a = \rho_c[1 - (d + \Delta d)^2(L + \Delta L)/(d^2 L)] \quad (6)$$

Ignore the high order small terms; then:

$$\Delta\rho_{ac} = -3\rho_a\alpha_c\Delta T_{ac} \quad (7)$$

So, after decoupling, the reconstruction process from point A to point E is: iso–mass heating from A to C, then iso–thermal depressurization from C to D, and then iso–mass heating from D to E.

The specified temperature and density differences between the start and the end points of each iso–mass heating process can be used to plan the start point by the end point. The temperature and pressure of the end point as the control targets are known, and its density can be obtained by finding the iso–density curve according to Equation (5). Then, the temperature, pressure and density of the start point can be determined by Equation (7) according the differences of temperature and density.

4.4. P-T Preservation

Some actions of the SERCT will cause changes in the environment inside the chambers: (1) the push rod extends or the valves close. These actions will increase the pressure and require drainage. (2) The push rod retracts or the valves open. These actions will cause pressure drop and water supplement is required. Because the above two actions have different impacts on the environment, the system handles them in different ways.

Figure 5 shows the control paths of P-T preservation. Assuming the initial stable state is at point D, when the push rod extends or the valves close, the pressure rises to D_1. Set the fluctuation thresholds of temperature ε_t and pressure ε_p. When the pressure fluctuation reaches ε_p, the push rod or valve stops and the pressure relief valve starts to work until the pressure returns to P_d. This process hardly requires water supplement and has little impact on temperature.

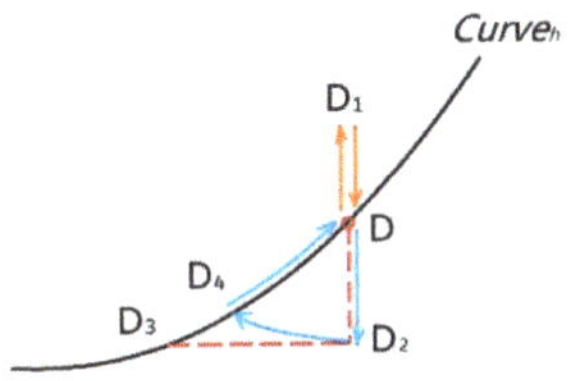

Figure 5. The control paths of P-T preservation.

When the push rod retracts or the valves open, water will be replenished. If the amount of water supplement is too much, the temperature will fluctuate greatly. Therefore, in this process, the water inflow is limited by controlling the moving distance of the push rod or the valve, so as to control the fluctuations of pressure and temperature. In Figure 5, DD_2 is a vertical line and D_2D_3 is a horizontal line. When the pressure drops to point

D_2 which satisfies the condition of Equation (8), stop the movement of the push rod or the valve.

$$(T_d - T_{d3} = \varepsilon_t \ \& \ P_d - P_{d2} \leq \varepsilon_p) \ || \ (T_d - T_{d3} \leq \varepsilon_t \ \& \ P_d - P_{d2} = \varepsilon_p) \tag{8}$$

After the push rod or the valve stops moving, the booster valve starts to replenish water into the chamber, which makes the temperature drop while the pressure rise. Assuming the temperature and pressure run along a P-T curve D_2D_4 which is located inside the triangle DD_2D_3, when $D_4(P_{d4}, T_{d4})$ satisfies Equation (5), it returns to the iso–density curve where point D is located. Then, stop adding water and start to heat, entering an iso–density temperature control process until the state returns to point D. Because the temperature fluctuation and the amount of water added each time are very small, the density change from D_4 to D can be ignored, and the heating process can be regarded as an iso–density heating process.

The moving distance of the push rod or the valve gate can be controlled by monitoring the pressure change. However, we use the following method to determine this distance, which is stable and reduces the complexity of the control system.

According to Equation (1), when temperature is given and remains constant, the relationship between density of water and pressure is determined. When P_d and its allowable fluctuation are given, its density ρ and allowable change $\Delta\rho$ can be obtained. Ignoring the influence of temperature, the maximum distance of each movement of the push rod or the valve can be obtained by Equation (9):

$$l = \frac{V \cdot \Delta\rho}{\rho \cdot A} \tag{9}$$

where V is the internal volume of the working chamber, and A is the sectional area of the push rod or the valve gate.

5. Fuzzy-PID Dual Mode Pressure Control

The structure diagram of pressure control is shown in Figure 6. In Figure 6, Inlet is the entrance of water. Drive Entrance is the pneumatic source that drives the piston to pressurize the water under the control of the pressurization valves. High Pressure Outlet is the exit of high-pressure water leading to the chamber. Unloading Port is the pressure relief outlet. The system collects pressure signals through 1 and 2, and obtains control variables for the pressurization valves and pressure relief valves by pressure control algorithm. The pressure is then controlled by PLC to pressurize through 5 and 6 or reduce pressure through 3 and 4. The traditional PID control is prone to overshoot. In the research, a fuzzy-PID dual mode method is adopted to reduce the response time and the overshoot.

As shown in Figure 7, pressure error e and its change rate ec are the input variables, and the control quantity u of the valve is the output variable. When e is small, u is mainly decided by the PID algorithm to ensure high control accuracy, while when e is large, u is mainly given by the fuzzy control algorithm to ensure quick dynamic response. The final value of u is obtained by the weighted sum of the outputs by the PID control and the fuzzy control. The weight coefficient w_2 of the fuzzy control is determined by Equation (10), and the weight coefficient of PID control is decided accordingly by $w_1 = 1 - w_2$.

$$\begin{cases} w_2 = 1 & |e| > |e_0| \\ w_2 = \frac{1-\cos\left(\left|\frac{e}{e_0}\right| \cdot \pi\right)}{2} & |e| \leq |e_0| \end{cases} \tag{10}$$

where e_0 is the initial deviation of pressure.

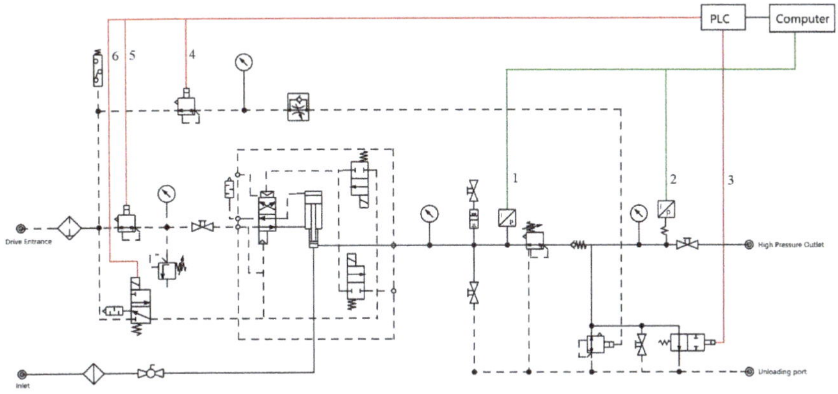

Figure 6. The structure diagram of the pressure control.

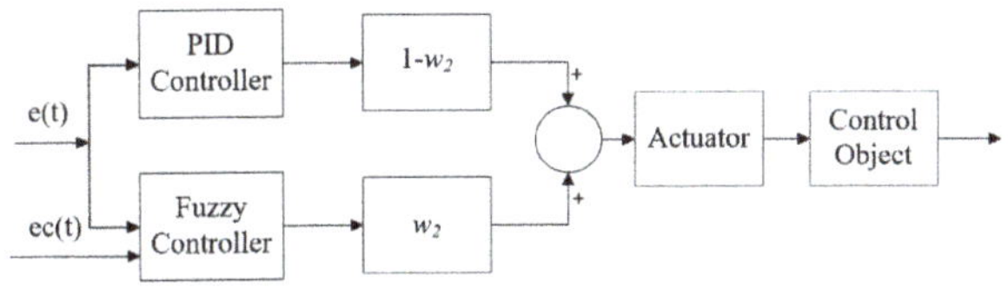

Figure 7. Fuzzy–PID dual mode pressure control.

The method of the fuzzy control is as follows:

1. Define *E* in the domain of discourse of fuzzy discrete set to represent the deviation, *EC* to represent the deviation change, and *U* to represent the output;
2. Set the domain of discourse of *E* and *EC* as {−6, −5, −4, −3, −2, −1, 0, 1, 2, 3, 4, 5, 6}, and the domain of discourse of *U* as {−3, −2.5, −2, −1.5, −1.0, −0.5, 0, 0.5, 1.0, 1.5, 2.0, 2.5, 3};
3. Seven fuzzy linguistic variables are used, namely PB (positive big), PM (positive middle), PS (positive small), ZO (zero), NS (negative small), NM (negative middle) and NB (negative big);
4. Triangular membership function is adopted, as shown in Figure 8;
5. The main principles for determining *U* according to *E* and *EC* are as follows:
   (a) When *E* is big, *U* should be big to speed up the system response;
   (b) When *E* is medium and *EC* is small, *U* should be medium to slow down the control;
   (c) When *E* and *EC* are both small, *U* should be small.
6. Center-of-gravity defuzzification is used on *U* to get its precise output.

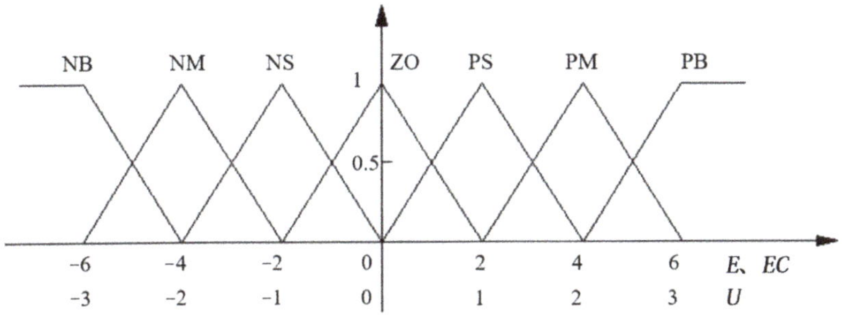

Figure 8. Triangular membership function.

The inference rules are shown in Table 1.

Table 1. The inference rules of U.

U		EC						
		NB	**NM**	**NS**	**ZO**	**PS**	**PM**	**PB**
	NB	PB	PB	PM	PM	PS	ZO	ZO
	NM	PB	PB	PM	PS	PS	ZO	NS
	NS	PM	PM	PM	PS	ZO	NS	NS
E	ZO	PM	PM	PS	ZO	NS	NM	NM
	PS	PS	PS	ZO	NS	NS	NM	NM
	PM	PS	ZO	NS	NM	NM	NM	NB
	PB	ZO	ZO	NM	NM	NM	NB	NB

6. Fuzzy PID Temperature Control Based on Grey Prediction Model

6.1. Study on Uniformity of Electric Heating Temperature Field

The non-uniformity of the internal temperature field of a horizontal cylindrical chamber can be presented by several temperatures at different heights on the cross section of the chamber [29]. As shown in Figure 9, in order to improve the uniformity of the temperature field, we divide the whole electric heating device covering the external surface of a chamber into 3 segments along the axial direction, and 8 groups along the circumferential direction, so there are 24 heating pieces in total. To monitor temperatures at different heights, five temperature-monitoring points (MPs) are uniformly distributed along the vertical diameter in the chamber.

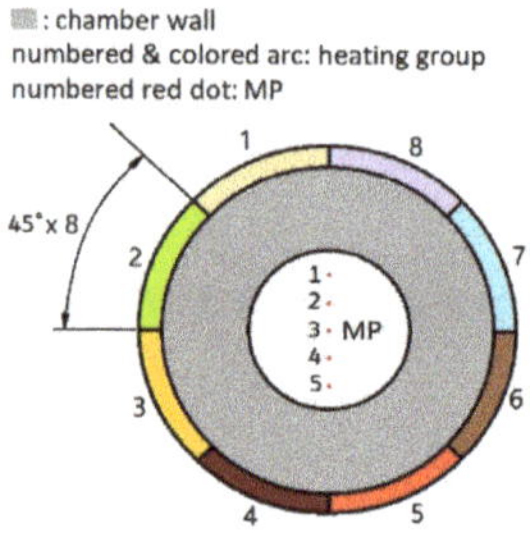

(**a**)

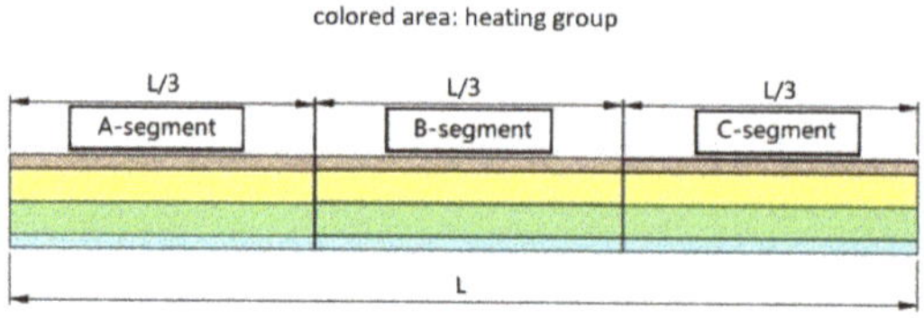

(**b**)

Figure 9. Segmented and grouped heating method; (**a**) 8 heating groups; (**b**) 3 heating segments.

A variable UI defined by Equation (11) is used as the temperature field uniformity index, being obtained by recording the temperatures of m MPs at n time points during P temperature control experiments with different target temperatures.

$$UI = \frac{1}{P}\sum_{k=1}^{P} \min_{1\leq i\leq n}\left(1 - \frac{s_k^i}{\overline{T}_k^i}\right) \tag{11}$$

in which,

$$s_k^i = \sqrt{\frac{\sum_{j=1}^{m}\left(T_{jk}^i - \overline{T}_k^i\right)^2}{m-1}}$$

$$\overline{T}_k^i = \frac{\sum_{j=1}^{m} T_{jk}^i}{m}$$

where T_{jk}^i is the temperature of the jth MP at time i in the kth temperature control experiment, $\overline{T}_k^i$ represents the average temperature of m MPs at time i in the kth experiment, and s_k^i is the standard deviation of temperatures of m MPs at time i in the kth experiment.

6.2. Simulation of Electric Heating Temperature Field

The simulation model takes 25 °C as the initial temperature, the temperature of MP 3 as the reference, and the chamber wall as the heat source. According to whether heating is on or off, the boundary condition of the chamber wall is set as heat flow density [30] or natural convection heat transfer.

As shown in Figure 10, four heating modes are simulated. The target temperature T_t is set from 40 °C to 80 °C at an interval of 10 °C, and the heat flow density of 5 kW/m^2 is used as the boundary condition.

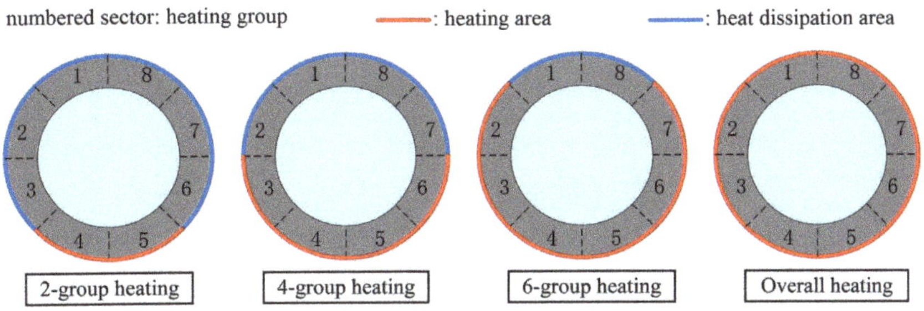

Figure 10. Four heating modes.

Figure 11 shows the temperature simulation curve with T_t = 60 °C. When the temperature of MP 3 is lower than T_t, start heating immediately, and stop when higher than T_t. The temperature control process is divided into three stages, i.e., heating stage, overshoot cooling stage and steady state. The error of the steady state is controlled within ±0.5 °C. The *UI*s of heating stage and steady state under different heating modes and the durations of cooling stage are shown in Table 2.

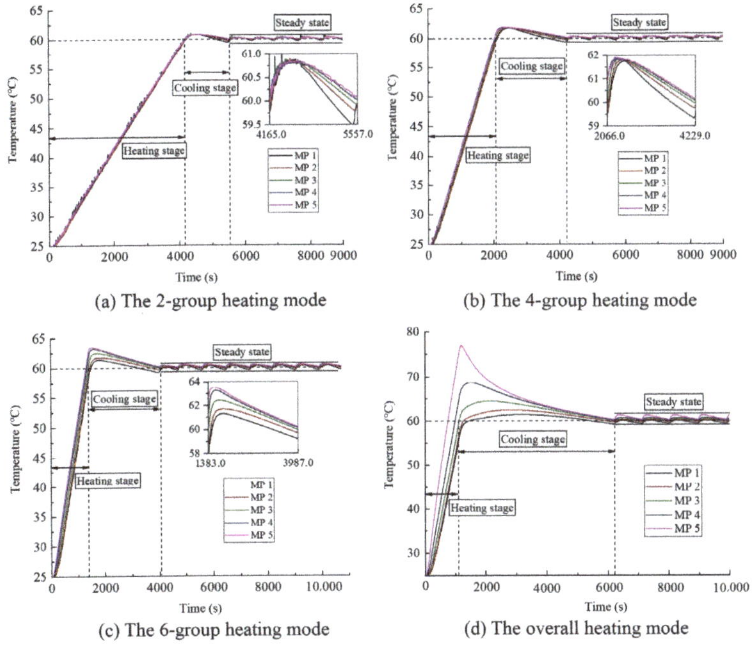

Figure 11. The temperature simulation curves.

Table 2. *UI*s in different stages and cooling durations of different heating modes.

Heating Mode	*UI*/%		Duration of Cooling Stage/min
	Heating Stage	Steady State	
2-group	98.29	99.66	27.88
4-group	97.36	99.71	44.52
6-group	93.24	99.51	55.21
overall	84.75	98.96	98.26

From the simulation results, it can be seen that:

1. In the heating stage, the less the heating groups, the better the temperature uniformity. The temperature field uniformity of the 2-group heating mode is the best, while that of the overall heating mode is the worst. In the steady state, the uniformities of temperature field of different heating modes are all improved, and the 4-group heating mode has the best result;
2. The more the heating groups, the longer the cooling duration is;
3. 4-group heating mode has a better overall performance in terms of temperature uniformity and cooling speed.

6.3. Fuzzy PID Temperature Control Based on Grey Prediction Model

The temperature control system of the SERCT is a nonlinear, time-varying, large time delay system. Conventional PID control and fuzzy PID control can hardly avoid the overshoot and ensure the stability of the system. In our research a grey prediction model is adopted, which replaces the input of the PID method with the prediction value instead of the feedback value to reduce the overshoot and improve the stability of the system [31,32].

6.3.1. Grey Prediction Model

GM(1,1) model is adopted for grey prediction. GM(1,1) model establishes a first-order ordinary differential equation (ODE) by the accumulation sequence of the original data sequence, as shown in Equation (12), then solves the ODE and obtain the prediction values by inverse accumulated generating operation(IAGO) on the solution sequence.

$$\frac{dX^{(1)}(t)}{dt} + aX^{(1)}(t) = b \tag{12}$$

where $X^{(1)} = \left\{x^{(1)}(k), (k = 1, \ldots, n)\right\}$ is the accumulation sequence of the original data sequence $X^{(0)} = \left\{x^{(0)}(k), (k = 1, \ldots, n)\right\}$, with $x^{(1)}(k) = \sum_{i=1}^{k} x^{(0)}(i), k = 1, \cdots, n$. In this study, the dimension n of the data sequence is fixed as 15.

The solution of the ODE (12) is:

$$\hat{x}^{(1)}(k+m) = \left[x^{(0)}(1) - \frac{b}{a}\right]e^{-a(k+m-1)} + \frac{b}{a} \tag{13}$$

And the solution for $X^{(0)}$ can be obtained by IAGO:

$$\hat{x}^{(0)}(k+m) = \left[x^{(0)}(1) - \frac{b}{a}\right](1 - e^{a})e^{-a(k+m-1)} \tag{14}$$

where $\hat{x}^{(0)}(k+m)$ is the prediction value at the time point of $k + m$.

The coefficients a and b in Equation (12) can be calculated by the data sequence. Calculate the weighted nearest neighbor sequence $Z^{(1)} = \left\{z^{(1)}(k), k = 2, \cdots, n\right\}$ of $X^{(1)}$, with $z^{(1)}(k) = \frac{1}{2}x^{(1)}(k-1) + \frac{1}{2}x^{(1)}(k)$, then the ODE (12) can be discretized into a difference equation as Equation (15).

$$x^{(0)}(k) + az^{(1)}(k) = b \tag{15}$$

Because $X^{(0)}$ and $Z^{(1)}$ are given, a and b can be obtained by the least square method.

6.3.2. Grey-Prediction-Based Fuzzy PID Controller

Figure 12 shows the schematic diagram of the controller, in which the inputs of the fuzzy controller are the difference e between the target value $r(k)$ and the result $y'(k)$ calculated by the grey prediction model and its change rate e_c. The outputs of the fuzzy controller are the correction values, i.e., ΔK_p, ΔK_i and ΔK_d, of the PID parameters K_p, K_i and K_d, respectively. The PID parameter tuning is achieved by the following formula:

$$\begin{aligned} K_p &= K'_p + \Delta K_p \\ K_i &= K'_i + \Delta K_i \\ K_d &= K'_d + \Delta K_d \end{aligned} \quad (16)$$

where K'_p, K'_i and K'_d are PID parameters before correction.

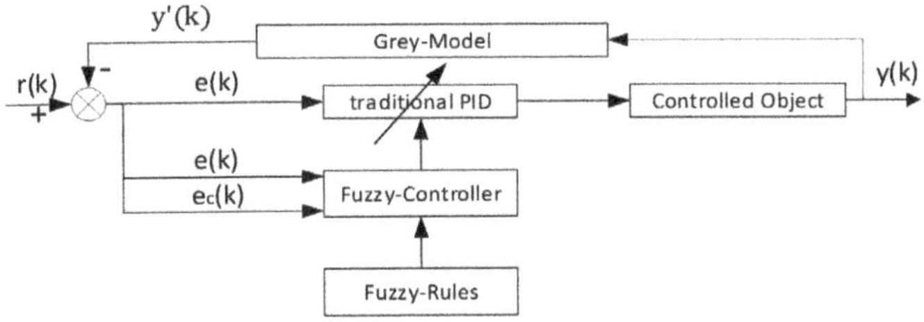

Figure 12. Schematic diagram of fuzzy PID controller based on grey prediction model.

The fuzzy linguistic variables of temperature control are the same as the fuzzy pressure control. The domain of discourse E of e and EC of e_c, ΔK_p, ΔK_i and ΔK_d, are all $[-3, 3]$. The main task of the fuzzy controller is to construct inference rules of ΔK_p, ΔK_i and ΔK_d by E and EC, as shown in Table 3. The center-of-gravity method is used for defuzzification.

Table 3. Inference rules of ΔK_p, ΔK_i and ΔK_d.

u ($\Delta K_p/\Delta K_i/\Delta K_d$)		*EC*						
		NB	**NM**	**NS**	**ZO**	**PS**	**PM**	**PB**
E	NB	PB/NB/PS	PB/NB/NS	PM/NM/NB	PM/NM/NB	PS/NS/NB	ZO/ZO/NM	ZO/ZO/PS
	NM	PB/NB/PS	PB/NB/NS	PM/NM/NB	PS/NS/NM	PS/NS/NM	ZO/ZO/NS	NS/ZO/ZO
	NS	PM/NB/ZO	PM/NM/NS	PM/NS/NM	PS/NS/NM	ZO/ZO/NS	NS/PS/NS	NS/PS/ZO
	ZO	PM/NM/ZO	PM/NM/NS	PS/NS/NS	ZO/ZO/NS	NS/PS/NS	NM/PM/NS	NM/PM/ZO
	PS	PS/NM/ZO	PS/NS/ZO	ZO/ZO/ZO	NS/PS/ZO	NS/PS/ZO	NM/PM/ZO	NM/PB/ZO
	PM	PS/ZO/PM	ZO/ZO/PS	NS/PS/PS	NM/PS/PS	NM/PM/PS	NM/PB/PS	NB/PB/PS
	PB	ZO/ZO/PB	ZO/ZO/PM	NM/PS/PM	NM/PM/PM	NM/PM/PS	NB/PB/PS	NB/PB/PS

7. Experiment Results and Discussion

7.1. *Experiment of the Fuzzy-PID Dual Mode Pressure Control*

In all pressure experiments, water was distilled and boiled to minimize the impact of impurities and dissolved air in the water. Figure 13 shows the results of 70 MPa pressure test on the storage chamber of the SERCD. The internal volume of the chamber is 35.33 L. The maximum output pressure of the booster valve is 425 MPa with the flow per stroke being 3.93 mL. The simple PID control and the fuzzy-PID dual mode control were tested. The steady-state errors of both methods were less than F.S. 1%. When the PID parameters K_p, K_i and K_d of both methods were 300, 12 and 1.5, it can be seen that compared with the simple PID control, the response speed of the fuzzy-PID dual mode control was faster and the overshoot was smaller.

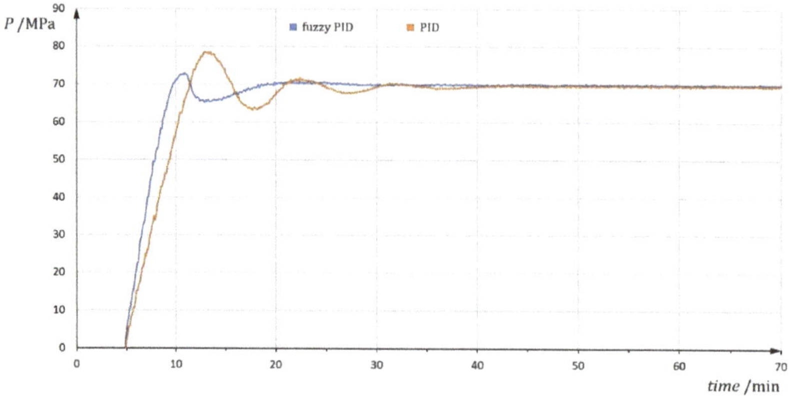

Figure 13. The results of 70 MPa pressure test on the storage chamber.

7.2. Experiment of the Uniformity of Temperature Field

In the heating experiment, the silicone heating tapes were wound outside the storage chamber and covered with insulating cotton for heat insulation, as shown in Figure 14. The power supply was DC 24 V for each heating group. The heating power was 835 W for each two groups. Each heating group could be powered on or off by a solid-state relay. Five PT100 temperature sensors were mounted on the positions MP1~MP5 as shown in Figure 9a.

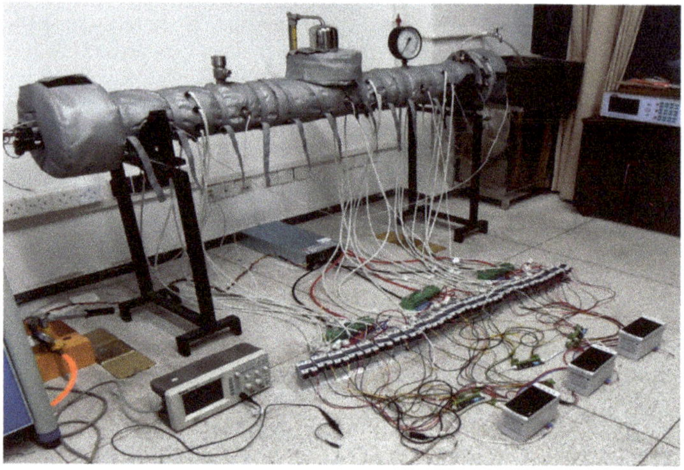

Figure 14. The heating experiment setup.

The experimental results are shown in Table 4. It can be seen that the 2-group and the 4-group heating modes had good temperature uniformity (>99%) in the heating stage and the steady state, which verifies the simulation results. The duration of heating stage of the 2-group heating mode was twice that of the 4-group heating mode, with the overall time to reach the steady state being the longest and the heating efficiency being the worst. The 4-group heating mode had the best temperature uniformity (99.23%) in the steady state. Therefore, the 4-group heating mode was selected as the preferred heating mode of the SERCT.

Table 4. Experimental results of temperature uniformity and durations of different heating modes.

Heating Mode	UI/%		Duration/min	
	Heating Stage	Steady State	Heating Stage	Cooling Stage
2-group	99.20	99.12	90.23	23.54
4-group	99.07	99.23	43.50	44.52
6-group	98.14	98.96	30.24	71.15
overall	91.30	98.46	32.23	79.71

7.3. Experiment of the Fuzzy PID Temperature Control Based on Grey Prediction Model

Figure 15 shows the temperature curves of the storage chamber using the fuzzy PID control and the grey-prediction-based fuzzy PID control with the target temperature of 85 °C. te MPa, tempB and tempC are the temperatures of A-segment, B-segment and C-segment of the chamber, respectively. In the experiment the 4-group heating mode was adopted. Table 5 shows the experiment results of 75 °C, 85 °C and 95 °C. It can be seen that compared with the fuzzy PID control, the overshoot and steady-state errors of the grey-prediction-based fuzzy PID control were relatively lower, with the steady-state errors less than ±0.13% and the overshoots less than 0.22%.

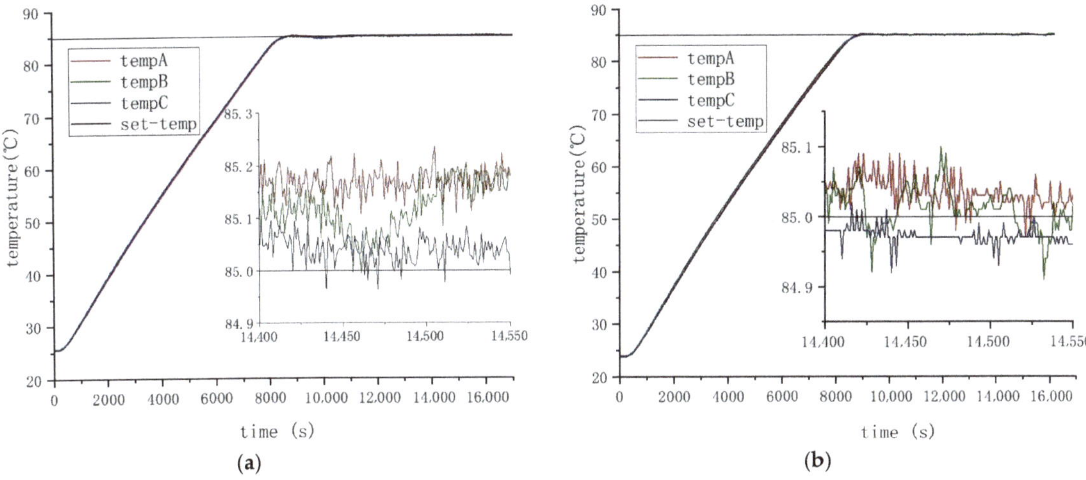

Figure 15. Temperature curves of heating experiments of 85 °C; (**a**) Fuzzy PID control; (**b**) Grey-prediction-based Fuzzy PID Control.

Table 5. Comparison of experimental results.

Target Temp.	Performance	Fuzzy PID			Grey Prediction Based Fuzzy PID		
		Sect. A	Sect. B	Sect. C	Sect. A	Sect. B	Sect. C
75 °C	Overshoot/%	0.14	0.25	0.48	0.07	0.10	0.13
	Steady-state error/°C	−0.20	0.28	0.17	0.10	−0.11	0.12
85 °C	Overshoot/%	0.19	0.19	0.14	0.09	0.14	0.18
	Steady-state error/°C	0.29	0.25	0.13	0.13	−0.10	−0.10
95 °C	Overshoot/%	0.28	0.29	0.20	0.17	0.22	0.10
	Steady-state error/°C	0.33	−0.26	0.14	0.13	0.12	0.13

7.4. Experiment of the Temperature and Pressure Decoupling Control

In the process of initial environment reconstruction, the water in the storage chamber was heated from 25 °C and 0.1 MPa to 95 °C and 70 MPa. As shown in Figure 16, the decoupling control path ABCDE consists of four steps:

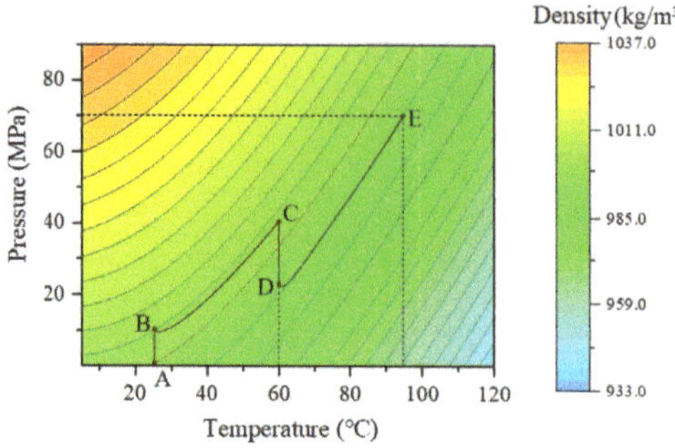

Figure 16. The planning of the P-T decoupling control path.

Step 1. Iso–thermal pressurizing from A (25 °C, 0.1 MPa) to B (25 °C, 10 MPa). During the heating process from 25 °C to 95 °C, the water pressure reduction caused by the expansion of the chamber is about 6 MPa. Therefore, in order to reduce the possible water supplement operation during the reconstruction, the system was pressurized to 10 MPa in advance.

Step 2. Iso–mass heating from B (25 °C, 10 MPa) to C (60 °C, 40.3 MPa).

Step 3. Iso–thermal depressurizing from C(60 °C, 40.3 MPa) to D(60 °C, 22.7 MPa).

Step 4. Iso–mass heating from D (60 °C, 22.7 MPa) to E (95 °C, 70 MPa).

Where C and D were planned by B and E, respectively, according to Equation (7).

Figure 17a shows the temperature and the pressure curves during the process and Figure 17b shows the P-T curve, in which B′, C′, D′ and E′ were the real values of target points B, C, D and E, respectively. When the system was stable at points B′, C′ and D′, the temperature and pressure values were B′(25 °C, 10.1 MPa), C′(60.2 °C, 38.2 MPa), D′(60.2 °C, 22.6 MPa) and E′(95.2 °C, 68.4 MPa), respectively. It can be seen that there were errors on the control points. Besides the accuracy of the control algorithm, there were many others factors that might cause these steady-state errors; for example, the physical characteristics of water might change under different pressures and temperatures, the non-uniformity of the temperature field in the chamber might have an impact on the relationship between temperature and pressure and the actual thermal deformation of the chamber might be different from the theoretical one. To improve the accuracy of the system, after the reconstruction process reached point E′, an iso–thermal pressure fine-tuning was carried out to ensure that the system is stable at E(94.9 °C, 70.1 MPa).

In the process of P-T preservation, the pressure and temperature changes during the push rod pushing out and retracting were examined. With the internal volume of the storage chamber being 35.33 L and the diameter of the push rod being 50 mm, according to Equation (9) when the push rod moves 10 mm each time, the pressure fluctuation can be controlled within 1.5 MPa, less than 2%. The speed of the push rod was 0.5 mm/s. The test steps were as follows: (1) let the push rod move out by 10 mm; (2) stopped the push rod and waited till the system got stable; (3) then pulled the push rod back by 10 mm; (4) stopped the push rod and waited till the system got stable again. The test was repeated 10 times. Figure 18 shows the curve obtained by averaging the pressure values of the 10 tests at 85 °C. It can be seen that the pressure fluctuation was controlled within 1.5 MPa.

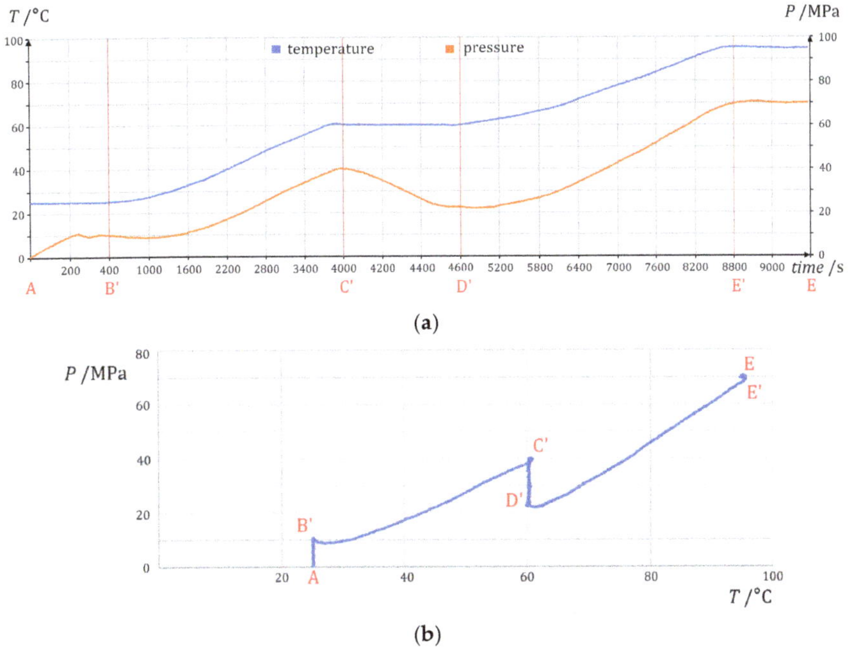

Figure 17. Results of the experiment of initial environment reconstruction. (**a**) The temperature curve and the pressure curve; (**b**) The temperature–pressure curve.

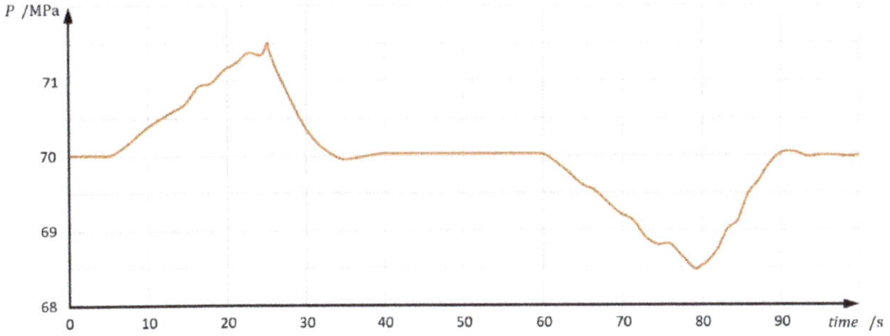

Figure 18. The pressure curve during the push rod movement.

There were always temperature fluctuations when the push rod moved, but these fluctuations had no obvious regularity. This might be related to the disturbance of the push rod movement to the uniformity of the temperature field, or to the change of the temperature conduction characteristics in the chamber due to the movement of the metal push rod. However, because of the preheating mode adopted by the SERCT, even in the process of water replenishment, the water temperature in the chamber did not change significantly, and the temperature errors were controlled within 1%.

8. Conclusions

In this paper, the structure of the SERCT and the principle of its two-layer temperature and pressure control are given. A P-T interpolation decoupling control algorithm based on the iso–density P-T curves of water is proposed for its high-temperature and high-pressure coupling control problem. The control path is divided into two kinds of independent interpolation paths, namely, iso–thermal pressure control and iso–mass temperature control. The decoupled pressure control adopts fuzzy PID dual mode control, which reduces the dynamic response time and the overshoot. The phenomenon of temperature stratification of water in the chamber during the heating process is studied, and a three-segment eight-group electric heating method is proposed to improve the uniformity of the temperature field inside the chamber. In view of the low cooling efficiency of the electric heating method, the fuzzy PID temperature control algorithm based on the grey prediction model is adopted in this study to achieve a very small overshoot and low static error.

Future works mainly focus on further improving the capacity of the SERCT to 140 MPa and 150 °C, and studying the P-T control under the environment of such high temperature and ultra-high pressure, exploring other heating methods that can achieve better temperature uniformity and higher heating and cooling efficiency at the same time.

Author Contributions: Conceptualization, X.P. and X.L.; methodology, X.P. and X.L.; software, L.W. and H.Z.; validation, S.Y. and M.W.; investigation, X.P. and X.L.; manuscript writing and review, X.P. and X.L.; visualization, S.Y. and J.W.; project administration, H.X. All authors have read and agreed to the published version of the manuscript.

Funding: The research was supported by National Natural Science Foundation of China (Grant No. 51827901), Shenzhen Key Technology Research and Development Program (JSGG20220831105002005) and Shenzhen Natural Science Fund (the Stable Support Plan Program 20220807145745001).

Institutional Review Board Statement: Not applicable.

Informed Consent Statement: Not applicable.

Data Availability Statement: Not applicable.

Conflicts of Interest: The authors declare no conflict of interest.

References

1. Lu, Y.C.; He, Z.Q.; Wang, Y.W.; Dai, Z.X.; Wang, Z.J. Mining-induced mechanics behavior in the deep mine with an overkilometer depth. *J. China Coal Soc.* **2019**, *44*, 1326–1336.
2. Xie, H.P.; Li, C.B.; Gao, M.Z.; Zhang, R.; Gao, F.; Zhu, J.B. Conceptualization and preliminary research on deep in situ rock mechanics. *Chin. J. Rock Mech. Eng.* **2021**, *40*, 217–232.
3. Zhang, Z.P.; Xie, H.P.; Zhang, R.; Zhang, Z.T.; Gao, M.Z.; Jia, Z.Q.; Xie, J. Deformation damage and energy evolution characteristics of coal at different depths. *Rock Mech. Rock Eng.* **2019**, *52*, 1491–1503. [CrossRef]
4. Xie, H.P.; Gao, M.Z.; Zhang, R.; Chen, L.; Liu, T.; Li, C.B.; Li, C.; He, Z.Q. Study on concept and progress of in situ fidelity coring of deep rocks. *Chin. J. Rock Mech. Eng.* **2020**, *39*, 865–876.
5. Li, C. *Reliability Analysis of Deep-Sea Ultra-High Pressure Environment Simulation System*; SOA: Beijing, China, 2013.
6. Zhang, J.N. Study on Acoustic Testing System for Pressure Environment Simulation of Seabed Sediment. Master's Thesis, Guangdong University of Technology, Guangzhou, China, 2021.
7. Molfino, P.; Nervi, M.; Rossi, M.; Malgarotti, S.; Odasso, A. Design and development of a module for the construction of reversible HVDC submarine deep-water sea electrodes. *IEEE Trans. Power Deliv.* **2017**, *32*, 1682–1687. [CrossRef]
8. Gauthey, J.R.; Ventriglio, F.J. *Naval Ship Systems Command Research and Development Program on Pollution Abatement*; American Society of Mechanical Engineers: New York, NY, USA, 1973; Volume 95, p. 69.
9. McInroy, J.E.; Neat, G.W.; O'Brien, J.F. A robotic approach to fault-tolerant, precision pointing. *IEEE Robot. Autom. Mag.* **1999**, *6*, 24–31. [CrossRef]
10. AMSTEC. Facilities and Equipment in Yokosuka Headquarters. 2003. Available online: https://www.jamstec.go.jp/e/about/equipment/yokosuka/chugata_kouatsu_jikken.html (accessed on 22 May 2023).
11. Qing, X. Design and Finite Element Analysis of a Super High Pressure Cylinder. Master's Thesis, Sichuan University, Chengdu, Chian, 2017; pp. 3–40.
12. Wang, W.T. Study on Pressure Retaining Transfer Device for Deep-Sea Sediments. Master's Thesis, Zhejiang University, Hangzhou, China, 2015.
13. Zeng, R.Y.; Chan, Z.H. Progress in research and development techniques on deep sea microorganism resource. *Chin. Bull. Life Sci.* **2012**, *24*, 991–996.
14. Ross, P.S.; Bourke, A.; Fresia, B. A multi-sensor logger for rock cores: Methodology and preliminary results from the Matagami mining camp, Canada. *Ore Geol. Rev.* **2013**, *53*, 93–111. [CrossRef]

15. Schultheiss, P.J.; Francis, T.J.G.; Holland, M.; Roberts, J.A.; Amann, H.; Thjunjoto, R.J.; Parkes, R.J.; Martin, D.; Rothfuss, M.; Tyunder, F.; et al. *Pressure Coring, Logging and Subsampling with the Hyacinth System*; Geological Society: London, UK, 2006; Volume 267, pp. 151–163.
16. Liu, J.B. Study on Pressure Maintaining System of Gas Hydrate Transfer Device. Master's Thesis, Zhejiang University, Hangzhou, China, 2016.
17. Liu, H.; Lee, J.C.; Li, B.R. High precision pressure control of a pneumatic chamber using a hybrid fuzzy PID controller. *Int. J. Precis. Eng. Manuf.* **2007**, *8*, 8–13.
18. Yu, L.; Lim, J.G.; Fei, S.M. An improved single neuron self-adaptive PID control scheme of superheated steam temperature control system. *Int. J. Syst. Control. Inf. Process.* **2017**, *2*, 1–13. [CrossRef]
19. Chew, I.M.; Wong, F.; Bono, A.; Nan, D.J.; Wong, K.I. Genetic algorithm optimization analysis for temperature control system using cascade control loop model. *Int. J. Comput. Digit. Syst.* **2020**, *9*, 119–128.
20. Shakeri, E.; Latif-Shabgahi, G.; Abharian, A.E. Design of an intelligent stochastic model predictive controller for a continuous stirred tank reactor through a Fokker-Planck observer. *Trans. Inst. Meas. Control.* **2018**, *40*, 3010–3022. [CrossRef]
21. Shi, H.Y.; Li, P.; Wang, L.M.; Su, C.L.; Yu, J.X.; Cao, J.T. Delay-range-dependent robust constrained model predictive control for industrial processes with uncertainties and unknown disturbances. *Complexity* **2019**, *2019*, 2152014. [CrossRef]
22. Aguilar-López, R.; Mata-Machuca, J.L.; Godinez-Cantillo, V. A tito control strategy to increase productivity in uncertain exothermic continuous chemical reactors. *Processes* **2021**, *9*, 873. [CrossRef]
23. Dorigo, M.; Maniezzo, V.; Colorni, A. Ant system: Optimization by a colony of cooperating agents. *IEEE Trans. Syst. Man Cybern. Part B* **1996**, *26*, 29–41. [CrossRef] [PubMed]
24. Wang, Y.B.; Chen, W.N.; Wang, X.D.; Wang, D.C. Overview of Pressure Control System Based on PID Algorithm. *Proc. First Pearl River Sci. Assoc. Forum* **2011**, 128–132.
25. Qian, X.; Huang, K.J.; Jia, S.K.; Chen, H.S.; Yuan, Y.; Zhang, L.; Wang, S.F. Temperature difference control and pressure-compensated temperature difference control for four-product extended Petlyuk dividing-wall columns. *Chem. Eng. Res. Des.* **2019**, *146*, 263–276. [CrossRef]
26. Pan, H.; Wu, X.; Qiu, J.; He, G.C.; Ling, H. Pressure compensated temperature control of Kaibel divided-Wall column. *Chem. Eng. Sci.* **2019**, *203*, 321–332. [CrossRef]
27. Zheng, Y.G.; Liu, M.; Wu, H.; Wang, J. Temperature and Pressure Dynamic Control for the Aircraft Engine Bleed Air Simulation Test Using the LPID Controller. *Aerospace* **2021**, *8*, 367. [CrossRef]
28. The International Association for the Properties of Water and Steam, IAPWS R6-95(2018), Revised Release on the IAPWS Formulation 1995 for the Thermodynamic Properties of Ordinary Water Substance for General and Scientific Use, 2018. Available online: http://www.iapws.org/relguide/IAPWS-95.html (accessed on 22 May 2023).
29. Li, X.J.; Wu, M.W.; Wan, L.H.; Wu, J.J.; Zhang, H.Y. Simulation and experimental study of uniformity of temperature field of water by electric heating. *J. Shenzhen Univ. Sci. Eng.* **2022**, *39*, 314–323. [CrossRef]
30. Ghani, A.A.; Farid, M.M. Numerical simulation of solid-liquid food mixture in a high pressure processing unit using computational fluid dynamics. *J. Food Eng.* **2007**, *80*, 1031–1420. [CrossRef]
31. Zhang, Y.B.; Wei, Z.Y.; Lin, Q.Y.; Zhang, L.; Xu, J. MBD of gray prediction fuzzy-PID irrigation control technology. *Desalination Water Treat.* **2018**, *110*, 328–336. [CrossRef]
32. Kayacan, E.; Kaynak, O. An adaptive gray PID-type fuzzy controller design for a non-linear liquid level system. *Trans. Inst. Meas. Control.* **2009**, *31*, 33–49. [CrossRef]

applied sciences

MDPI

Article

Structural Improvement of Differential Motion Assembly in In Situ Pressure-Preserved Coring System Using CFD Simulation

Da Guo [1,2,3], Jianan Li [2,*], Dingming Wang [2,3], Yiwei Zhang [2,3], Xin Fang [2,3] and Heping Xie [2,3]

1 School of Mechanical Engineering, Sichuan University, Chengdu 610065, China
2 MOE Key Laboratory of Deep Underground Science and Engineering, College of Water Resource and Hydropower, Sichuan University, Chengdu 610065, China
3 Guangdong Provincial Key Laboratory of Deep Earth Sciences and Geothermal Energy Exploitation and Utilization, Institute of Deep Earth Sciences and Green Energy, College of Civil and Transportation Engineering, Shenzhen University, Shenzhen 518060, China
* Correspondence: lijn2013@163.com

Abstract: In situ pressure-preserved coring (IPP-Coring) is one of the most efficient methods for identifying the scale of the oil and gas content. However, the differential motion assembly of the IPP-Coring system often undergoes ball and ball seat seal failure and sticking due to surface erosion, and a greater pressure drop may unexpectedly trigger the assembly. This paper addresses these issues by improving the hydraulic structure of an assembly based on a deep understanding of the flow characteristics in the assembly, thus increasing the success rate of the IPP-Coring. Computational fluid dynamics (CFD) was employed to investigate flows in a differential motion assembly. The effects of the diameter and outlet structure of the ball seat on the fluid status, velocity, and pressure distribution were thoroughly analyzed. When the ball seat diameter increased from 30 to 40 mm, the maximum velocity and pressure drop decreased to 0.55 and 0.2 times their original values, respectively. There was a severe vortex area in the differential motion assembly due to the presence of the ball seat, but changing the outlet structure in the ball seat to an arc structure decreased the length of the vortex area and the fluid velocity near the wall to 0.7 and 0.4 times, respectively, compared with those with the original right-angled structure. In addition, the pressure drop decreased to 0.33 times the original value. Thus, the hydraulic structure of the assembly was improved, and a 40 mm diameter ball seat and an arc-shaped ball seat outlet were selected. Particle trajectory and erosion calculation results showed that the improved structure has a lower particle velocity and less impact on the wall, and the average erosion rate is only 0.42 times the value of the original structure. Due to the better erosion resistance and smaller pressure drop, the improved structure shows promise for field performance.

Keywords: differential motion assembly; in situ coring; erosion; flow characteristics; computational fluid dynamics

1. Introduction

With the exhaustion of resources at shallow depths in the earth, the development of resources is gradually occurring at greater depths [1–3]. At present, the depth of coal mining exceeds 1500 m, metal mining has reached 4350 m, and oil and gas resource mining has reached 7500 m [4–7]. The exploitation and utilization of deep resources require accurate knowledge of reservoir scale and properties. Coring is a vital method used in exploration; it can obtain core samples from subsurface formations. By analyzing core samples, reliable information about the rock and fluid properties can be obtained, and then the scale of the reservoir content can be identified [3,8]. However, for conventional coring technology, the change in pressure during tripping can expel fluid and gas components from the core sample, resulting in a large error between the reserve assessment values and the real situation of the deep resource [9–13]. Field tests conducted by Bjorum et al. have shown that for conventional coring technology, more than 50% of the fluid and gas can be lost from a sample due to fluid expulsion during tripping [14].

To overcome this issue, in situ pressure-preserved coring (IPP-Coring) technology has been introduced for deep exploration [15–19]. This technology avoids fluid expulsion by maintaining the core pressure at the bottom hole pressure, thereby making it possible to accurately assess the scale of the reservoir contents [20–23]. At present, scholars around the world have performed much research on in situ pressure-preserved coring technology and developed many types of IPP-Coring equipment. For example, to obtain cores from offshore gas hydrates for research, the pressure core barrel (PCB), advanced piston corer (APC), pressure core sampler (PCS), hydrate autoclave coring equipment system (HY-ACE), and pressure temperature core sampler (PTCS) have been developed by different countries and institutions in the past few years [24–30]. For onshore coring for deep oil and gas exploration, the GWY194-70BB and GW-CP194-80A pressure coring systems are two typical types of IPP-Coring equipment; their pressure preservation capacities can reach 20 and 60 MPa, respectively [31,32]. In current IPP-Coring devices, their pressure preservation principle is mainly the closure of a ball valve or flap valve to form a sealed chamber to maintain the in situ pressure of the core sample. The closure of the valves depends on the relative movement between the core (inner) pipe and the outer pipe through a mechanical device such as an overshot assembly or a hydrodynamic-pressure lifting device such as a differential motion assembly. In onshore deep oil and gas exploration, due to the small inner diameters of common oil drill pipes, tripping the mechanical device in the hole has been a problem; usually, it is necessary to use specialized drill pipes, which wastes considerable effort and cost. Therefore, relative movement between the core tube and outer tube often depends on the hydrodynamic-pressure lifting device in onshore deep oil and gas explorations, namely, the differential motion assembly in this study [32].

The working principle of the differential motion assembly used to realize the pressure preservation operation of the IPP-Coring system for onshore oil and gas explorations is shown in Figure 1. In the coring operation, the upper section of the IPP-Coring system is successively connected to the drill collars and drill pipes in the bottom hole assembly. When coring begins, the drilling fluid passes through the inside of the differential motion assembly, and the valve cover in the valve assembly stays open due to the constraint of the inner pipe. At the end of drilling, the rock core enters the in situ pressure-preserved core chamber. At this time, a steel ball is dropped into the hole and dropped onto the ball seat, which changes the drilling fluid path from the interior to the outer part of the differential motion assembly, as shown by the red arrow. Under the action of hydrodynamic pressure, two limit pins are cut off, and the differential motion assembly is lifted to drive the inner pipe up over the valve cover. Then, the valve cover automatically closes under the action of gravity to maintain the in situ pressure. According to this working principle, the differential motion assembly plays a vital role in the process of IPP-Coring during onshore oil and gas exploration, and it directly determines the success rate of IPP-Coring. Unfortunately, in the field service process, due to the complex deep well environment characterized by high pressure and temperature, high flow rates, and solids content of the drilling fluid, the differential motion assembly is often faced with the failure of the seal of the ball and ball seat as well as sticking caused by surface erosion. In addition, in the case of large positive displacement pumps, the differential motion assembly may be lifted at the wrong time (the pin is cut off before the ball is dropped) due to the greater pressure drop, which contributes to the failure of IPP-Coring. Therefore, it is necessary to improve the hydraulic structure of the differential motion assembly to decrease the surface erosion and pressure drop to further increase its reliability and service life.

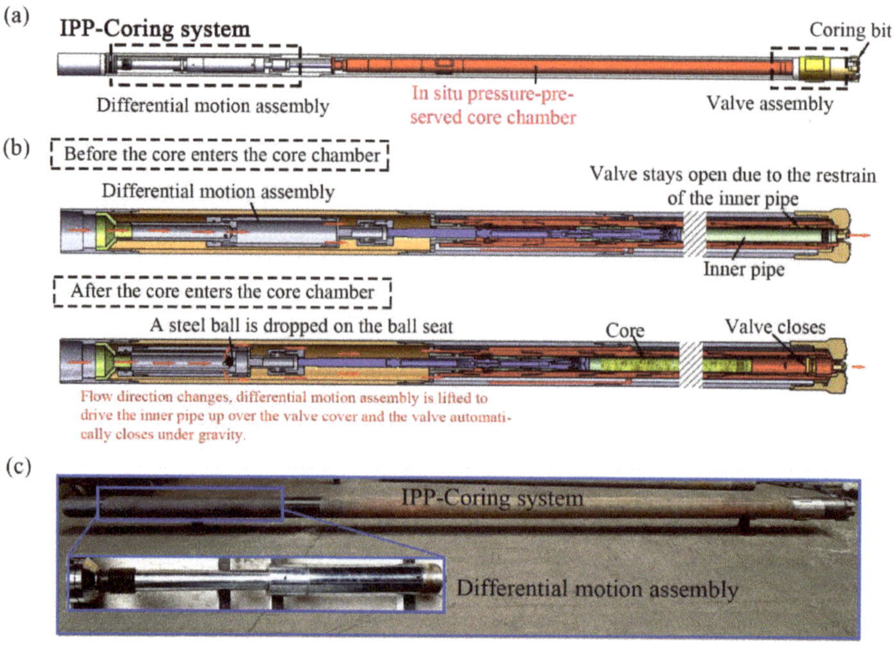

Figure 1. (**a**) Schematic diagram of the IPP-Coring system. (**b**) Schematic diagram of the working principle of the IPP-Coring system and the differential motion assembly. (**c**) Photographs of the IPP-Coring system and the differential motion assembly.

To improve the hydraulic structure, it is necessary to have a deep insight into the flow characteristics of the drilling fluid in the differential motion assembly. Computational fluid dynamics (CFD) can effectively analyze the flow characteristics of downhole tools [33–38]. However, there has been little research on flow characteristics in differential motion assemblies in the IPP-Coring systems used in deep oil and gas exploration. The effects of the internal size and structure of the differential motion assembly on the flow velocity and pressure distribution are unclear, and it is impossible to target the design of the hydraulic structure to reduce erosion and pressure drop. As a result, the operational reliability and service life of differential motion assemblies have been low, which would result in a low success rate of the IPP-Coring. To increase the operational reliability and service life of differential motion assemblies and increase the success rate of IPP-Coring, this study employed CFD with the standard k-ε turbulence model to study the characteristics of flows with different rates in a differential motion assembly during IPP-Coring. The effects of the diameter of the ball seat and ball seat outlet structure on the fluid status, velocity, and pressure distribution were analyzed. Further, the hydraulic structure of the differential motion assembly was improved, and field experiments demonstrated the erosion resistance of the improved structure.

2. Numerical Simulation

2.1. Mathematical Model

2.1.1. Liquid Phase Model

During running, the drilling fluid flows through the differential motion assembly. The continuity equations and momentum equations are as follows [39]:

$$\frac{\partial \rho}{\partial t} + \nabla \cdot \left(\rho \vec{u} \right) = 0 \tag{1}$$

$$\frac{\partial}{\partial t}\left(\rho \vec{u}\right)+\nabla\cdot\left(\rho \vec{u}\vec{u}\right)=-\nabla P+\nabla\cdot\left\{\mu\left[\left(\nabla \vec{u}+\nabla \vec{u}^{T}\right)-\frac{2}{3}\nabla\cdot\vec{u}I\right]\right\}+\rho\vec{g}+\vec{s}_{M} \quad (2)$$

where ρ is the liquid phase density, $\vec{u}$ represents the instantaneous velocity vector, P is pressure, μ is the molecular viscosity, I is the unit tensor, $\rho\vec{g}$ is the gravitational body force, and S_M is the added momentum caused by the discrete phase.

The standard k-ε model is very popular in industrial flow and heat transfer simulations because of its robustness and economy, and it has shown reasonable accuracy for fully developed turbulent flow conditions [40]. For the differential motion assembly, during the IPP-Coring process for deep oil and gas exploration, the drilling fluid, which is characterized by a high velocity (pump displacement can reach 20~40 L/s), high pressure, and high solid particle content, circulates through it. Due to the high velocity and the resulting high Reynolds number, the flow in the differential motion assembly is usually turbulent. Thus, the standard k-ε model, which has reasonable accuracy for a wide range of turbulent flows and a fast convergence rate [40], was employed in this study to gain an insight into the flow characteristics in the differential motion assembly. The equations are as follows [39,41,42]:

$$\frac{\partial(\rho k)}{\partial t}+\frac{\partial(\rho k u_i)}{\partial x_i}=\frac{\partial}{\partial x_j}\left[\left(\mu+\frac{\mu_T}{\sigma_k}\right)\frac{\partial k}{\partial x_j}\right]+P_k-\rho\varepsilon+S_k \quad (3)$$

$$\frac{\partial(\rho \varepsilon)}{\partial t}+\frac{\partial(\rho \varepsilon u_i)}{\partial x_i}=\frac{\partial}{\partial x_j}\left[\left(\mu+\frac{\mu_T}{\sigma_\varepsilon}\right)\frac{\partial \varepsilon}{\partial x_j}\right]+C_{\varepsilon1}\frac{\varepsilon}{k}P_k-C_{\varepsilon2}\rho\frac{\varepsilon^2}{k}+S_\varepsilon \quad (4)$$

$$P_k=\mu_T\nabla\vec{u}\cdot\left(\nabla\vec{u}+\nabla\vec{u}^{T}\right)-\frac{2}{3}\nabla\vec{u}\left(3\mu_T\nabla\cdot\vec{u}+\rho k\right) \quad (5)$$

$$\mu_T=\rho C_\mu\frac{k^2}{\varepsilon} \quad (6)$$

where μ_T is the turbulent eddy viscosity; k and ε are the turbulent kinetic energy and the turbulent dissipation rate, respectively; u_i denotes the velocity component in the i-direction; x_i and x_j are the coordinates in space; $C_{\varepsilon1}, C_{\varepsilon2}$, and C_μ are model constants; S_k and S_ε represent the source terms defined by the discrete phase caused by the particle damping and turbulence eddies; σ_k and σ_ε denote the turbulent Prandtl numbers; and P_k is the kinetic energy of the turbulence caused by the mean velocity gradients. In the standard k-ε model, $C_\mu = 0.99, C_{\varepsilon1} = 1.44, C_{\varepsilon2} = 1.92, \sigma_k = 1.0$, and $\sigma_\varepsilon = 1.3$ [40,43]. After the velocity and pressure fields in the fluid domain were solved by the momentum equation, the k-ε model was used to obtain the turbulent kinetic energy and its dissipation rate. Then, the results of the k-ε model were incorporated into the momentum equation to account for the effect of turbulence and the flow characteristics were obtained.

2.1.2. Particle Motion Model

During IPP-Coring, the motion trajectories of the particles in the drilling fluid can be obtained by solving the motion equation in the Lagrangian domain, and the motion governing equation of the particles can result from Newton's second law [42,44]:

$$m_p\frac{d\left(\vec{v_p}\right)}{dt}=\vec{F_d}+\vec{F_g}+\vec{F_b}+\vec{F_p}+\vec{F_{vm}} \quad (7)$$

where m_p denotes the particle mass, $\vec{v_p}$ is the particle velocity, and $\vec{F_d}$, $\vec{F_g}$, $\vec{F_b}$, $\vec{F_p}$, and $\vec{F_{vm}}$ are the drag force, gravity force, buoyancy, pressure gradient force, and added mass force, respectively. Those forces can be expressed as [41,44]:

$$\vec{F_d}=\frac{3\mu C_D R_{e_r}}{4\rho_p {d_p}^2}m_p\left(\vec{u}-\vec{v_p}\right) \quad (8)$$

$$\vec{F_g} = m_p \vec{g} \tag{9}$$

$$\vec{F_b} = \frac{\pi {d_p}^3}{6}(\rho_p - \rho) \tag{10}$$

$$\vec{F_p} = \frac{\pi d_p^3 \rho}{6}\frac{Du}{Dt} \tag{11}$$

$$\vec{F_{vm}} = \frac{1}{12}\pi d_p^3 \rho_p \frac{d\vec{v_p}}{dt} \tag{12}$$

where C_D is the drag coefficient, R_{e_r} is the relative Reynolds numbers, ρ_p is the density of the particle, and d_p is the diameter of the particle [41].

2.1.3. Erosion Model

Due to the impingement of the particles in the drilling fluids on the surface of the differential motion assembly, erosion is inevitable. In this study, the E/CRC model was used to calculate the erosion rate, and the equations are as follows [45,46]:

$$E = CF_s(BH)^{-0.59}v^n F(\alpha) \tag{13}$$

$$F(\alpha) = 5.40\alpha - 10.11\alpha^2 + 10.93\alpha^3 - 6.33\alpha^4 + 1.42\alpha^5 \tag{14}$$

where E is the erosion rate, C is a coefficient of the erosion model, F_s is a coefficient of the particle shape, BH is the Brinell hardness of the material, v is the impact velocity of the particles, and α is the incidence angle of the particles colliding against the wall. In this study, the round sands were set as the erosion particles, and 42CrMo steel was the material used for the differential motion assembly. Therefore, $C = 15.59 \times 10^{-7}$, $F_s = 0.2$, $BH = 240$, and $n = 1.73$. After the impact velocity and angle of the particles were calculated by the above turbulence and particle motion model, the erosion rate can be quantified using Equations (13) and (14) in CFD.

2.2. Computational Domain

In this paper, the CFD module in COMSOL Multiphysics was used to conduct the CFD simulation of the flow channel of the differential motion assembly. According to the structure of the differential motion assembly, a 3D computational domain was built. Because of the symmetry of the fluid domain of the motion assembly and considering the cost of computational time, 1/4 of the fluid domain of the differential motion assembly was selected as the computational domain. Figure 2 shows the mesh and boundary conditions of the flow domain of the differential motion assembly. Hexahedral grids with high accuracy were built using sweep algorithms. The density of the drilling fluid was set as 1000 kg/m^3. To study the effect of the fluid viscosity, fluid viscosities of 1000, 100, 10, and 1 mPa·s were employed. The mass flow rate of the particles was set to 0.5 kg/s, and the density and the diameter of the sand particles were set as 2850 kg/m^3 and 6×10^{-5} m, respectively. According to the real working conditions of the differential motion assembly, the boundary conditions were set as follows:

Inlet: The boundary condition of the inlet was set as "fully developed flow", and flow rates of 0.01, 0.02, 0.03, and 0.04 m^3/s were set at the inlet to study the flow characteristics.

Wall: The inner surface of the differential motion assembly was set as the wall, no slip was selected for the wall, and the wall roughness parameter and the roughness height were set as 0.26 and 3.2 μm, respectively. In addition, the wall boundaries were set as "bounce" for the particles.

Outlet: The boundary condition of the outlet was set as the pressure condition, and according to the pump pressure in the field, the value of the pressure at the outlet was set as 30 MPa. In addition, the wall condition of the outlet for the particles was set as "Freeze".

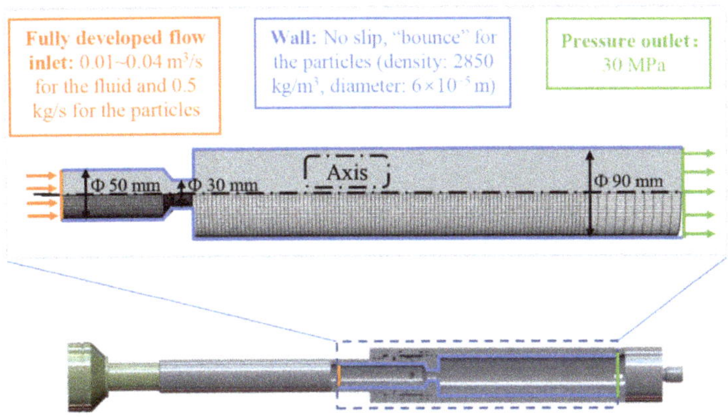

Figure 2. Mesh and boundary conditions of the flow domain in the differential motion assembly.

The velocity distributions along the radial direction at a line 150 mm away from the inlet under a flow rate of 0.04 m^3/s and fluid viscosity of 100 mPa·s were used to analyze the grid independency. The results of the grid independence study are shown in Figure 3; it shows that when the number of grids is more than 108,134, the solution is grid independent.

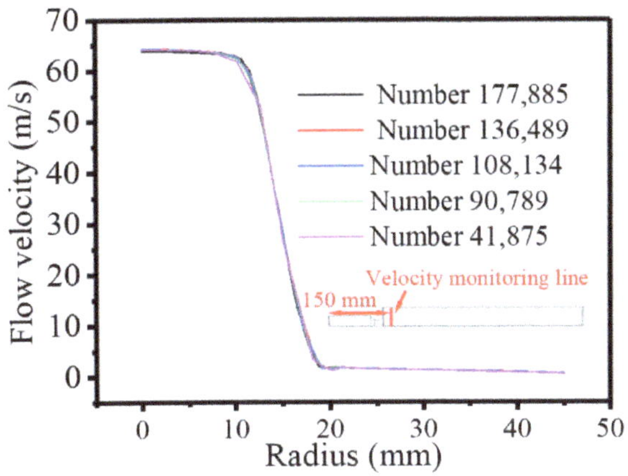

Figure 3. Grid independence study.

3. Results and Discussion

3.1. Flow Characteristics in the Differential Motion Assembly

The viscous effect is significant, and it is of great concern to the dynamic response of structures. Thus, in this study, the flow characteristics in the differential motion assembly with different fluid viscosities were studied first. The velocity streamlines in the differential motion assembly with different fluid viscosities are shown in Figure 4. It can be seen that a vortex area appeared in the differential motion assembly, and that the size of the vortex area increased as the viscosity of the fluid decreased from 1000 mPa·s to 1 mPa·s. To quantify the effect of the fluid viscosity on the flow velocity, we extracted the velocity at a monitoring line 220 mm away from the flow inlet, as shown in Figure 5. As seen in Figure 5, the maximum velocity in the monitoring line increased with the increase in the fluid viscosity, and the maximum in the monitoring line was 68 m/s for a fluid viscosity of 1000 mPa·s. These results demonstrate that increased fluid viscosity can increase the local velocity of the flow and decrease the size of the vortex area.

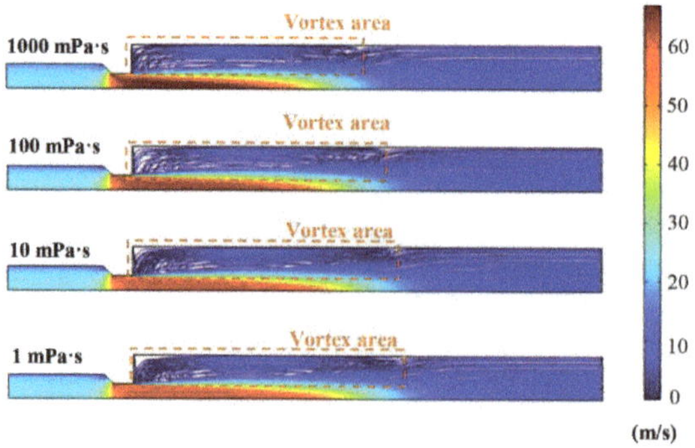

Figure 4. Velocity streamlines in the differential motion assembly with different fluid viscosities; the flow rate was 0.04 m^3/s.

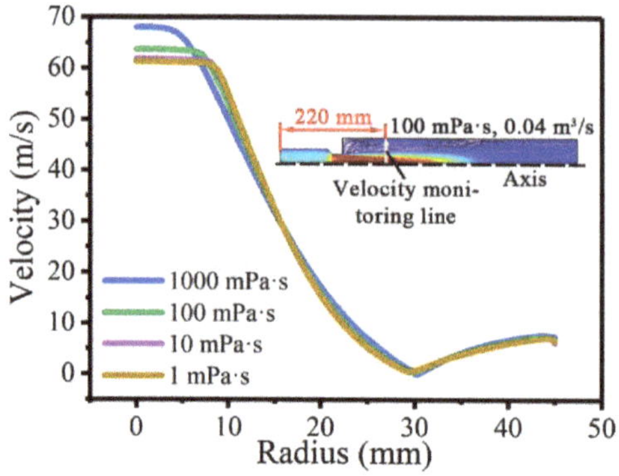

Figure 5. Velocity distributions at the monitoring line with different fluid viscosities; the flow rate was 0.04 m^3/s.

For the real working condition of the differential motion assembly, the fluid viscosity is usually about 100 mPa·s. Thus, we set the fluid viscosity as 100 mPa·s to study the effect of the flow rate and the inner structure. The flow characteristics of drilling fluid in the differential motion assembly, such as flow velocity and pressure distribution, directly affect the operational reliability and life of the assembly. Figure 6 shows the velocity streamlines in the differential motion assembly for different inlet flow rates. As the inlet flow rate increased, the velocity of the fluid in the differential motion assembly increased remarkably. The maximum velocity of 65 m/s appeared at the inlet of the ball seat for an inlet flow rate of 0.04 m^3/s. Although the diameter of the flow domain increased abruptly from 30 to 90 mm after the drilling fluid flowed through the ball seat, the drilling fluid near the axis still flowed a distance of about 200 mm at a relatively large velocity (e.g., at approximately 64 m/s when the inlet flow rate was 0.04 m^3/s) before the velocity of the fluid gradually decreased. However, due to the abrupt increase in the diameter of the flow domain at the outlet of the ball seat, a severe vortex was present near the wall of the differential motion assembly. The size of the vortex area showed almost no change for different inlet flow rates, which may be attributed to the same inner hydraulic structure. A vortex is a harmful flow characteristic that causes drilling fluid, which carries particles such as barite, to continuously impact and severely erode the inner wall of the differential motion assembly. Unfortunately, the inner wall with a diameter of 90 mm is a motion surface, and after the ball is dropped to trigger the differential motion assembly, this wall moves upward under hydrodynamic pressure to realize in situ pressure preservation. The erosion of this wall causes sticking when the differential motion assembly moves upward and leads to the failure of the IPP-Coring system.

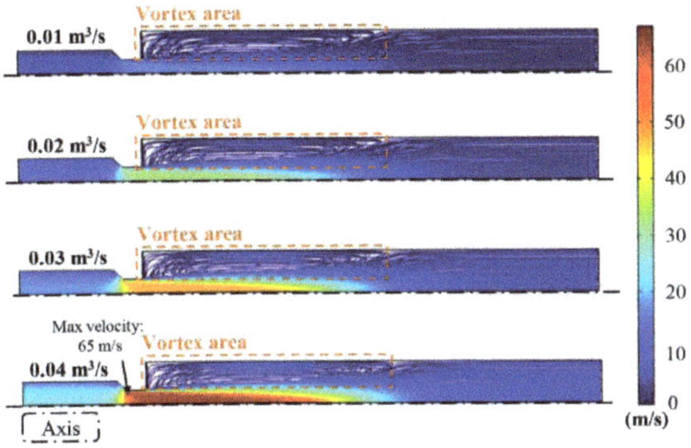

Figure 6. Velocity streamlines in the differential motion assembly with different inlet flow rates (0.01~0.04 m^3/s); the fluid viscosity was set as 100 mPa·s.

To further study the drilling fluid velocity distributions at the vortex area, we extracted the velocity at a monitoring line 220 mm away from the flow inlet, as shown in the inset illustration of Figure 7. The velocity distributions at the monitoring line with different inlet flow rates are shown in Figure 7. Along the radial direction, the flow area could be divided into the central jet area and vortex area according to the flow characteristics of the drilling fluid. In the central jet area, the velocity was stable at a larger value in the area with a radius less than 7 mm, such as 64 m/s for the inlet flow rate of 0.04 m^3/s. As the inlet flow rate decreased from 0.04 to 0.01 m^3/s, this velocity value gradually decreased to 16 m/s. With increasing radius, the velocity started to decrease and then gradually entered the vortex area where the velocity gradually decreased to nearly 0 m/s with increasing radius and then increased slowly. This trend conformed to the typical characteristics of the vortex. Near the wall with a diameter of 90 mm, the velocity of the vortex was relatively slow, less than 7.3 m/s. As the inlet flow rates decreased from 0.04 to 0.01 m^3/s, the velocity near the wall decreased from 7.3 to 1.9 m/s. At low velocity and small impact angles, the particles in the drilling fluid could still remove material from the wall with a diameter of 90 mm by plowing, which resulted in erosion [47]. As the flow rate increased from 0.01 to 0.04 m^3/s, although the size of the vortex area did not increase, the vortex velocity near the wall increased by 3.8-fold, which may lead to more severe surface erosion.

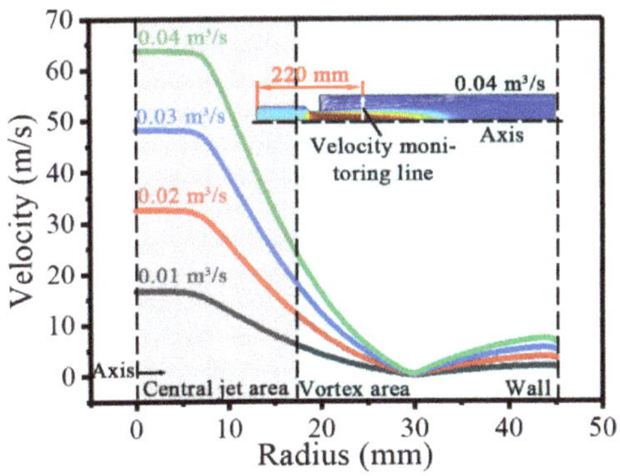

Figure 7. Velocity distributions at the monitoring line with different inlet flow rates; the fluid viscosity was set as 100 mPa·s.

Pressure contours in the differential motion assembly with different inlet flow rates are shown in Figure 8. There was an obvious pressure drop when the drilling fluid flowed through the differential motion assembly. In this study, the outlet pressure was set to 30 MPa during the calculation. With an increase in the inlet flow rate from 0.01 to 0.04 m^3/s, the inlet pressure increased from 30.1 to 31.4 MPa, and the pressure drop ΔP between the inlet and outlet of the differential motion assembly increased by 14-fold. Due to the greater pressure drop of 1.4 MPa when the inlet flow rate was 0.04 m^3/s, under the long-term impact of the drilling fluid, there is a risk of cutting the pins before the ball is dropped, which may trigger the differential motion assembly at the wrong time and result in the failure of the IPP-Coring process. Therefore, when a deep oil and gas IPP-Coring operation is conducted under large pump displacement, it is necessary to replace the pins with those of greater shear strength or diameter. In addition, the lowest pressure of 28.3 MPa (inlet flow rate 0.04 m^3/s) occurred at the inlet of the ball seat of the differential motion assembly where the flow velocity was extremely fast, up to 65 m/s. Therefore, severe erosion may occur in this zone due to the complex flow characteristics. In general, there was a severe vortex area in the differential motion assembly due to the presence of the ball seat and, with the increase in inlet flow rate, the velocity of the drilling fluid and the pressure drop between the inlet and outlet increased remarkably. These conditions may increase the erosion rate on the inner surface of the differential motion assembly and the risk of cutting the pin at the wrong time, which would damage the differential motion assembly and lead to the failure of the IPP-Coring process.

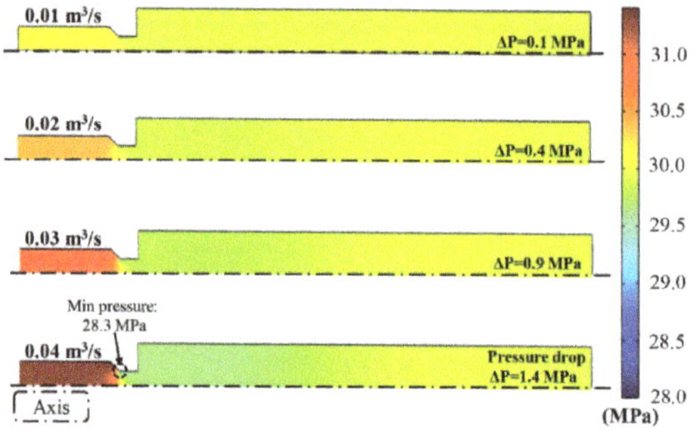

Figure 8. Pressure contours in the differential motion assembly with different inlet flow rates (0.01~0.04 m^3/s); the fluid viscosity was set as 100 mPa·s.

3.2. Effect of the Diameter of the Ball Seat on the Flow Characteristics

According to the analysis of the flow characteristics of the drilling fluid in the differential motion assembly, the flow had a higher velocity at the inlet of the ball seat, a severe vortex was present at the outlet of the ball seat near the wall, and the pressure drop reached 1.4 MPa when the inlet flow rate was 0.04 m^3/s. These characteristics will reduce the reliability and service life of the differential motion assembly. To improve these characteristics and further increase the success rate of IPP-Coring operations in deep oil and gas exploration, it is necessary to improve the local structure of the differential motion assembly.

Section 3.1 shows that the change in the flow status was largest at the ball seat. Therefore, we studied the effect of the diameter of the ball seat on the flow characteristics for ball seat diameters of 30, 35, and 40 mm. Figure 9 shows the effect of the diameter of the ball seat on the flow velocity. With the increase in the ball seat diameter, the velocity of the drilling fluid in the differential motion assembly decreased remarkably. The maximum velocity in the differential motion assembly with a 40 mm ball seat diameter decreased to 36 m/s, which was only 0.55 times that of the original assembly with a 30 mm ball seat diameter. In addition, the position of the maximum velocity changed; it was no longer at the inlet of the ball seat. This meant that the erosion at the inlet of the ball seat could be improved more after the diameter of the ball seat was increased to 40 mm. In addition, in Figure 9, the axial length of the vortex area decreased to 0.85 times that of the original differential motion assembly with a 30 mm ball seat diameter when the ball seat diameter increased to 40 mm. To further study the velocity distributions in the vortex area, we extracted the velocity at the monitoring line for ball seats with different diameters, as shown in Figure 10. As the ball seat diameter increased from 30 to 40 mm, the velocity at the axis decreased from 64 to 35 m/s, and the velocity in the central jet area markedly decreased. Moreover, the distance of the vortex center (the place the velocity was near 0 m/s) with the axis increased from 29 to 33 mm. This meant that the radial length of the vortex area also decreased. Therefore, it can be concluded that the increase in the diameter of the ball seat decreased the size of the vortex area. Figure 10 also shows that when the diameter of the ball seat increased from 30 to 40 mm, the velocity near the wall in the vortex area decreased to 0.67 times that of the model with the original ball seat diameter. The decreases in the size of the vortex area and the vortex velocity near the wall would reduce erosion by drilling fluid and the risk of sticking when the differential motion assembly was triggered.

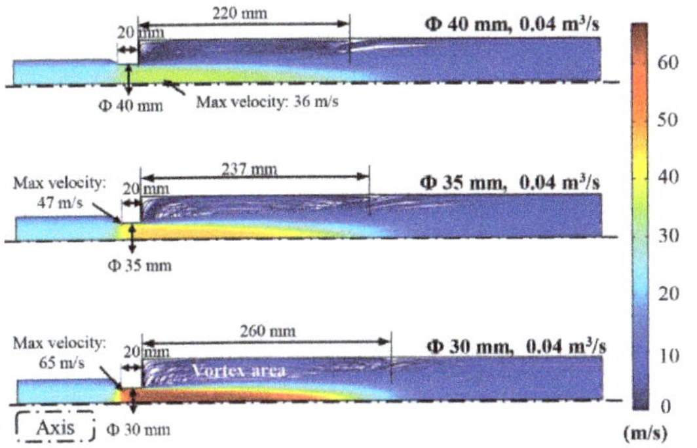

Figure 9. Effect of the diameter of the ball seat on the flow velocity; the fluid viscosity was set as 100 mPa·s.

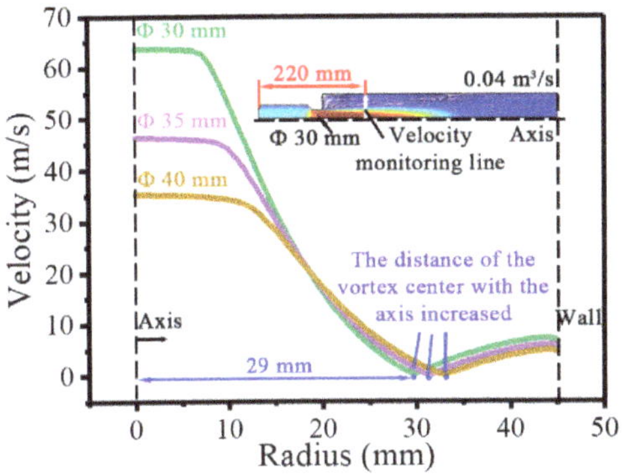

Figure 10. Velocity distributions at the monitoring line for ball seats with different diameters; the fluid viscosity was set as 100 mPa·s.

In addition to velocity changes, pressure changes also affect the service performance of the differential motion assembly. The larger pressure drop not only increases the load on the drilling pump and further results in unnecessary costs but can also increase the risk of cutting the pin before the ball is dropped, which would unexpectedly trigger the differential motion assembly and cause the IPP-Coring process to fail. Therefore, we studied the effect of the diameter of the ball seat on the pressure distribution. As shown in Figure 11, as the diameter of the ball seat increased from 30 to 40 mm, the pressure at the inlet of the differential motion assembly decreased from 31.4 to 30.3 MPa, and the pressure drop ΔP of the differential motion assembly with a 40 mm ball seat diameter was only 0.2 times that of the assembly with a 30 mm ball seat diameter. In summary, when the ball seat diameter increased from 30 to 40 mm, the maximum velocity decreased to 0.55 times that of the original differential motion assembly with a ball seat diameter of 30 mm. The axial length of the vortex area and the vortex velocity near the wall decreased to 0.85 times and 0.67 times that for the original ball seat diameter, respectively. In addition, the pressure drop of the differential motion assembly with a ball seat diameter of 40 mm was only 0.2 times that of the original assembly. Thus, increasing the diameter of the ball seat could effectively reduce the erosion of the drilling fluid on the inner surface of the differential motion assembly and the risk of cutting the pin before the ball is dropped, thereby improving the reliability and service life of the differential motion assembly. Notably, the larger diameter of the ball seat in the differential motion assembly means that a larger drop ball should be used to trigger the differential motion assembly when a core enters the IPP-Coring system. However, due to the constraint of the inner diameter of the drilling tool, the diameter of the drop ball should not be too large; otherwise, it will be difficult to smoothly drop the ball onto the ball seat. As shown in Figure 2, the diameter of the inlet of the differential motion assembly was only 50 mm; therefore, a ball seat with a diameter of 40 mm may be the most appropriate.

3.3. *Effect of the Outlet Structure of the Ball Seat on the Flow Characteristics*

Increasing the diameter of the ball seat improved the flow status of the drilling fluid. However, due to the abrupt change of the diameter in the ball seat outlet, a severe vortex and turbulence occurred within the differential motion assembly. To reduce these behaviors, it is necessary to improve the outlet structure of the ball seat.

To study the effect of the outlet structure of the ball seat on the flow characteristics, and considering machining and structural strength factors, three outlet structures of the ball seat—arc, cone, and original right-angled structure—were designed, as shown in Figure 12. Their effect on the velocity is shown in Figure 13. The internal velocity distribution of the differential motion assembly of the cone outlet at the ball seat was similar to that of the original right-angled outlet. Their maximum velocities in the differential motion assembly were both 36 m/s at the axis behind the ball seat outlet. Notably, the arc ball seat outlet structure greatly decreased the fluid velocity in the differential motion assembly, and the maximum velocity was only 34 m/s at the ball seat inlet. In addition, the axial length of the vortex area in the differential motion assembly with a cone outlet structure at the ball seat was 211 mm, which was only 9 mm less than that for the original right-angled outlet. However, the axial vortex length in the differential motion assembly with the arc outlet structure decreased to 0.7 times that with the original right-angled outlet.

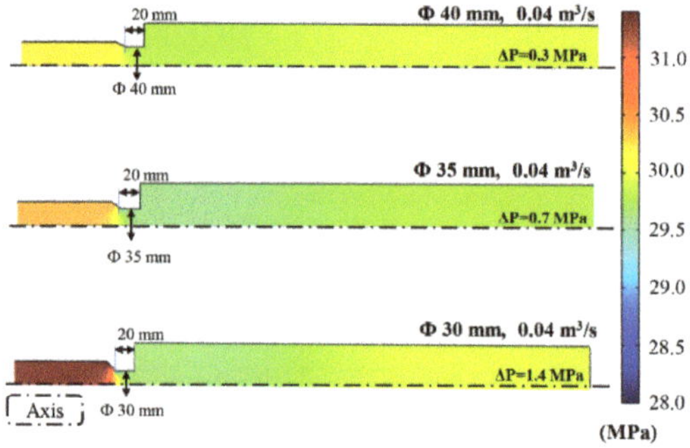

Figure 11. Effect of the ball seat diameter on the pressure distribution; the fluid viscosity was set as 100 mPa·s.

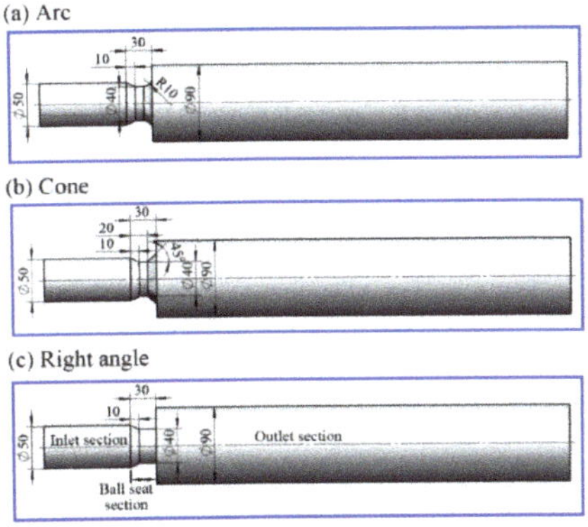

Figure 12. Differential motion assembly with different ball seat outlet structures: (**a**) arc, (**b**) cone, and (**c**) right angle.

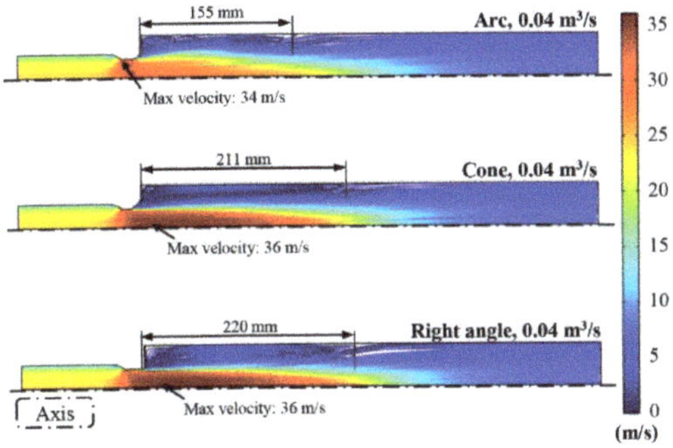

Figure 13. Effect of the outlet structure of the ball seat on the flow velocity; the fluid viscosity was set as 100 mPa·s.

To quantitatively study the effect of the outlet structure of the ball seat on the velocity distribution in the differential motion assembly, we set two velocity monitoring lines (shown in black and white) along the axial and radial directions, respectively. The velocity distributions at the two monitoring lines for different outlet structures at the ball seat are shown in Figure 14. In Figure 14a, according to the structural characteristics of the differential motion assembly, the computational domain of the differential motion assembly was divided into the inlet, ball seat, and outlet sections. The change in the outlet structure at the ball seat had almost no effect on the axial velocity distribution of the inlet section. However, when the drilling fluid entered the ball seat and outlet sections, the velocity of the arc structure was significantly less than that of the cone structure and the original right-angled structure. Notably, in the ball seat section of the arc structure, the drilling fluid first rose to 33 m/s and then started to decrease at the arc of the ball seat section. However, for the cone and original right-angled structure, the fluid continued to accelerate in the ball seat section. After entering the outlet section, the fluid continued to advance at a velocity greater than 35 m/s for approximately 130 mm before the velocity began to gradually decrease. In addition, as shown in Figure 14b, the maximum velocity of the central jet zone of the arc structure was only 28 m/s, which was 0.8 times that of the cone and the right-angled structure, and the vortex velocity near the wall of the arc structure was only 0.4 times that of the cone and right-angled structures. Therefore, it can be concluded that the arc structure in the ball seat outlet effectively decreased the fluid velocity in the differential motion assembly and improved the severe vortex and turbulence behaviors in the differential motion assembly. Furthermore, the erosion of the inner surface of the differential motion assembly by the drilling fluid could be improved.

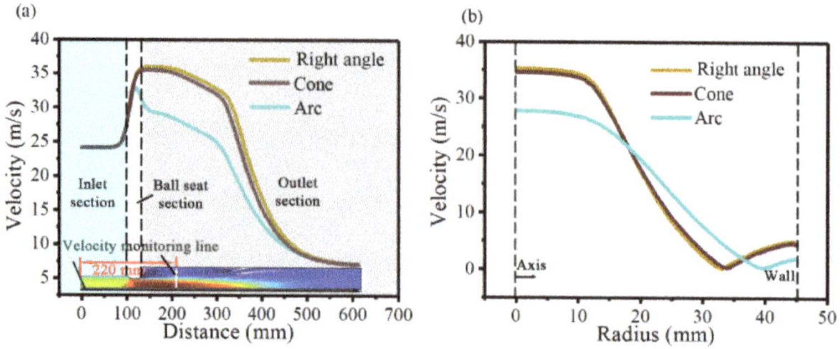

Figure 14. (**a**) Velocity distributions at the black velocity monitoring line with different diameters of the ball seat; (**b**) velocity distributions at the white velocity monitoring line with different diameters of the ball seat; the fluid viscosity was set as 100 mPa·s.

Figure 15 shows the effect of the outlet structure of the ball seat on the pressure distribution. There was a low-pressure zone in the ball seat section of the differential motion assembly with the arc ball seat outlet structure because the flow status changed at the arc. In addition, the pressure drops at the inlet and outlet of the differential motion assembly with the arc ball seat outlet structure were only 0.1 MPa, which was only 0.33 times that of the cone outlet and the right-angled outlet. In summary, the arc outlet ball seat not only greatly reduced the velocity of the drilling fluid and the severe vortex and turbulence behaviors in the differential motion assembly but also decreased the pressure drops in the differential motion assembly. Therefore, this outlet structure of the ball seat can reduce erosion by the drilling fluid and the risk of cutting the pin before the ball is dropped, which would improve the reliability and service life of the differential motion assembly as well as the success rate of the IPP-Coring procedure in deep oil and gas exploration.

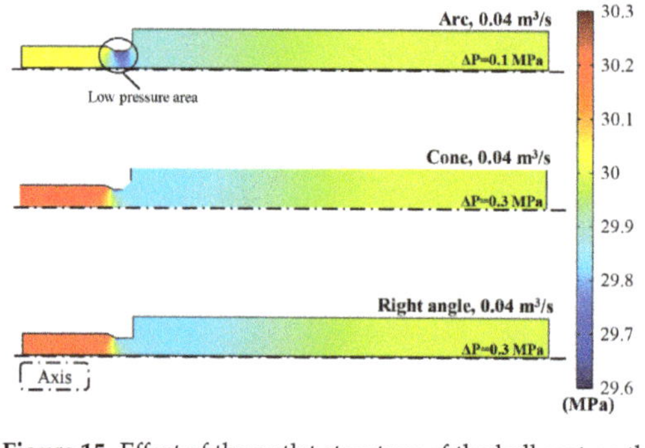

Figure 15. Effect of the outlet structure of the ball seat on the pressure distribution; the fluid viscosity was set as 100 mPa·s.

3.4. Structural Improvement of the Differential Motion Assembly of the IPP-Coring System

From the above results, the differential motion assembly with a 40 mm diameter ball seat and the arc structure in the ball seat outlet shows the lowest pressure drop and fluid velocity. To increase the operational reliability and service life of the differential motion assembly and further increase the success rate of IPP-Coring, this structure was chosen as the improved structure of the differential motion assembly. To quantitatively analyze the erosion of the improved structure, we further calculated the particle trajectories and the erosion of the original and improved differential motion assemblies when the fluid viscosity was set as 100 mPa·s and the inlet flow rate was 0.04 m^3/s. As shown in Figure 16, compared with the original structure, the particles in the improved structure have a lower velocity and less impact on the wall. Therefore, the improved structure shows lower surface erosion, and the average erosion rate is only 0.42 times the value of the original structure. Due to the lower pressure drop and erosion rate, the improved structure has a smaller risk of sticking and triggering the assembly at the wrong time.

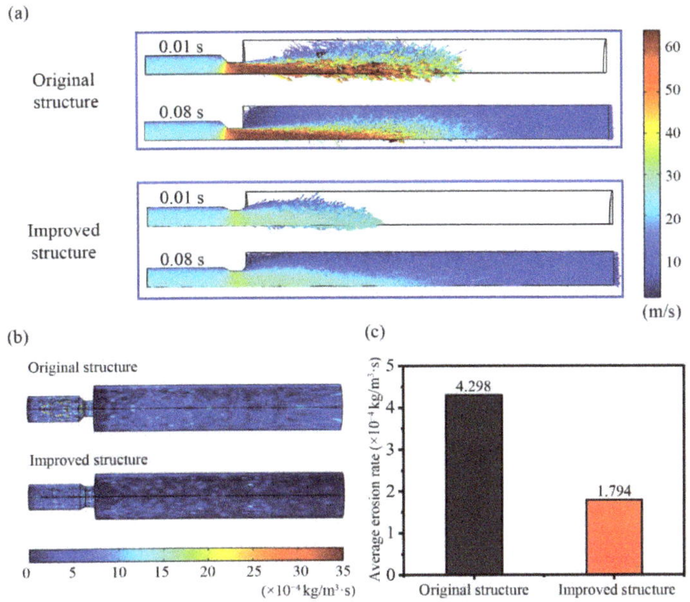

Figure 16. (**a**) Particle trajectories of the original and improved differential motion assembly; (**b**) the erosion contours of the original and improved differential motion assembly; (**c**) the average erosion rate of the original and improved differential motion assembly; the fluid viscosity was set as 100 mPa·s and the inlet flow rate was 0.04 m^3/s.

3.5. Field Validation Experiments

According to the CFD simulation results obtained above, the differential motion assembly was redesigned and manufactured. To validate the simulation results, field experiments were conducted in an experimental well in Tangshan, Hebei, China. During the experiments, the differential motion assembly with original and improved structure was installed in the IPP-Coring system, respectively, and then it was lowed into the well with a depth of 30 m. After that, the pump was turned on and the coring operation was conducted. The solid phase in the drilling fluid is mainly quartz sand and the field experimental conditions were summarized in Table 1.

Table 1. Field experimental conditions.

Parameter	Value
Flow rate (m^3/s)	0.01
Density of the drilling fluid (kg/m^3)	1050
Funnel viscosity of the drilling fluid (s)	60–70

The photographs of the outlet of the ball seat of the original and improved differential motion assemblies after the experiments are shown in Figure 17. It can be seen that there was obvious erosion damage at the outlet of the ball seat of the original differential motion assembly, while the outlet of the ball seat of the improved differential motion assembly was relatively smooth and no obvious surface damage can be observed. In addition, the circulation pump pressure of the system with the improved differential motion assembly decreased from 0.2 MPa to nearly 0 MPa compared with that of the system with the original differential motion assembly. Therefore, it can be validated that the improved differential motion assembly shows the best erosion resistance and the lower pressure drop; thus, it has better promise for field performance.

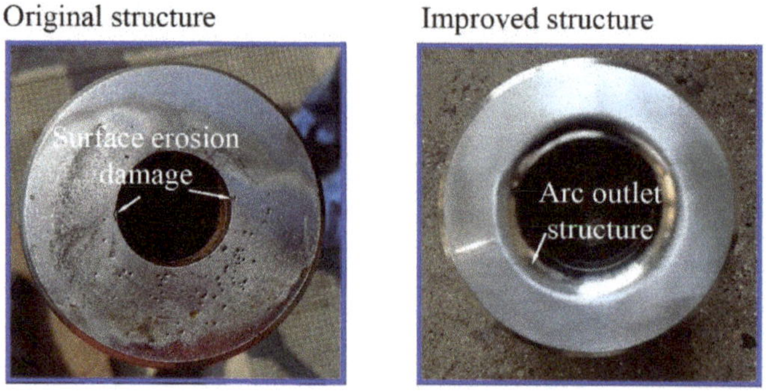

Figure 17. Photographs showing the outlet of the ball seat of the original and improved differential motion assemblies after the experiments.

4. Conclusions

In this study, CFD simulations were performed to investigate the flow characteristics in a differential motion assembly during the IPP-Coring process with different flow rates. The effects of the diameter of the ball seat and the structure of the ball seat outlet on the fluid status, velocity, and pressure distribution were thoroughly investigated. Thus, the hydraulic structure of the differential motion assembly was improved. The specific conclusions are presented as follows:

1. There was a severe vortex area in the differential motion assembly due to the presence of the ball seat. Increased fluid viscosity can increase the local velocity of the flow and decrease the size of the vortex area. In addition, as the inlet flow rate increased from 0.01 to 0.04 m^3/s, the vortex velocity near the wall and the pressure drops between the inlet and outlet of the differential motion assembly increased by 3.8- and 14-fold, respectively.
2. With the increase in the ball seat diameter from 30 to 40 mm, the maximum velocity in the differential motion assembly decreased to 0.55 times that of the original assembly. The axial length of the vortex area and the vortex velocity near the wall decreased to 0.85 and 0.67 times the values of the original assembly. In addition, the pressure drop decreased to 0.2 times that in the original assembly with a 30 mm ball seat diameter.
3. Compared with the cone and original right-angled structures, the arc structure at the ball seat outlet of the differential motion assembly showed the best hydraulic properties. Its axial vortex length and vortex velocity near the wall in the differential motion assembly decreased, respectively, to 0.7 and 0.4 times the values for the system with the original right-angled structure at the ball seat outlet. The pressure drop was only 0.33 times that of the system with the original right-angled structure at the ball seat outlet.
4. Considering the above results, the ball seat with a 40 mm diameter was selected for the differential motion assembly, and the outlet of the ball seat was set as the arc structure. The calculated results of the particle trajectories and the erosion show that the improved structure has lower particle velocity and less impact on the wall, and the average erosion rate decreased to 0.42 times the original structure. Due to the

lower pressure drop and erosion rate, the improved differential motion assembly may have better promise for field performance.

Author Contributions: Conceptualization, D.G. and J.L.; methodology, D.G., D.W. and Y.Z.; software D.G. and X.F.; validation, D.G., J.L. and D.W.; formal analysis, D.G. and X.F.; investigation, D.G. and Y.Z.; resources, H.X.; data curation, D.G.; writing—original draft preparation, D.G.; writing—review and editing, D.G., J.L. and H.X.; visualization, D.G.; supervision, H.X.; project administration, H.X.; funding acquisition, H.X. All authors have read and agreed to the published version of the manuscript.

Funding: The authors are grateful for the financial support from the National Natural Science Foundation of China (No. 51827901), the National Science Fund for Distinguished Young Scholars (No. 52225403) and the Sichuan Science and Technology Program (2023NSFSC0780).

Institutional Review Board Statement: Not applicable.

Informed Consent Statement: Not applicable.

Data Availability Statement: Raw or processed data required to reproduce these findings cannot be shared at this time, as the data also form part of an ongoing study.

Conflicts of Interest: The authors declare no conflict of interest.

References

1. Xie, H.P.; Zhu, J.B.; Zhou, T.; Zhang, K.; Zhou, C.T. Conceptualization and Preliminary Study of Engineering Disturbed Rock Dynamics. *Geomech. Geophys. Geo-Energy Geo-Resour.* **2020**, *6*, 34. [CrossRef]
2. Gao, M.Z.; Zhang, R.; Xie, J.; Peng, G.Y.; Yu, B.; Ranjith, P.G. Field Experiments on Fracture Evolution and Correlations between Connectivity and Abutment Pressure under Top Coal Caving Conditions. *Int. J. Rock Mech. Min. Sci.* **2018**, *111*, 84–93. [CrossRef]
3. Guo, D.; Xie, H.; Chen, L.; Zhou, Z.; Lu, H.; Dai, L. In-Situ Pressure-Preserved Coring for Deep Exploration: Insight into the Rotation Behavior of the Valve Cover of a Pressure Controller. *Pet. Sci.* 2023, *in press*. [CrossRef]
4. Xu, M.; Li, Y.; Chen, L.; Yang, X.; Duan, Z.; Fu, C.; Wang, D. Structural Design and Dynamic Simulation Optimization of the Triggering Device in a Pressure-Holding Controller for Deep In Situ Coring. *Appl. Sci.* **2022**, *12*, 4961. [CrossRef]
5. Xie, H.P.; Gao, F.; Ju, Y. Research and Development of Rock Mechanics in Deep Grounp Engineering. *Chin. J. Rock Mech. Eng.* **2015**, *34*, 2161–2678. [CrossRef]
6. Xie, H.P.; Gao, F.; Ju, Y.; Gao, M.Z.; Zhang, R.; Gao, Y.N.; Liu, J.F.; Xie, L.Z. Quantitative Definition and Investigation of Deep Mining. *J. China Coal Soc.* **2015**, *40*, 1–10. [CrossRef]
7. Xie, H.P.; Zhou, H.W.; Xue, D.J.; Wang, H.W.; Zhang, R.; Gao, F. Research and Consideration on Deep Coal Mining and Critical Mining Depth. *J. China Coal Soc.* **2012**, *37*, 535–542. [CrossRef]
8. Ashena, R.; Thonhauser, G. *Coring Methods and Systems*; Springer: Berlin/Heidelberg, Germany, 2018; ISBN 9783319777337.
9. Li, C.; Pei, J.L.; Wu, N.H.; Liu, G.K.; Huang, W.; Dai, Z.X.; Wang, R.Z.; Chen, Z.F.; Long, W.C. Rotational Failure Analysis of Spherical-Cylindrical Shell Pressure Controllers Related to Gas Hydrate Drilling Investigations. *Pet. Sci.* **2022**, *19*, 789–799. [CrossRef]
10. Xie, H.P.; Liu, T.; Gao, M.Z.; Chen, L.; Zhou, H.W.; Ju, Y.; Gao, F.; Peng, X.B.; Li, X.J.; Peng, R.D.; et al. Research on In-Situ Condition Preserved Coring and Testing Systems. *Pet. Sci.* **2021**, *18*, 1840–1859. [CrossRef]
11. Li, J.N.; Wang, J.; Hu, Y.Q.; You, Z.X.; Xu, M.; Wang, Y.W.; Zou, Z.J.; Kang, Q.Y. Contact Performance Analysis of Pressure Controller's Sealing Interface in Deep in-Situ Pressure-Preserved Coring System. *Pet. Sci.* **2022**, *19*, 1334–1346. [CrossRef]
12. He, Z.Q.; Yang, Y.; Yu, B.; Yang, J.P.; Jiang, X.B.; Tian, B.; Wang, M.; Li, X.Y.; Sun, S.Q.; Sun, H. Research on Properties of Hollow Glass Microspheres/Epoxy Resin Composites Applied in Deep Rock in-Situ Temperature-Preserved Coring. *Pet. Sci.* **2022**, *19*, 720–730. [CrossRef]
13. Hu, Y.Q.; Xie, J.; Xue, S.N.; Xu, M.; Fu, C.H.; He, H.L.; Liu, Z.Q.; Ma, S.M.; Sun, S.Q.; Wang, C.L. Research and Application of Thermal Insulation Effect of Natural Gas Hydrate Freezing Corer Based on the Wireline-Coring Principle. *Pet. Sci.* **2022**, *19*, 1291–1304. [CrossRef]
14. Bjorum, M. A New Coring Technology to Quantify Hydrocarbon Content and Saturation. In Proceedings of the Society of Petroleum Engineers-SPE Canadian Unconventional Resources Conference 2013-Unconventional Becoming Conventional: Lessons Learned and New Innovations, Calgary, AB, Canada, 5–7 November 2013; Volume 2, pp. 1159–1162. [CrossRef]
15. Hyland, C.R. Pressure Coring-an Oilfield Tool. In Proceedings of the Proceedings-SPE Annual Technical Conference and Exhibition, San Francisco, CA, USA, 5–8 October 1983. [CrossRef]
16. Zhu, H.; Liu, Q.; Deng, J.; Wang, G.; Xiao, X.; Jiang, Z.; Zhang, D. Pressure and Temperature Preservation Techniques for Gas-Hydrate-Bearing Sediments Sampling. *Energy* **2011**, *36*, 4542–4551. [CrossRef]
17. Liu, G.K.; Gao, M.Z.; Yang, Z.W.; Chen, L.; Fu, M.Q.; Xie, H.P. The Innovative Design of Deep in Situ Pressure Retained Coring Based on Magnetic Field Trigger Controller. *Adv. Civ. Eng.* **2020**, *2020*, 8873628. [CrossRef]

18. Merey, Ş. Drilling of Gas Hydrate Reservoirs. *J. Nat. Gas Sci. Eng.* **2016**, *35*, 1167–1179. [CrossRef]
19. Sun, Y.; Wang, Y.; Lü, X.; Jia, R.; Guo, W. Hole-Bottom Freezing Method for Gas Hydrate Sampling. *J. Nat. Gas Sci. Eng.* **2015**, *25*, 271–283. [CrossRef]
20. Li, C.; Xie, H.P.; Gao, M.Z.; Chen, L.; Zhao, L.; Li, C.B.; Wu, N.; He, Z.; Li, J. Novel Designs of Pressure Controllers to Enhance the Upper Pressure Limit for Gas-Hydrate-Bearing Sediment Sampling. *Energy* **2021**, *227*, 120405. [CrossRef]
21. He, Z.Q.; Chen, L.; Lu, T.; Xie, J. The Optimization of Pressure Controller for Deep Earth Drilling. *Therm. Sci.* **2019**, *23*, S877–S885. [CrossRef]
22. Chen, J.W.; Fan, W.; Bingham, B.; Chen, Y.; Gu, L.Y.; Li, S.L. A Long Gravity-Piston Corer Developed for Seafloor Gas Hydrate Coring Utilizing an in Situ Pressure-Retained Method. *Energies* **2013**, *6*, 3353–3372. [CrossRef]
23. Abid, K.; Spagnoli, G.; Teodoriu, C.; Falcone, G. Review of Pressure Coring Systems for Offshore Gas Hydrates Research. *Underw. Technol.* **2015**, *33*, 19–30. [CrossRef]
24. Kvenvolden, K.A.; Barnard, L.A.; Cameron, D.H. Pressure Core Barrel: Application to the Study of Gas Hydrates, Deep Sea Drilling Project Site 533, Leg 76. *Initial. Rep. DSDP* **1983**, *76*, 367–375. [CrossRef]
25. Milkov, A.V.; Dickens, G.R.; Claypool, G.E.; Lee, Y.J.; Borowski, W.S.; Torres, M.E.; Xu, W.; Tomaru, H.; Tréhu, A.M.; Schultheiss, P. Co-Existence of Gas Hydrate, Free Gas, and Brine within the Regional Gas Hydrate Stability Zone at Hydrate Ridge (Oregon Margin): Evidence from Prolonged Degassing of a Pressurized Core. *Earth Planet. Sci. Lett.* **2004**, *222*, 829–843. [CrossRef]
26. Dickens, G.R.; Paull, C.K.; Wallace, P. Direct Measurement of in Situ Methane Quantities in a Large Gas-Hydrate Reservoir. *Nature* **1997**, *385*, 426–428. [CrossRef]
27. Dickens, G.R.; Schroeder, D.; Hinrichs, K.-U. *The Pressure Core Sampler (PCS) on ODP Leg 201: General Operations and Gas Release. Texas: Ocean Drilling Program*; Texas A&M University: College Station, TX, USA, 2003; pp. 1–22.
28. Schultheiss, P.; Holland, M.; Humphrey, G. Wireline Coring and Analysis under Pressure: Recent Use and Future Developments of the HYACINTH System. *Sci. Drill.* **2009**, *7*, 44–50. [CrossRef]
29. Amann, H.; Hohnberg, H.J.; Reinelt, R. HYACE—A Novel Autoclave Coring Equipment for Systematic Offshore Gas Hydrate Sampling. *Dtsch. Wiss. Ges. Erdgas Kohle E.V.* **1997**, *9706*, 37–49.
30. Wakishima, R.; Imazato, M.; Nara, M.; Aumann, J.T.; Hyland, C. The Development of a Pressure Temperature Core Sample (PTCS) for the Recovery of in-Situ Methane Hydrates. In Proceedings of the International Symposium on Methane Hydrates; JNOC-TRC: Chiba, Japan, 1998; p. 107.
31. Yang, L.W.; Sun, W.T.; Luo, J.; Wang, G.Y.; Wang, J.M. Study and Application of GWY194-70BB Heat and Pressure Preservation Coring Tool. *OIL Drill. Prod. Technol.* **2014**, *36*, 58–61.
32. Yang, L.W.; Su, Y.; Luo, J.; Sun, S.L. Development and Application of GW-CP194-80A Pressure-Maintaining Coring Tool. *Nat. Gas Ind.* **2020**, *40*, 91–96.
33. Messa, G.V.; Yang, Q.; Adedeji, O.E.; Chára, Z.; Duarte, C.A.R.; Matoušek, V.; Rasteiro, M.G.; Sean Sanders, R.; Silva, R.C.; Souza, F.J. De Computational Fluid Dynamics Modelling of Liquid–Solid Slurry Flows in Pipelines: State-of-the-Art and Future Perspectives. *Processes* **2021**, *9*, 1566. [CrossRef]
34. Wang, Q.; Huang, Q.; Wang, N.; Wen, Y.; Ba, X.; Sun, X.; Zhang, J.; Karimi, S.; Shirazi, S.A. An Experimental and Numerical Study of Slurry Erosion Behavior in a Horizontal Elbow and Elbows in Series. *Eng. Fail. Anal.* **2021**, *130*, 105779. [CrossRef]
35. Quan, J.; Liu, X.; Wang, C.; Gu, Y.; Wang, C.; Jin, H. A Study on Corrosion Failure of the Circulation Line with Valve Openings in Atmospheric Tower Based on CFD. *Eng. Fail. Anal.* **2022**, *141*, 106633. [CrossRef]
36. Tang, Y.; Zhao, P.; Li, X.; Fang, X.; Yang, P. Numerical Simulation and Experimental Test of the Sliding Core Dynamics of a Pressure Controlled Jet Crushing Tool for Natural Gas Hydrate Exploitation. *Processes* **2022**, *10*, 1033. [CrossRef]
37. Tang, Y.; Jing, X.; Li, W.; He, Y.; Yao, J. Analysis of Influence of Different Convex Structures on Cooling Effect of Rectangular Water Channel of Motorized Spindle. *Appl. Therm. Eng.* **2021**, *198*, 117478. [CrossRef]
38. Alghurabi, A.; Mohyaldinn, M.; Jufar, S.; Younis, O.; Abduljabbar, A.; Azuwan, M. CFD Numerical Simulation of Standalone Sand Screen Erosion Due to Gas-Sand Flow. *J. Nat. Gas Sci. Eng.* **2021**, *85*, 103706. [CrossRef]
39. Zhao, J.; Zhang, G.; Xu, Y.; Wang, R.; Zhou, W.; Yang, D. Experimental and Theoretical Evaluation of Solid Particle Erosion in an Internal Flow Passage within a Drilling Bit. *J. Pet. Sci. Eng.* **2018**, *160*, 582–596. [CrossRef]
40. Zheng, C.; Liu, Y.; Wang, H.; Zhu, H.; Liu, Z.; Ji, R.; Shen, Y. Structural Optimization of Downhole Fracturing Tool Using Turbulent Flow CFD Simulation. *J. Pet. Sci. Eng.* **2015**, *133*, 218–225. [CrossRef]
41. Feng, C.; Liu, W.; Gao, D. CFD Simulation and Optimization of Slurry Erosion of PDC Bits. *Powder Technol.* **2022**, *408*, 117658. [CrossRef]
42. Yang, S.; Fan, J.; Zhang, L.; Sun, B. Performance Prediction of Erosion in Elbows for Slurry Flow under High Internal Pressure. *Tribol. Int.* **2021**, *157*, 106879. [CrossRef]
43. Pei, J.; Lui, A.; Zhang, Q.; Xiong, T.; Jiang, P.; Wei, W. Numerical Investigation of the Maximum Erosion Zone in Elbows for Liquid-Particle Flow. *Powder Technol.* **2018**, *333*, 47–59. [CrossRef]
44. Zheng, C.; Liu, Y.; Wang, H.; Zhu, H.; Liu, Z.; Cai, B.; Shen, Y. Numerical Study on Improving the Erosion Life of Ball Seat for Oil and Gas Reservoir Fracturing. *Eng. Fail. Anal.* **2016**, *60*, 188–198. [CrossRef]
45. Ahlert, K.R. Effects of Particle Impingement Angle and Surface Wetting on Solid Particle Erosion of AISI 1018 Steel. Ph.D. Thesis, University of Tulsa, Tulsa, OK, USA, 1994.

46. Zhang, Y.; Reuterfors, E.P.; McLaury, B.S.; Shirazi, S.A.; Rybicki, E.F. Comparison of Computed and Measured Particle Velocities and Erosion in Water and Air Flows. *Wear* **2007**, *263*, 330–338. [CrossRef]
47. Javaheri, V.; Porter, D.; Kuokkala, V.T. Slurry Erosion of Steel-Review of Tests, Mechanisms and Materials. *Wear* **2018**, *408–409*, 248–273. [CrossRef]

applied sciences

MDPI

Article

Development of an In-Situ Simulation Device for Testing Deep Pressure-Preserving Coring Tools under High-Temperature and Ultrahigh-Pressure Conditions

Wei Huang [1], Heping Xie [1,2,3], Jianan Li [2], Yang Yang [2], Cong Li [2,3], Zhiqiang He [2,3], Yihang Li [2] and Zetian Zhang [2,*]

1 School of Mechanical Engineering, Sichuan University, Chengdu 610065, China
2 College of Water Resource & Hydropower, Sichuan University, Chengdu 610065, China
3 Guangdong Provincial Key Laboratory of Deep Earth Sciences, Geothermal Energy Exploitation and Utilization, Institute of Deep Earth Sciences and Green Energy, College of Civil and Transportation Engineering, Shenzhen University, Shenzhen 518060, China
* Correspondence: zhangzetian@scu.edu.cn

Abstract: With the increasing mining depth of deep mineral resources, the underground temperature and pressure also increase, which requires more advanced mining equipment. Therefore, to adapt to the special application scenario of the research and development of pressure-preserving coring tools under the extreme environmental conditions of deep strata, in this study, an in-situ simulation device under high-temperature and ultrahigh-pressure conditions is developed. The principles and methods of applying temperature and pressure to the device are expounded. Furthermore, the two main modules of the device are analyzed and studied experimentally. On the one hand, a segmented simulated coring test cabin is constructed, and pressure testing of the test cabin is carried out. The results show that the test cabin with inner diameters of 150 mm and 500 mm runs stably under the working condition of a pressure up to 190 MPa (considering the influence of temperature of 150 °C), and the cabin remains in the stage of elastic deformation. There is no leakage of pressure or fluid in the whole test process. On the other hand, the performance of the driving module is tested. The results show that the driving module can provide a stable rotation speed of up to 150 r/min when the sealing pressure is 140 MPa. Therefore, the device can be applied to carry out simulated coring test and is suitable for the research and development of pressure-preserving coring tools in deep extreme environments, which may promote the development of deep mining engineering.

Keywords: coring simulation device; high-temperature; ultrahigh-pressure; pressure-preserving coring tools

1. Introduction

With the continuous exploitation of global resources, the number of deep and ultradeep holes is increasing, and the pressure and temperature of the occurrence environment at the bottom of holes are also increasing [1–4]. Because the physical and chemical properties of rocks in deep in-situ environments are quite different from those under normal temperature and pressure [5], it is very important to obtain in-situ rock samples and study their related properties to realize effective evaluation of deep resources [6–8]. At the same time, a high-temperature and high-pressure environment will impact the engineering of deep drilling projects. When the resource mining depth exceeds 1000 m, a series of mining accidents will occur because existing rock theory cannot provide theoretical support for the development of deep mining technology [9,10]. Therefore, it is urgent to evaluate rock theory in a deep in-situ state to promote the development of deep mining technology.

During the exploration of deep rock, it is important to retrieve cores with their in-situ pressure conditions to more accurately simulate the occurrence environment (temperature and pressure) of deep rock samples [11–14]. According to cores obtained in recent decades, deep cores undergo cracking and destruction as they are brought to the surface, which changes their original composition and characteristics. This phenomenon is caused by the lack of means necessary to maintain the pressure environment of the core as it is raised from the bottom of the hole to the surface and exposed on the ground; this changes the environment of the core, results in the release of internal stress, and alters the composition [15–21]. Therefore, it is of great significance to study the physical and mechanical properties of bottom-hole rock with deep cores for which the in-situ pressure is preserved. To achieve this goal, it is necessary to simulate the deep temperature and pressure environment first, because this provides an experimental environment for the development of coring tools compatible with high pressures and solves the problems of high-risk and high-cost for on-site coring tests.

The simulation of a high-temperature and ultrahigh-pressure environment can be used to verify the performance of a pressure-preserving coring tools in deep environments. At present, research institutions have carried out considerable research on downhole simulation test devices and have made some progress [22–26]. Ekei et al. used an indoor micro-drill to conduct drilling tests on rock samples subjected to lithostatic pressure, pore pressure, and drilling fluid column pressure at the same time, and studied the effects of fluid properties and pressure on the drilling speed of rock samples [27]. Schlumberger Cambridge Research Center in the UK has established a drilling simulation test facility that can be used to study the mechanical properties of drill bits and rocks [28]. This facility can provide a pressure environment with a maximum overburden pressure of 17.9 MPa, a lithostatic pressure of 103.5 MPa, and a pore pressure and drilling fluid column pressure of 69 MPa, and achieve the highest simulation temperature of 200 °C. Terra Tek, Inc. [29,30] has developed a full-scale simulation drilling test device to simulate downhole pressure, which is as follows: overburden pressure of 207 MPa, lithostatic pressure of 138 MPa, pore pressure of 27.6 MPa, and liquid column pressure of 103 MPa. A series of important conclusions in the field of drilling have been obtained by using standard tricone bits to drill rock samples. The simulation test device manufactured by the Comprehensive Research Institute of Resources and Environment Technology of the Ministry of Industry and Technology of Japan can complete the simulation of temperature and pressure environment of the stratum with a depth of 6000 m at the bottom of the well [31], in which the compressive stress of overlying strata can be simulated to be 135 MPa, pore pressure and liquid column pressure to be 50 MPa, and lithostatic pressure to be 100 MPa. The test unit can simulate the drilling of rock samples with a diameter of 215.9 mm or less. The full-size drilling simulation test device developed by the Belm Branch of the Drilling Technology Research Institute of the former Soviet Union in Russia used a rock sample with a diameter of 260 mm and a length of 1500 mm in the simulation drilling test [31,32]. The device can simulate the temperature and pressure environment of rock occurrence at the bottom of the well at 20,000 m, mainly used for the study of rock physical characteristics. The Institute of Exploration Technology of the Ministry of Geology and Mineral Resources developed the M150 simulation wellbore with a maximum simulated pressure of 2.45 MPa and a simulated temperature of 150 °C [33]. The China National Petroleum Corporation (CNPC) has established a drilling tool test system at the Daguang Oilfield [34], which is mainly used to test the reliability of drilling tools. Its maximum simulated temperature is 180 °C, and its maximum pressure is 60 MPa. Wei Linshan et al. [35] designed a set of high-temperature and high-pressure simulation test systems for instrument development and used them to test the safety and reliability of sensitive instrumental components in high-temperature and high-pressure environments. Pang Dongxiao et al. [36] developed a high-temperature and high-pressure experimental device for downhole tools, and it performed loading and torsion tests on tools inside the wellbore. The high-temperature and high-pressure downhole tool experimental device developed by Xu Dingjiang et al. [37] was used to conduct performance evaluation experiments on various downhole tools, such as packers and throttles. Zhang Weihong et al. [38] developed a simulation test device for downhole tools in vertical holes, and it simulates the working conditions under formation temperature and pressure. The device can simulate test functions for downhole tools with different specifications, including heating, loading, pressurization, and circulation of oil casings. Though these studies were designed by research groups in different fields for different purposes and requirements, all of them have important value. However, most studies have only simulated the downhole pressure environment, and few have simulated the temperature. Meanwhile, these devices are mainly used to study rock properties and bit performance. Very few are dedicated to the development of coring tools, and even fewer are dedicated to the research of pressure-preserving coring tools. Therefore, the development of an in-situ high-temperature and ultrahigh-pressure device for deep pressure-preserving coring tools is described in this paper. The goal is to build a test system capable of simulating a maximum pressure of 140 MPa and a maximum temperature of 150 °C to carry out experimental research on pressure-preserving coring tools in deep extreme environments. The research and development of such a device is of great significance to the mining engineering of deep resources.

2. Principle and Structure of the In-Situ Simulation Device for Deep Coring Tools

2.1. The Structure and Design Principle of the Device

A high-temperature and ultrahigh-pressure simulation test for deep coring tools must have a strictly controlled working environment. The simulation test device is a comprehensive test system that comprises two parts: a high-temperature and ultrahigh-pressure simulation test cabin and a driving module for simulating coring tests, as shown in Figure 1. High-temperature and ultrahigh-pressure simulation test cabins can be used to simulate the in-situ occurrence environment of underground rock. The driving module for simulating coring tests provides a power source for the coring tools and allows it to realize rotation and downward vertical action and ultrahigh-pressure dynamic sealing. The key design specifications of the in-situ simulation device were as follows:

(1) Maximum working pressure of the test cabin: 140 MPa;
(2) Maximum operating temperature of the test cabin: 150 °C;
(3) Maximum working pressure of the driving module: 140 MPa;
(4) Maximum rotation speed of the driving module: 150 r/min;
(5) Inner diameter of the rock cabin: 500 mm;
(6) Inner diameter of the drill pipe cabin: 150 mm.

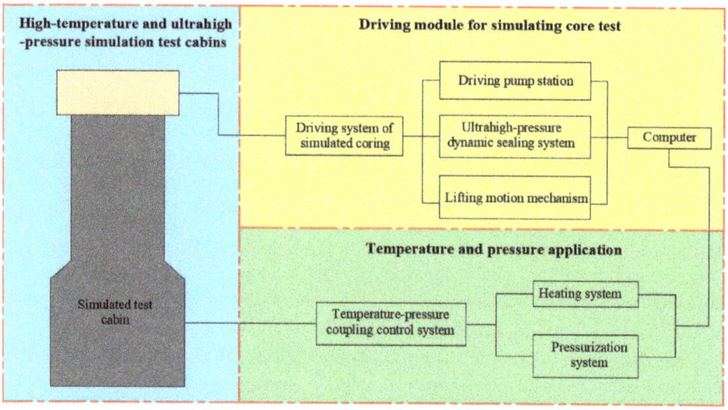

Figure 1. Schematic diagram of the in-situ simulation device.

In addition to meeting the requirements for the temperature, pressure, and size parameters described above, the simulation device should follow these design principles [22–24]: (1) safety and reliability; (2) economy (the costs of design, materials, processing, and manufacturing should be reduced as much as possible, as long as the components meet the use requirements); (3) easy maintenance; and (4) simple application (the design and manufacture of the whole test chamber system should adopt existing structural forms and processing technology as much as possible, with simple application as the goal).

2.2. Principle of Temperature and Pressure Application

(1) Analysis of the stress state of underground rock

In the deep earth environment, rocks are mainly subjected to multidirectional compressive stress. In the actual drilling and coring process, the pressure on bottom-hole rock in a high-temperature environment is due to four compressive stresses: overburden pressure, lithostatic pressure, pore pressure, and drilling fluid column pressure. The stress state of rock is illustrated in Figure 2 [31].

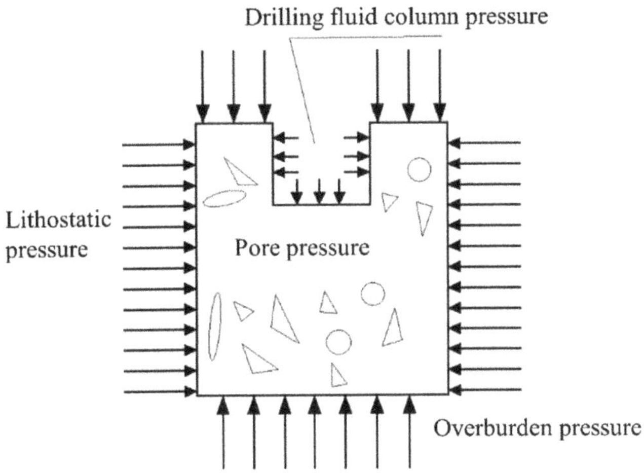

Figure 2. Stress state of rock at the bottom of the hole.

The overburden pressure is caused by the vertical downward pressure exerted by rocks in the upper strata. Lithostatic pressure is the lateral pressure exerted by rocks in the surrounding strata. Due to the presence of pores in the rock, the fluid in the pores provides pore pressure. Fluid column pressure is caused by the unavoidable use of drilling fluid during drilling, which exerts pressure on the rock.

(2) Temperature and pressure application method

The principle for applying temperature and pressure is shown in Figure 3. To apply overburden pressure on rock samples, a pressure oil cylinder is added in the lower part of the rock cabin, the pressurized hydraulic oil enters the lower end face of the piston, and the piston applies the overburden pressure on the upper face of the rock sample. The overburden pressure can be adjusted by adjusting the oil pressure on the lower end of the piston, and finally, an overburden pressure of 140 MPa is applied to the rock sample.

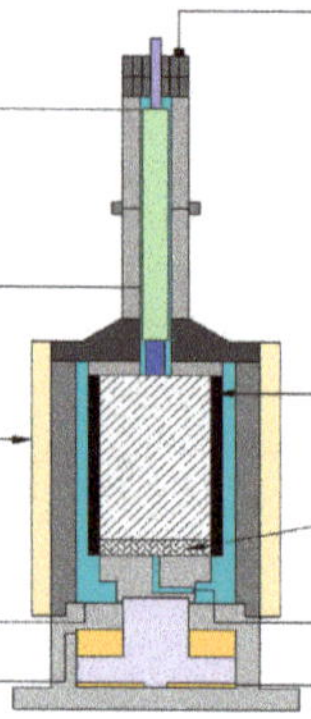

Figure 3. Schematic diagram of temperature-pressure application.

A special rubber sleeve is used to wrap the rock sample, and the outer cylindrical surface of the rock sample and the inner wall of the rock cabin form a closed pressurized space. Then, the high-pressure pump forces high-temperature and high-pressure water into the space. The rock sample rubber sleeve applies pressure perpendicular to the sample surface, which provides lithostatic pressure on the rock sample. To apply pore pressure, the high-temperature and high-pressure water added by the high-pressure pump is injected into a hole through a pore in the middle of the upper cover of the piston, flows to the porous bottom plate, and then penetrates upward from the bottom of the rock sample. The drilling fluid column pressure is added by regulating the back pressure with a throttle valve installed in a high-pressure line in the return hole of the first drill pipe cabin.

The outer layer of the rock sample chamber is wrapped with a layer of heating material to apply heat to the rock sample. Although the pressurized oil in the bottom oil cylinder is at normal temperature, the lithostatic pressure, pore pressure, and drilling fluid column pressure are established with a high-temperature and high-pressure water with a temperature of 150 °C, which also applies heat to the whole test cabin. Additionally, the use of clear water as a heating and pressurizing medium reflects the actual drilling process.

3. Analysis and Design of Key Components

3.1. High-Temperature and Ultrahigh-Pressure Simulation Test Cabin

With the requirements of high-pressure resistance and a large pressure vessel, the material and structure of the pressure vessel must be strictly controlled. In practical engineering, vessels with design pressures between 10 and 100 MPa are generally called high-pressure vessels, and those with design pressures exceeding 100 MPa are called ultrahigh-pressure vessels. The maximum working pressure of the coring simulation test chamber proposed in this paper is 140 MPa, so it belongs to the category of ultrahigh-pressure vessels.

3.1.1. Overall Structure of the Simulation Test Cabin

The high-temperature and ultrahigh-pressure simulation test chamber is used to create the downhole environment and accommodate large rock samples, and it must also meet operating space requirements for the coring tester. The overall structure is shown in Figure 4. The chamber consists of two main parts. The first part is the rock sample chamber, which contains a ∅480 × 1500 mm rock sample to be drilled. Based on the application space needed for control of the four pressures and the temperature acting on the rock sample, the inner diameter of the rock sample chamber is set at 500 mm, and the length is 2400 mm. The second part is the drill pipe cabin located in the upper part of the core cabin. Based on the operational size requirements of the core, the drill pipe cabin is divided into two sections. The length of the first drill pipe cabin is 2 m, the length of the second drill pipe cabin is 3 m, and both are 150 mm in diameter. During simulation tests, the coring device is put into the drill pipe cabin to simulate the coring of rock samples in the rock cabin. In addition, an intermediate transition cabin and the bottom oil cylinder are included.

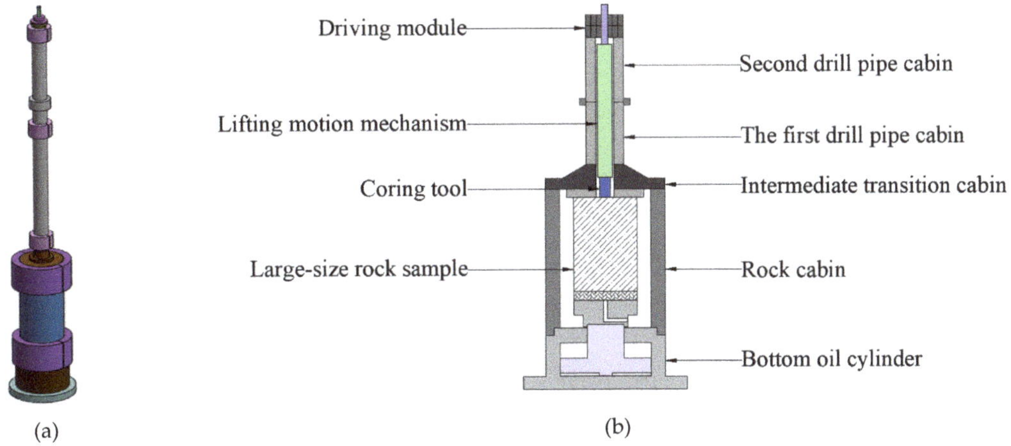

Figure 4. Overall structure of the simulation test cabin. (**a**) 3D model. (**b**) Two-dimensional cross-section.

3.1.2. The Structural Form of the Cabin

The maximum working pressure of the simulation test chamber designed in this paper is 140 MPa, and the maximum working temperature is 150 °C. Therefore, there are many design differences between this simulation test cabin and a cylinder under normal temperature and pressure, including the structural form, material, and wall thickness. At present, many research institutions have adopted various cylindrical structures for simulation test devices. The most commonly used structures are single-layer integral forged thick-walled cylinders, integral forged self-reinforcing thick-walled cylinders, double-layer and multilayer thick-walled cylinders, wire-wound cylinders, split block cylinders, and interlayer charging cylinders [30]. The bearing capacities for cylinders with different structural forms are not the same; the bearing capacity of a double-layer or multilayer cylinder is higher than that of a single-layer cylinder, and self-reinforced or prestressed structures carry higher loads than structures that are not self-reinforced or prestressed. Each cylinder structure has corresponding advantages and limiting factors. Therefore, in designing the structural form of the cylinder, all factors should be fully considered to choose a correct and reasonable structural form that meets usage requirements and is economical.

Figure 5 [39] shows the relationships between the ratio of the outer diameter to the inner diameter of cylinders with various structural forms and the pressures they bear. Based on Figure 5, the simulation test chamber in this paper was designed with a single-layer cylindrical structure to meet the usage requirements. The ranges and characteristics of various cylinder forms are listed in Table 1 [39]. Based on a comparison of various types of cylinder structures and economic considerations for manufacturing, a single-layer integral forged thick-walled cylinder was chosen for the test cabin.

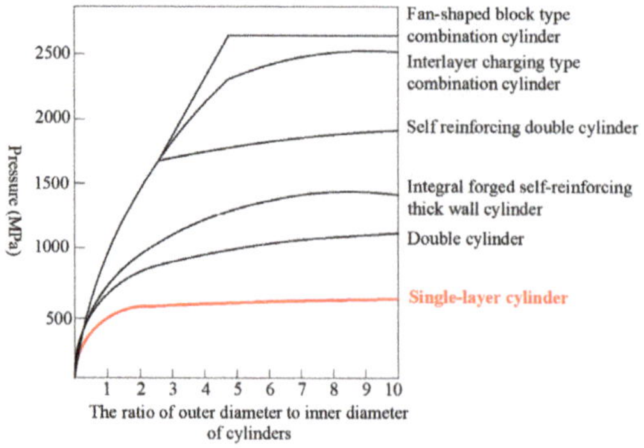

Figure 5. Bearing capacities of various cylindrical structures.

Table 1. Structural characteristics and application range for each cylinder form.

Structural Style		Characteristic	Scope of Application
Single-layer cylinder	Integral forging	Due to the limitation of forging conditions and high cost, it is suitable for steel with poor welding performance	The diameter of the cylinder is between 300 mm and 800 mm, and the length does not exceed 12 m
	Roll-welded cylinder	Simple process, short cycle, high efficiency; however, it cannot be used when the cylinder diameter is too small	The diameter of the cylinder is greater than 400 mm, and the maximum thickness is 110 mm
	Segmentally welded cylinder	Does not need large coil equipment; low productivity	The larger the diameter is, the longer the manufacturing time
	Seamless tubular cylinder	The source of raw materials is convenient, the manufacturing efficiency is high, and the cycle is short	The diameter of the cylinder should not exceed 500 mm

3.1.3. Analysis and Calculation of Wall Thickness

(1) Material selection

The materials used in the design and manufacture of the simulation test cabin must be provided by the manufacturer with the required material parameters. Key parameters for materials used in ultrahigh-pressure vessels have been stipulated in the literature [40] and are shown in Table 2.

Table 2. Material property specifications for ultrahigh-pressure vessels.

Percent Elongation after Fracture	Charpy Impact Work	Fracture Toughness	Area Reduction
≥16%	≥41 J	≥120 MPa	≥40%

According to the requirements for materials used in the simulation test cabin and the need for economy, the material chosen for the test chamber designed in this paper was 35CrNi3MoVR. The mechanical properties of the material at room temperature are shown in Table 3, and the mechanical properties at 150 °C are shown in Table 4 [40].

Table 3. Mechanical properties of 35CrNi3MoVR at room temperature.

Yield Strength, MPa	Strength of Extension, MPa	Percent Elongation after Fracture	Area Reduction	Shock Absorption Energy	Lateral Expansion, mm
≥960	1070–1230	≥16	≥45	≥47	≥0.53

Table 4. Mechanical properties of 35CrNi3MoVR at 150 °C.

Mark	Intensity Index	Date
35CrNi3MoVR	Yield strength Strength of extension	≥857 MPa ≥1060 MPa

According to the performance parameters given for 35CrNi3MoVR in Tables 3 and 4, the wall thickness of the rock cabin and drill pipe cabin were designed to provide a room temperature yield strength of $R_{p0.2}$ = 960 MPa and a tensile strength of R_m = 1070 MPa. At a design temperature of 150 °C, the yield strength and tensile strength were
$R^t_{p0.2}$ = 857 MPa and R^t_m = 1060 MPa, respectively. In this paper, the tensile test data for materials were used to calculate the thickness of the cylinder. The strength reduction coefficient of materials at 150°C was calculated as shown in Equation (1), which is 0.9.

$$\phi = 1 - \frac{T - 50}{1000} \quad (1)$$

where ϕ is the strength reduction coefficient of materials, and T is the temperature.

(2) Calculation of wall thickness

The failure criteria for pressure vessels mainly include elastic failure, plastic failure, and blasting failure criteria. The elastic failure criterion has been widely used and is poorly understood. Container elastic failure indicates that when the cylinder is subjected to internal pressure or other complex working loads, the stress on the cylinder wall is higher than the yield strength, and the container cannot continue to work normally. Plastic failure refers to the condition that, even though the local stress of the cylinder has exceeded the yield strength of the material and the material has undergone plastic deformation, as long as the cylinder material has not entered the full yield state, the container is not considered to have failed. Only when the whole container wall has completely undergone plastic deformation will the container fail [41,42].

The material properties of a single-layer integral forged thick-walled cylinder include high strength and good plasticity. When all materials in the cylinder yield, the increase in plastic deformation of the material leads to strain hardening and wall thinning. When the effect of strain hardening is stronger than the effect of wall thinning, the bearing capacity of the cylinder is enhanced. When the two effects are equivalent, the bearing capacity of the cylinder reaches the limit. If the load is increased further, the influence of wall thinning is more significant, which results in a decreased bearing capacity of the cylinder. When a certain pressure is reached, the container bursts, and blasting failure occurs. The materials used in ultrahigh-pressure vessels are generally high-strength materials rather than ideal plastic materials; with increases in the internal pressure of the container, the material gradually yields and then enters the plastic deformation phase. Due to material strain hardening, the container carrying capacity increases until blasting, and the bearing pressure at this time is called the burst pressure. The blasting failure process for container materials is illustrated in Figure 6 [39].

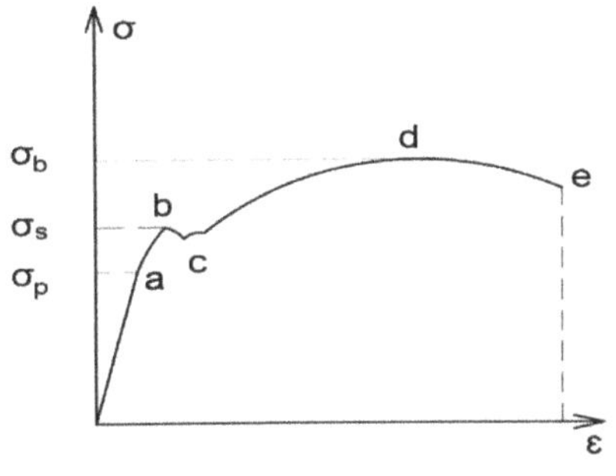

Figure 6. Failure process for nonideal plastic materials.

Although there are many methods for calculating the blasting failure criterion for a thick-walled pressure vessel, the Faupel formula is most widely used in practical engineering, and its derivation proceeds is as follows [43–46]:

The yield pressure of the vessel in the full yield state is:

$$p_s = \frac{2}{\sqrt{3}} R_{p0.2} \ln(K) \tag{2}$$

where p_s is the full yield pressure, MPa; $R_{p0.2}$ is the yield strength of the material at room temperature, MPa; and K is the ratio of the outside diameter to the inside diameter of the container.

Therefore, the bursting pressure can be written as:

$$p_b = \frac{2}{\sqrt{3}} R_m \ln(K) \tag{3}$$

where p_b is the blasting pressure, MPa and R_m is the tensile strength of the material at room temperature, MPa.

The formula for the calculation of burst pressure can be modified as follows:

$$p_b = \frac{R_{p0.2}}{R_m}(\frac{2}{\sqrt{3}} R_m \ln(K)) + (1 - \frac{R_{p0.2}}{R_m})(\frac{2}{\sqrt{3}} R_{p0.2} \ln(K)) \tag{4}$$

The final burst pressure is:

$$p_b = (2 - \frac{R_{p0.2}}{R_m})\frac{2}{\sqrt{3}} R_{p0.2} \ln(K) \tag{5}$$

The wall thickness of the simulation test cabin designed in this paper was calculated with the Faupel formula (Equation (5)). Because the simulation test chamber operates in a high-temperature and ultrahigh-pressure environment, all cylinders are subjected to high temperature and high pressure at the same time. Therefore, when calculating the thickness of the test chamber wall, the thermal load should be converted into a certain pressure and included in the design pressure, which can be converted as shown in Equation (6).

$$P_D = \phi(\frac{p_b}{n_b}) \tag{6}$$

In this formula, P_D is the design pressure; because the design pressure of the cabin body should not be lower than its maximum working pressure, 1.08 times the working pressure should be used as the design pressure. ϕ is the strength reduction coefficient of the material at the design temperature, which is calculated to be 0.9 according to Equation (1). n_b is the blasting safety factor of the cabin, which should be greater than or equal to 2.2 when calculated from tensile test data. Considering the economy of equipment manufacturing and the safety of use, the blasting safety factor of the rock cabin designed in this paper is 2.5. As the total length of drill pipe cabin is 5 m, to avoid the instability of equipment caused by large axial deformation during operation, its blasting safety factor is further increased to 3. Therefore, the wall thickness calculation formula can be derived as follows [39].

$$\ln(K) = \frac{P_b}{\frac{2}{\sqrt{3}} R_{P0.2}(2 - \frac{R_{P0.2}}{R_m})} = \ln(\frac{R_i + \delta}{R_i}) \tag{7}$$

where R_i is the inner radius, mm and δ is the wall thickness, mm.

Therefore,

$$\delta = \frac{D_i}{2}\left[\exp(\frac{\sqrt{3} n_b P(D)}{2\phi R_{P0.2}(2 - \frac{R_{P0.2}}{R_m})}) - 1\right] \tag{8}$$

where D_i is the inner diameter, mm.

The wall thickness required for a rock cabin with an inner diameter of 500 mm was calculated with Equation (8) as follows:

$$\delta = \frac{D_i}{2}\left[\exp(\frac{\sqrt{3}n_b P(D)}{2\phi R_{P0.2}(2-\frac{R_{P0.2}}{R_m})})-1\right] = \frac{500}{2}\left[\exp(\frac{\sqrt{3}\times 2.5\times 140\times 1.08}{2\times 0.9\times 960\times(2-\frac{960}{1070})})-1\right] = 102.49\text{mm}$$

The wall thickness required for a drill pipe cabin with an inner diameter of 150 mm was calculated as follows:

$$\delta = \frac{D_i}{2}\left[\exp(\frac{\sqrt{3}n_b P(D)}{2\phi R_{P0.2}(2-\frac{R_{P0.2}}{R_m})})-1\right] = \frac{150}{2}\left[\exp(\frac{\sqrt{3}\times 3\times 140\times 1.08}{2\times 0.9\times 960\times(2-\frac{960}{1070})})-1\right] = 38.27\text{mm}$$

Therefore, when 1.08 times the maximum working pressure was taken as the design pressure and blasting failure was adopted as the design criterion, the wall thickness of the rock cabin was 102.49 mm and that of the drill pipe cabin was 38.27 mm. In actual working conditions, the influence of added thickness and manufacturing deviations should be considered, so the thickness of rock cabin should be increased to 107.5 mm and that of drill cabin was rounded up to 40 mm.

Therefore, the inner diameter of the rock cabin is 500 mm and that the outer diameter is 715 mm. The inside diameter of the drill pipe cabin is 150 mm, and the outside diameter is 230 mm. In the calculations of wall thickness for each section of the cabin, the thermal load and pressure on the test cabin were considered simultaneously. Theoretically, the calculated wall thickness can bear an ultrahigh pressure of 140 MPa and a temperature of 150 °C at the same time.

3.2. *Driving Module for Simulating Coring Tests*

The driving module consists of two parts: a dynamic system and a lifting motion mechanism. The dynamic system provides weight on bit, torque and speed for simulated coring tests and provides a dynamic sealing function for the upper part of the device. The lifting motion mechanism is used to connect the power system to the pressure-preserving coring tool, to transfer weight on bit and torque, and to assist in the function of the coring tool.

3.2.1. Structure and Working Principle of the Lifting Motion Mechanism

In an actual field coring process, rotational and vertical downward coring movements must be completed. To maintain the core pressure after the core enters the core barrel, it must be pulled into the core device, which provides similar environmental conditions. Because the rotary drive pump station can provide only rotary coring motion, it cannot provide the downward feeding motion. Therefore, the lifting mechanism in the cabin was designed independently to realize the vertical downward coring motion and core lifting motion after drilling. The lifting mechanism in the cabin was mainly composed of a rotating shaft, rotating piston, core lifting mechanism, rotating piston joint, and corer joint, as shown in Figure 7.

The working principle of the lifting motion mechanism is as follows: The rotation shaft is driven by the rotating pump station, and a spline connection is placed between the rotating piston and the rotating drive shaft, so the rotating shaft causes the piston to rotate. Additionally, the rotary piston is driven by the drilling pressure and moves downward in a straight line. Furthermore, power is transferred to the upper part of the corer by rotating the piston joint and the upper part of the corer, thus initiating the coring motion. After the coring motion is completed, the drilling pressure is reduced, and the piston is moved upward by the pressure difference; the corer joint and coring device form a threaded connection, and the rotating piston joint and coring device jointly adopt the form of a spline connection to release the spline. This part of the rotating piston connection moves upward, driving up the core-lifting mechanism to complete the coring motion.

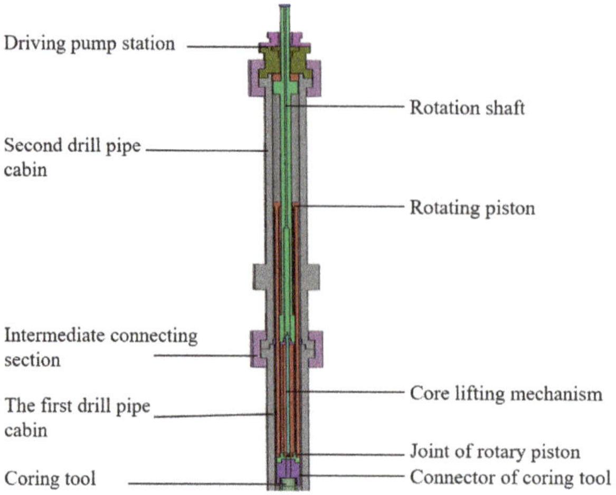

Figure 7. Structure of the lifting motion mechanism.

3.2.2. Composition of the Dynamic System

This system includes the driving pump station and an ultrahigh-pressure rotary dynamic sealing system [6], and the main function is to provide a power source for simulated coring tests and activation of the pressure seal inside the cabin. The ultrahigh-pressure rotary sealing structure consists of three groups of sealing rings, as shown in Figure 8. Each set of sealing rings comprise an "O"-type rubber ring, a "Z"-type sealing ring with grooves on the inner surface, and a supporting sleeve. Among them, the "Z" ring is made of polytetrafluoroethylene (PTFE). PTFE has the advantages of a low friction coefficient and high wear resistance, and it can adapt to ultrahigh-pressure rotary dynamic sealing conditions. On this basis, a pair of combined grooves is provided on the main sealing surface and matched with the rotating axis of the "Z" ring. Combined grooves can cover impurities and prevent the sealing surface from being damaged. Additionally, lubricating oil can be stored inside the combined grooves and produce a lubricating oil film on the main sealing surface during operation and effectively prevent wear and destruction of the main sealing surface.

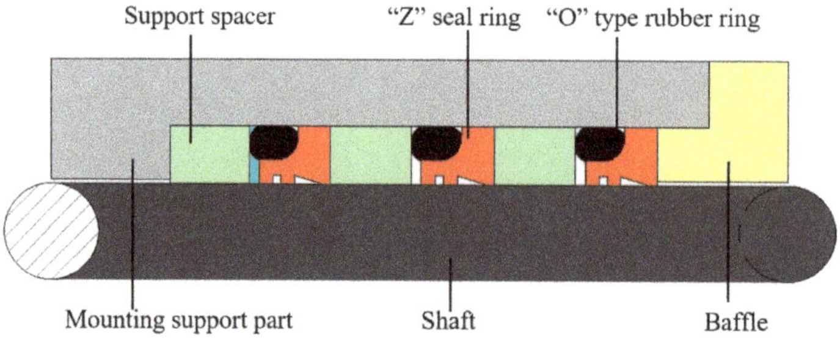

Figure 8. Ultrahigh-pressure rotary dynamic sealing structure.

4. Experimental Study and Results Analysis of the Device

The in-situ simulation device for testing deep coring tools is composed of two main modules. The high-temperature and ultrahigh-pressure simulation test cabin needs to operate under the ultrahigh-pressure of 140 MPa and the high-temperature of 150 °C, so the influence of temperature and pressure on the deformation of the cabin was taken into account during the experiment. However, the driving module is located at the upper end of the drill pipe cabin and far away from the rock cabin. Meanwhile, in Section 3.2.1 of this paper, the rotating piston set in the lifting motion mechanism can play a role in isolating the high-temperature fluid in the rock cabin. Therefore, the driving module mainly works under the ultrahigh-pressure of 140 MPa, and the influence of temperature on it can be ignored. In this section, experimental studies are carried out on the two modules of the device respectively. The results show that the design of the device is reasonable, and the stability of the working performance of the device in deep extreme environment is verified.

4.1. *Pressure Testing and Results Analysis of the Test Cabin*

In this study, a hydraulic pressure test was carried out with the rock cabin and drill pipe cabin, and the pressure pump of a Sichuan jet was used for pressure testing, as shown in Figure 9. Considering the influence of temperature and pressure on the cabin body, the minimum test pressure, P_t, was calculated with Equation (9) [40] below, and the minimum test pressure at room temperature was 189.70 MPa. Therefore, a test pressure of 190 MPa meets the use requirements.

$$P_t = 1.12 P_D \frac{R_{P0.2}}{R_{P0.2}^t} = 1.12 \times 140 \times 1.08 \times \frac{960}{857} = 189.70\text{MPa} \quad (9)$$

Figure 9. Pressure pump produced for a Sichuan jet.

4.1.1. Pressure Testing of the Rock Cabin

The inner diameter of the rock cabin was 500 mm, and the length was 2400 mm. During the experiment, hydraulic oil is injected into the interior of the cabin body through pressure testing pump to achieve pressure application, and the axial deformation of the rock cabin was detected. Due to the symmetrical structure of the rock cabin, deformation data for only one end face should be recorded when axial deformation is detected, and it should then be multiplied by 2 to obtain the total axial deformation. Therefore, in pressure tests of the rock cabin, an axial displacement detection meter was placed on the end face to measure axial deformation, as shown in Figure 10. The original reading of the displacement detector during the test and the data after modification are provided in Table 5.

Figure 10. Pressure system for testing the rock cabin.

Table 5. Axial deformation of the rock cabin.

Test Pressure, MPa	Axial Displacement Test Data, mm	Unilateral Axial Deformation, mm	Total Axial Deformation, mm
0	1.000	0	0
50	1.865	0.865	1.730
100	2.769	1.769	3.538
150	3.742	2.742	5.484
190	4.490	3.490	6.980

As shown in Table 5, the second column is the original reading of the axial displacement detector during the test. Because the initial reading of the axial displacement detector is 1 mm when the pressure is 0 MPa, the data recorded by the displacement detector should be subtracted from the initial readings to obtain the real axial displacement of one side, as shown in the second column of Table 5. Meanwhile, the axial displacement of one side should be multiplied by 2 to obtain the total axial deformation of the cabin, as shown in the third column of Table 5. The relation curves between the axial displacement and test pressure are shown in Figure 11.

According to Figure 11, with the gradual increase of the test pressure, the axial deformation of the rock cabin also increases gradually and presents a linear growth trend with the change of the pressure. When the highest pressure is 190 MPa, the total axial deformation reaches the maximum value of 6.980 mm, and the relative deformation is 0.291%. Therefore, in the process of the internal pressure of the rock cabin rising from 0 MPa to 190 MPa, the axial deformation of the cabin body is always in the stage of elastic deformation, and the deformation is small. At the same time, no leakage of pressure or flow was detected on the outer surface of the cabin during the test. Therefore, the design of the cabin is reasonable.

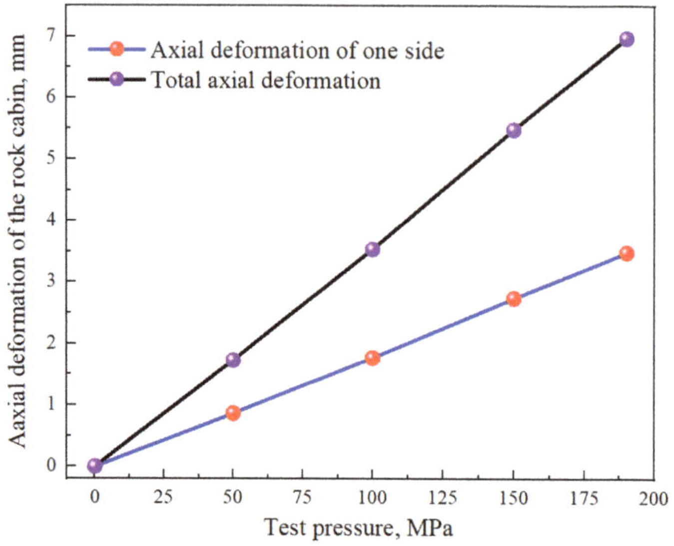

Figure 11. Axial deformation of the rock cabin.

4.1.2. Pressure Testing of the Drill Pipe Cabin

The drill pipe cabin had an inner diameter of 150 mm, an outer diameter of 230 mm, and a total length of 5000 mm. Because the inner diameter of the cabin was small, primarily axial displacement occurred during use. However, the design of the wall thickness was sufficient. Therefore, the main purpose of the pressure test on the drill pipe cabin was to detect axial deformation. Due to the asymmetrical structure of the two drill pipe cabins, axial displacement detector 1 should be placed on the lower end face of the first drill pipe cabin, and axial displacement detector 2 should be placed on the upper end face of the second drill pipe cabin to record the axial displacement of the drill pipe cabin during testing, as shown in Figure 12. In addition, the total axial deformation for each drill pipe cabin should be the sum of two deformations. The axial deformation data after processing are shown in Table 6. The plots of axial deformation vs. test pressure are shown in Figure 13.

Figure 12. Drill pipe cabin test system.

Table 6. Data for axial deformation of the drill pipe cabin.

Test Pressure, MPa	Axial Displacement 2, mm	Axial Displacement 1, mm	Total Axial Deformation, mm
0	0	0	0
50	0.285	0.350	0.635
100	0.567	0.630	1.197
150	0.873	0.932	1.805
190	1.115	1.194	2.309

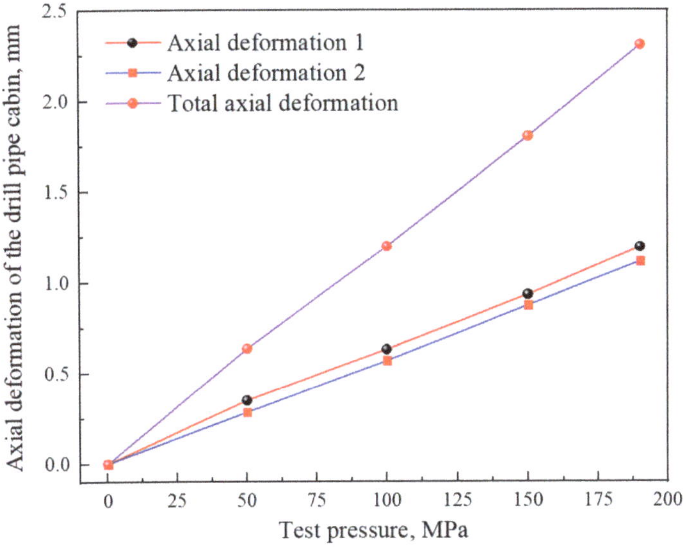

Figure 13. Axial deformation of the drill pipe cabin.

According to Figure 13, when the internal pressure of the drill pipe chamber rises, the axial deformation detected at both ends of the drill pipe cabin presents a linear increase trend with the increase of pressure, indicating that the drill pipe cabin was always in the elastic deformation stage under the pressure condition of 0 MPa to 190 MPa, and can operate safely and stably. Furthermore, it is found that the deformation data of the two detectors are close to each other, which indicates that the deformation of one end is half of the total axial deformation of the drill pipe cabin, as long as their structure is consistent, even if the length of the two drill pipe cabins is not consistent. Meanwhile, under the condition of maximum pressure of 190 MPa, the maximum deformation of the drill pipe cabin is 2.309 mm, and the relative deformation is 0.046%, which is greatly reduced compared with that of rock sample chamber, which is 0.291%. It is further explained that, in the calculation of the wall thickness of the drill pipe cabin in Section 3.1.3 of this paper, considering that the drill pipe cabins are slender tubes, it is reasonable to adjust the safety factor upward to 3 to ensure its small deformation under ultrahigh-pressure. Therefore, the drill pipe cabin can operate stably in the extreme environment of ultrahigh-pressure. Its structure selection is reasonable, and the calculation of wall thickness is reliable.

4.2. Experimental Study of the Driving Module

4.2.1. The Composition and Working Principle of the Experimental System

Because the high temperature load of 150 °C is mainly applied to the rock cabin, the driving module only works under the ultrahigh-pressure condition of 140 MPa, without the influence of high temperature. To verify the performance of the driving module, ultrahigh-pressure dynamic system experimental equipment was independently developed; it mainly comprised a driving pump station, an ultrahigh-pressure cabin, a rotating shaft, and an ultrahigh-pressure hydraulic station, as shown in Figure 14. At the same time, the ultrahigh pressure rotary dynamic sealing structure is installed between the inner surface of the ultrahigh pressure cabin and the rotating shaft (the diameter is 50 mm). The ultrahigh-pressure hydraulic station can provide a pressure of 140 MPa for high-pressure conditions. In the lifting motion mechanism in Section 3.2.1, a rotating piston is adopted to isolate the high-temperature fluid at the lower part, and normal temperature fluid is passed into the upper space of the rotary piston to complete the application of bit weight. Therefore, the driving module only works in the high-pressure environment of 140 °C, without considering the influence of temperature.

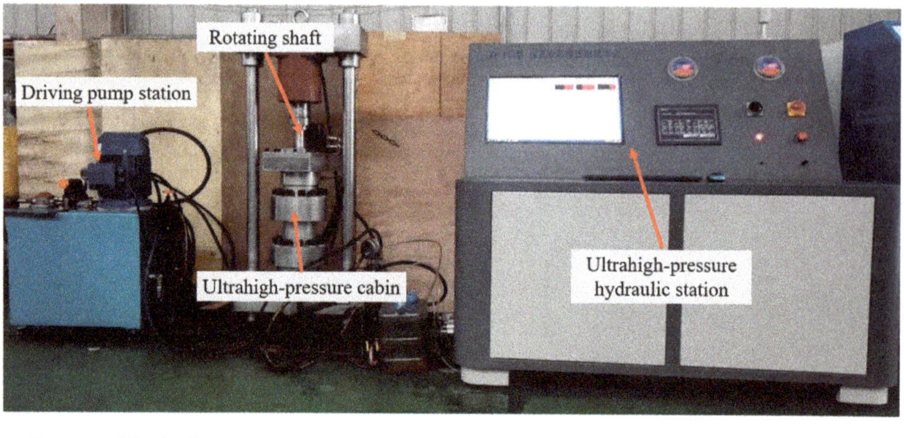

Figure 14. Ultrahigh-pressure dynamic system experimental equipment.

The performance of the driving module is studied experimentally with this system. The high-pressure fluid is injected into the ultrahigh-pressure cabin through the ultrahigh-pressure hydraulic station to achieve the pressure required by the experiment. Meanwhile, the driving pump station is used to provide power for the rotating shaft to complete the application of rotation speed.

4.2.2. Results and Analysis

In order to facilitate analysis, the test data were plotted as curves, as shown in Figures 15–17. Figure 15 shows the curve of test pressure changing with time, Figure 16 shows the curve of rotation speed changing with time, and Figure 17 shows the curve of rotation speed and test pressure.

As shown in Figures 15 and 16, both pressure and rotation speed are applied in two steps. In the first stage, the pressure is increased to 10 MPa and the rotation speed is increased to 60 r/min within 1 min, and the working condition is maintained for approximately 3 min. By observing the curve of test results, it is found that the pressure remains stable, and the rotation speed of the rotating shaft is basically unchanged. Therefore, under the condition of low pressure and low rotation speed, the test system can run normally, which preliminarily verifies the stability of the test system function.

On this basis, the pressure is further increased from 10 MPa to 140 MPa and the rotation speed from 60 r/min to 150 r/min within 1 min, and the stable running time is 105 min under this condition. There is no leakage of flow or pressure in the whole test process. Therefore, under the extreme conditions of ultrahigh-pressure of 140 MPa and rotation speed of 150 r/min, the driving pump station can provide a stable power source, and the sealing structure has good sealing performance.

Furthermore, the rotation speed was reduced from 150 r/min to 142 r/min and maintained for 15 min under the condition that the ultrahigh-pressure was maintained at 140 MPa. The test system can also run stably. The rotation speed was further reduced, as shown in Figure 17. No leakage of pressure or flow was detected during the test. Therefore, the driving module can operate safely and stably without pressure or flow leakage risk by reducing rotation speed under the condition of maintaining constant ultrahigh-pressure. It is suggested that the rotating speed should be reduced first and then the pressure should be reduced after the test with the in-situ deep simulation coring device.

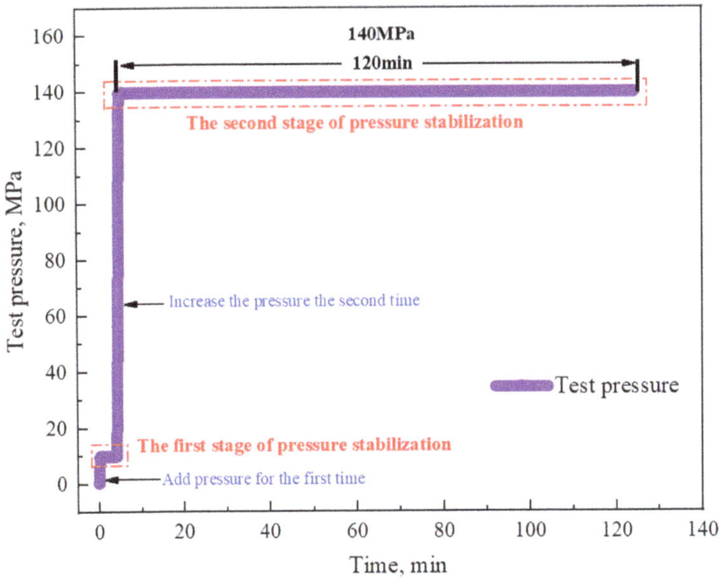

Figure 15. Test pressure vs. time.

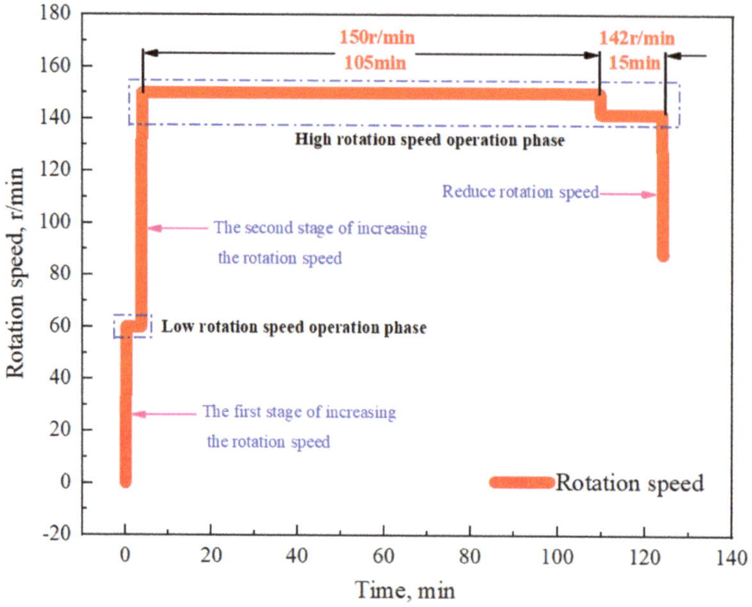

Figure 16. Rotation speed vs. time.

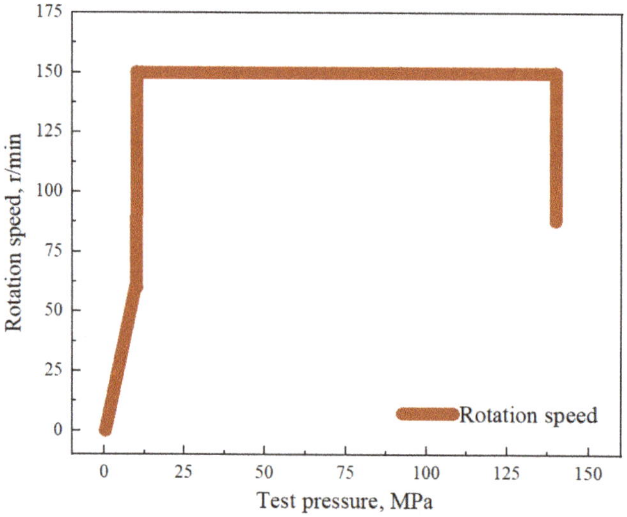

Figure 17. Rotation speed vs. test pressure.

5. Conclusions

In this study, an in-situ simulation device for testing deep pressure-preserving coring tools under high-temperature and ultrahigh-pressure was developed, and the simulation principle and method for this extreme environment were expounded. Furthermore, the high-temperature and ultrahigh-pressure simulation test cabin and the driving module of the device were analyzed and experimentally studied. The main conclusions are as follows:

(1) In this study, a simulated coring test system with a working pressure of 140 MPa and a temperature of 150 °C was established. On the basis of analyzing the stress state

of rock in deep extreme environments, the principle and method of constructing the temperature and pressure conditions of the test cabin are proposed.

(2) Based on the design standard of ultrahigh-pressure vessels, a segmented high-temperature and ultrahigh-pressure coring simulation test cabin was innovatively constructed. A pressure test was conducted on the cabin body by setting different pressure values. The results showed that the test cabin operated stably under the maximum pressure of 190 MPa (the effect of temperature of 150 °C has been translated into pressure for experiments), and there was no pressure or fluid leakage during the test. The test cabin exhibited good performance. Therefore, the design and manufacture of the cabin have high reliability, which has important reference value for the development of ultrahigh-pressure vessels for extreme environments.

(3) The experimental study of the driving module showed that this module could run stably for 105 min under the conditions that the axis diameter is 50 mm, the test pressure is 140 MPa, and the rotation speed is 150 r/min (the highest tested), which provides a stable power source for the coring simulation. When the pressure is maintained at 140 MPa, the driving module can operate safely and stably by reducing the rotation speed of the rotating shaft. Therefore, after the completion of the test with the in-situ simulation device, the safe operation mode of reducing the speed first and then depressurizing the pressure can be adopted.

(4) The in-situ simulation device innovatively developed in this study can realize the simulation of the in-situ extreme environment of deep rock occurrence. Further, it can be used for the research and development of deep pressure-preserving coring tools, which effectively avoids the problems of high risk and high cost in field testing of coring tools.

Author Contributions: Conceptualization, W.H. and Z.Z.; data curation, Y.Y. and Y.L.; methodology, W.H. and Z.H.; supervision, H.X.; writing—original draft preparation, W.H.; writing—review and editing, J.L. and C.L. All authors have read and agreed to the published version of the manuscript.

Funding: This research was funded by the Program for Guangdong Introducing Innovative and Entrepreneurial Teams (Grant No. 2019ZT08G315) and the National Natural Science Foundation of China (Grant No. 51827901, U2013603).

Institutional Review Board Statement: Not applicable.

Informed Consent Statement: Informed consent was obtained from all subjects involved in the study.

Data Availability Statement: The data presented in this study are available on request from the corresponding author.

Acknowledgments: The authors would like to thank the editors and reviewers for their valuable comments and constructive suggestions.

Conflicts of Interest: The authors declare that there is no conflict of interest.

References

1. Xie, H.P.; Konietzky, H.; Zhou, H.W. Special Issue "Deep Mining". *Rock Mech. Rock Eng.* **2019**, *52*, 1415–1416. [CrossRef]
2. Xie, H.P.; Gao, F.; Ju, Y. Research and development of rock mechanics in deep grand engineering. *Chin. J. Rock Mech. Eng.* **2015**, *34*, 2161–2178. [CrossRef]
3. Yang, J.P.; Chen, L.; Gu, X.B.; Zhao, Z.Y.; Fu, C.H.; Yang, D.S.; Tian, D.Z.; Chen, Z.S.; Xie, H.P. Hollow glass microspheres/silicone rubber composite materials toward materials for high performance deep in-situ temperature-preserved coring. *Pet. Sci.* **2022**, *19*, 309–320. [CrossRef]
4. He, Z.Q.; Yang, Y.; Yu, B.; Yang, J.P.; Jiang, X.B.; Tian, B.; Wang, M.; Li, X.Y.; Sun, S.Q.; Sun, H. Research on properties of hollow glass microspheres/epoxy resin composites applied in deep rock in-situ temperature-preserved coring. *Pet. Sci.* **2022**, *19*, 720–730. [CrossRef]
5. Zhang, Q.G.; Fan, X.Y.; Chen, P.; Ma, T.S.; Zeng, F.T. Geomechanical behaviors of shale after water absorption considering the combined effect of anisotropy and hydration. *Eng. Geol.* **2020**, *269*, 105547. [CrossRef]
6. Huang, W.; Feng, G.; He, H.L.; Chen, J.Z.; Wang, J.Q.; Zhao, Z. Development of an ultra-high pressure rotary combined dynamic seal and experimental study on its sealing performance in deep energy mining conditions. *Pet. Sci.* **2022**, *19*, 1305–1321. [CrossRef]
7. Xie, H.P. Research framework and anticipated results of deep rock mechanics and mining theory. *Adv. Eng. Sci.* **2017**, *49*, 1–16. [CrossRef]

8. Li, C.; Pei, J.L.; Wu, N.H.; Liu, G.K.; Huang, W.; Dai, Z.X.; Wang, R.Z.; Chen, Z.F.; Long, W.C. Rotational failure analysis of spherical-cylindrical shell pressure controllers related to gas hydrate drilling investigations. *Pet. Sci.* **2022**, *19*, 789–799. [CrossRef]
9. Gao, M.Z.; Yang, B.G.; Xie, J.; Ye, S.Q.; Liu, J.J.; Liu, Y.T.; Tang, R.F.; Hao, H.C.; Wang, X.; Wen, X.Y.; et al. The mechanism of microwave rock breaking and its potential application to rock-breaking technology in drilling. *Pet. Sci.* **2022**, *19*, 1110–1124. [CrossRef]
10. Wang, G.; Qin, X.J.; Han, D.Y.; Liu, Z.Y. Study on seepage and deformation characteristics of coal microstructure by 3D reconstruction of CT images at high temperatures. *Int. J. Min. Sci. Technol.* **2021**, *31*, 175–185. [CrossRef]
11. Xie, H.P.; Liu, T.; Gao, M.Z.; Chen, L.; Zhou, H.W.; Ju, Y.; Gao, F.; Peng, X.B.; Li, X.J.; Peng, R.D.; et al. Research on in-situ condition preserved coring and testing systems. *Pet. Sci.* **2021**, *18*, 1840–1859. [CrossRef]
12. Gao, M.Z.; Hao, H.C.; Xue, S.N.; Lu, T.; Cui, P.F.; Gao, Y.N.; Xie, J.; Yang, B.G.; Xie, H.P. Discing behavior and mechanism of cores extracted from Songke-2 hole at depths below 4500 m. *Int. J. Rock Mech. Min. Sci.* **2022**, *149*, 104976. [CrossRef]
13. Gao, M.Z.; Xie, J.; Gao, Y.N.; Wang, W.Y.; Li, C.; Yang, B.G.; Liu, J.J.; Xie, H.P. Mechanical behavior of coal under different mining rates: A case study from laboratory experiments to field testing. *Int. J. Min. Sci. Technol.* **2021**, *31*, 825–841. [CrossRef]
14. Zhang, Q.G.; Wang, Z.X.; Fan, X.Y.; Wei, N.; Zhao, J.; Lu, X.W.; Yao, B.W. A novel mathematical method for evaluating the wellbore deformation of a diagenetic natural gas hydrate reservoir considering the effect of natural gas hydrate decomposition. *Nat. Gas Ind. B* **2021**, *8*, 287–301. [CrossRef]
15. Sun, Y.H.; Wang, Y.; Lü, X.S.; Jia, R.; Guo, W. Hole-bottom freezing method for gas hydrate sampling. *J. Nat. Gas Sci. Eng.* **2015**, *25*, 271–283. [CrossRef]
16. Gao, M.Z.; Xie, J.; Guo, J.; Lu, Y.Q.; He, Z.Q.; Li, C. Fractal evolution and connectivity characteristics of mining-induced crack networks in coal masses at different depths. *Geomech. Geophys. Geo-Energy Geo-Resour.* **2021**, *7*, 9. [CrossRef]
17. Hu, Y.Q.; Xie, J.; Xue, S.N.; Xu, M.; Fu, C.H.; He, H.L.; Liu, Z.Q.; Ma, S.M.; Sun, S.Q.; Wang, C.L. Research and application of thermal insulation effect of natural gas hydrate freezing corer based on the wireline-coring principle. *Pet. Sci.* **2022**, *19*, 1291–1304. [CrossRef]
18. Li, J.N.; Wang, J.; Hu, Y.Q.; You, Z.X.; Xu, M.; Wang, Y.W.; Zou, Z.J.; Kang, Q.Y. Contact performance analysis of pressure controller's sealing interface in deep in-situ pressure-preserved coring system. *Pet. Sci.* **2022**, *19*, 1334–1346. [CrossRef]
19. Zhu, L.Y.; Liu, T.; Zhao, Z.Y.; Wu, Y.F.; Yang, D.S.; Shi, X.C.; Liu, Z.Q.; Lu, F.F.; Qin, P.; Gao, X.L. Deep original information preservation by applying in-situ film formation technology during coring. *Pet. Sci.* **2022**, *19*, 1322–1333. [CrossRef]
20. Gao, M.Z.; Zhang, Z.L.; Yin, X.G.; Xu, C.; Liu, Q.; Chen, H.L. The location optimum and permeability-enhancing effect of a low-level shield rock roadway. *Rock Mech. Rock Eng.* **2018**, *51*, 2935–2948. [CrossRef]
21. Gao, M.Z.; Zhang, J.G.; Li, S.W.; Wang, M.; Wang, Y.W.; Cui, P.F. Calculating changes in the fractal dimension of surface cracks to quantify how the dynamic loading rate affects rock failure in deep mining. *J. Cent. South Univ. Technol.* **2020**, *27*, 3013–3024. [CrossRef]
22. Xu, J.J. Design of High Temperature High Pressure Simulation Test Device Program. Master's Thesis, China University of Geosciences, Beijing, China, 2021.
23. Zheng, J.H.; Zong, Y.B.; Qian, D.R.; Wang, L.; Wang, Q. Development of downhole environment simulation test equipment. *Sci. Technol. Eng.* **2017**, *17*, 21–25. [CrossRef]
24. Liu, X. Design and Research on High Pressure Simulated Shaft Heating System. Master's Thesis, Northeast Petroleum University, Daqing, China, 2018.
25. Luo, Q. Design and Experimental Research of Down-Hole Tools Simulation Test Bench. Master's Thesis, Yangtze University, Jinzhou, China, 2015.
26. Kong, R.; Luan, J.F.; Wang, C.L. Stress evaluation and reliability analysis for high temperature and high-pressure vessel in the discontinuous zone. *Ind. Heat.* **2016**, *45*, 30–32. [CrossRef]
27. Morandi, A.C.; Karunakaran, D.; Dixon, A.T.; Baerheim, M. Comparison of Full-Scale Measurements and Time-Domain Irregular Sea Analysis for a Large Deepwater Jack-Up. In Proceedings of the Offshore Technology Conference, Houston, TX, USA, 2–5 May 1998. [CrossRef]
28. Hooker, P.R.; Brigham, W.E. Temperature and heat transfer along buried liquids pipelines. *J. Pet. Technol.* **1978**, *30*, 747–749. [CrossRef]
29. Quigley, M.S.; Dzialowski, A.K.; Zamora, M. A Full-Scale Wellbore Friction Simulator. In Proceedings of the IADC/SPE Drilling Conference, Houston, TX, USA, 27 February–2 March 1990. [CrossRef]
30. Kabir, C.S.; Hasan, A.R.; Jordan, D.L.; Wang, X.W. A wellbore/reservoir simulator for testing gas holes in high-temperature reservoirs. *SPE Form. Eval.* **1996**, *11*, 128–134. [CrossRef]
31. Yang, L.Q. Study of the Full-Scale Drilling Simulating Test Device under the Condition of Bottom Hole Pressures. Master's Thesis, Zhejiang University, Hangzhou, China, 2002.
32. Xue, J. Overview of several foreign high temperature and high pressure simulation drilling test equipment. *Foreign Geoexplor. Technol.* **1995**, *2*, 35–36.
33. Zhou, C.; Wang, X.D. Introduction of M150 simulated wellbore. *Drill. Eng.* **1993**, *3*, 16–17.
34. Zhang, F.M. Development of drilling tool test system in dagang oilfield. *Oil Field Equip.* **2009**, *384*, 72–78. [CrossRef]
35. Wei, L.S. Design of High Temperature and High Pressure Simulation Testing System for Instrument Development. Master's Thesis, Southwest Petroleum University, Chengdu, China, 2016.

36. Pang, D.X.; Wang, Z.M.; Pan, D. Development of high temperature and high pressure test equipment for downhole tools. *Hole Test.* **2017**, *26*, 45–48+51+77.
37. Xu, D.J.; Liu, H.; Wang, Y.; Zeng, L.X.; Wang, K.; Wang, X.J. The developing and using of downhole tools experimental facility under high temperature and high pressure condition. In *2018 the National Natural Gas Annual Symposium;* Natural Gas Professional Committee of Chinese Petroleum Society: Beijing, China, 2018. [CrossRef]
38. Zhang, W.H.; Zhang, H.T.; Wang, W.P. Development of high temperature and high pressure vertical hole simulation test device for downhole tools. *Mach. Des. Manuf. Eng.* **2020**, *49*, 31–34.
39. Ding, G.D. Design and Research on Simulation Test Shaft of High Temperature and High Pressure. Master's Thesis, China University of Petroleum, Beijing, China, 2014.
40. *GB/T 34019-2017;* Ultra-High Pressure Vessels. National Standards of People's Republic of China: Beijing, China, 2017.
41. Shao, G.H.; Wei, Z.C. *Ultra-High Pressure Vessel;* Chemical Industry Press: Beijing, China, 2002.
42. Wang, J.B. Safety Analysis and Accident Prevention of High Temperature and High Pressure Testing Equipment of Logging Lools. Master's Thesis, China University of Petroleum, Beijing, China, 2014.
43. Hu, X.M.; Wang, C.L.; Cai, X.L.; Li, Q.W.; Chen, B. Development of high-temperature and high-pressure reaction kettle system. *Mech. Eng. Autom.* **2013**, *3*, 153–155. [CrossRef]
44. Wang, Z.W.; Cai, R.L. *Pressure Vessel Design;* Chemical Industry Press: Beijing, China, 2005.
45. Liu, C.; Wu, S.L.; Yang, F.; Hong, K.; Zhang, S.; Liu, X.N. Precision comparison of calculation formulas for ultra-high pressure vessel burst pressure. *Press. Vessel Technol.* **2019**, *36*, 43–49+66. [CrossRef]
46. Chen, Z.W.; Li, T.; Yang, G.Y. Technical Progress in GB/T 34019—2017 Standard "Ultrahigh Pressure Vessel". *Press. Vessel Technol.* **2019**, *36*, 46–51.

applied sciences

MDPI

Article

Design and Dynamic Analysis of the Wire-Line Coring Robot for Deep Lunar Rocks

Yufeng Wen [1], Guoqing Zhang [1,*], Heping Xie [2], Mingzhong Gao [2], Xu Zhang [1], Yaohui Wang [1] and Cunbao Li [2]

1 College of Mechatronics and Control Engineering, Shenzhen University, Shenzhen 518060, China
2 Guangdong Provincial Key Laboratory of Deep Earth Sciences and Geothermal Energy Exploitation and Utilization, Institute of Deep Earth Sciences and Green Energy, College of Civil and Transportation Engineering, Shenzhen University, Shenzhen 518060, China
* Correspondence: zhanggq@szu.edu.cn; Tel.: +86-755-2653-6306; Fax: +86-755-2655-7471

Abstract: Deep lunar rocks carry geological information about the primitive Moon and are of great scientific value. In this paper, a coring robot for deep lunar rocks was proposed for the lunar environment based on the wire-line sampling device. This robot consists of the coring executor on the ground to assist in coring tube replacement and sample storage and the wireline self-excavating coring (WSC) robot for active drilling underground, which can provide autonomous deep coring on the moon. Subsequently, based on Prandtl's failure mechanism and the prediction equations of the mechanical properties of the lunar soil, the mathematical relationship between the ultimate support force and the depth of the support point of the WSC robot was constructed. Additionally, the drilling scheme of the WSC robot at different depths was also determined. The constraint model of the impact module was established, and the structural parameters were optimized through non-linear programming to achieve the maximum impact energy. Simulations of the impact process were then carried out in explicit dynamics. The simulation results show that the optimized impact module can effectively drill through the lunar rocks. This result validates, to some extent, the drilling capability of the WSC robot in lunar rocks. The research work can provide technical reference and theoretical support for deep coring lunar rocks.

Keywords: sampling device; impact mechanism; structure optimization; deep lunar rocks; wire-line sampling

1. Introduction

Sampling for extraterrestrial subsurface exploration is an important tool for human understanding of the solar system and the universe, and it can help humans understand the formation process of celestial bodies [1]. In addition, sampling can effectively probe the precious metals and rare elements in celestial bodies, which can provide a good foundation for humans to utilize celestial bodies in the future [2]. Additionally, sampling can provide the necessary guarantee for the establishment of permanent interstellar bases [3]. The moon is the closest extraterrestrial object to the Earth, and it is the preferred target for the sampling of celestial bodies.

In the 1960s and 1970s, the Soviet Union and the United States carried out lunar exploration missions, namely the Luna program and the Apollo program [4]. There was also no lack of lunar surface sample return missions, such as the Apollo 17 mission. China also obtained lunar soil and returned it to Earth in 2020 [5]. Among the successful coring return missions, the Luna16 swing arm shallow drilling and the Chang'e-5 fixed drilling both achieved surface lunar soil coring [6]. the Apollo project used the astronaut-held Apollo lunar surface drill (ALSD) to achieve subsurface lunar soil coring up to 3.05 m [7]. To understand the celestial bodies more deeply, researchers now continue to develop deep sampling devices.

The current deep sampling devices for celestial bodies can be classified into two categories: multi-rod drilling sampling devices and wire-line sampling [8]. The multi-rod drilling sampling device is mature and stable. It is commonly loaded with multiple drilling rods and sampling tubes and achieves deep drilling by multiple combinations [9]. Therefore, institutions and researchers have built various devices to achieve deep sampling, such as the pneumatic multi-rod drilling device for lunar sampling [10], the Micro Robots for Scientific Applications 2 (RoSA2) [11], the Deep Drilling Rig (DeeDri) [12], and the Mars Astrobiology Research and Technology Experiment (MARTE) drilling system [13]. As a rule, the impact effect is applied by sampling devices in order to penetrate the deep hard layers more effectively [14]. However, in multi-rod drilling sampling devices, the energy lost due to thermal and rebound between drilling rods exceeds the energy used to destroy the terrain. Additionally, this phenomenon is further exacerbated by the increase in the number of connected segments in the sampling rod [15]. This makes multi-rod drilling sampling devices require more power and mass to achieve deep sampling.

The wire-line sampling device is connected to the lander by the power cable and drills deeper by its own self-excavation capability. It is more prone to jamming and requires higher soil properties at the sampling site than the multi-rod drilling sampling device. At the same time, it is difficult to drill in shallow and loose layers since a stable anchorage cannot be achieved in this layer [8]. However, the wire-line sampling device has the advantages of a compact structure, high energy utilization, low reaction force, and lightweight. These advantages provide obvious benefits for wire-line sampling devices for deep sampling. The wire-line sampling device is also considered the preferred option for sampling devices when drilling over a 10 m depth. The wire-line drilling device is softly connected to the surface by cables, which makes it necessary to drill itself through the self-excavation capability. The self-excavation capability of wire-line drilling devices can be accomplished in various approaches, including anchored drilling, bionic mole, bionic inchworm, etc. The bionic mole and bionic inchworm are able to propel at depth in the subsurface without lifting the drill. The feature of the bionic mole and the bionic inchworm leads to the increased usage of in situ probe emplacements, such as the mole carried by insight with the bionic mole [16] and the inchworm drilling (ID) System with the bionic inchworm [17]. However, the sampling missions, especially the full profile sampling, are accomplished by multiple liftings of the drill and collecting samples from each drill. For example, the Autonomous Tethered Corer achieved the drilling and coring of 10 m of limestone by multiple liftings of the drill and the removal of core samples. The coring device weighs 7 kg and has 50–75 W of power [18]; Auto-Gopher (AG) II with an ultrasonic percussion drill obtained a core at a 7.52 m depth with gypsum as the drilling target and is expected to achieve more than 50 m drilling [19]. However, the current wire-line sampling device still cannot achieve fully autonomous deep coring, and all the above drilling approaches require human assistance to exchange the coring tubes. Therefore, the development of a deep coring robot with autonomous capability is necessary.

In this paper, a wire-line robot for deep coring lunar rocks was designed with low energy consumption and a small space as an entry point. In addition, this robot provides a prototype solution for the deep coring of other celestial bodies. Firstly, the wire-line scheme was proposed, and the coring executor was designed. Secondly, a rotating impact composite coring robot with functions of subsurface anchoring, in-hole change in direction, etc., was designed for the requirements of subsurface self-excavation coring functions. Subsequently, the anchoring support force model with depth was established for the anchor module, which provided theoretical support for the drilling scheme at different depths. Finally, the structure parameters of the impact module were optimized with the objective of maximum impact energy. The optimized structure parameters were also simulated to verify the drilling and breaking effect of the impact module on the lunar rocks. The flow chart of the research methodology is shown in Figure 1.

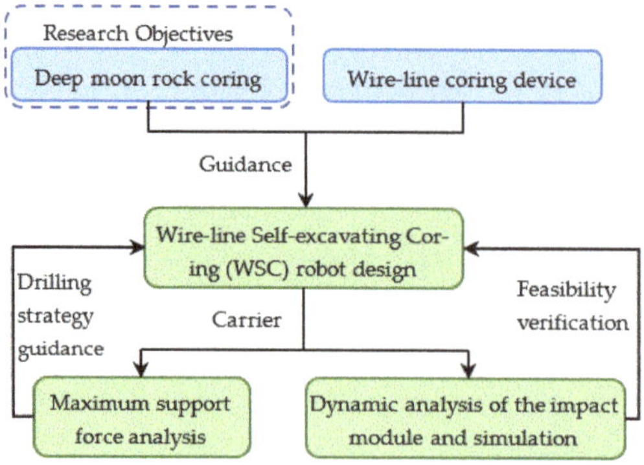

Figure 1. Methodological framework for the wire-line self-excavating coring robot research.

2. Design of the Wire-Line Coring Robot for Deep Lunar Rocks

With deep lunar rocks as the coring target, a wire-line coring robot incorporating a wire-line sampling device was proposed based on lightweight, low-power consumption design criteria and limited envelope space conditions. The wire-line coring robot can be divided into the coring executor and the wireline self-excavating coring (WSC) robot. The coring executor is responsible for replacing the coring tubes in the WSC robot and storing the core samples. The WSC robot is responsible for the underground autonomous drilling and coring work and is connected to the coring executor through an integrated cable.

2.1. Coring Executor

The coring executor consists of the X-Z linear displacement robot, the fidelity chamber, etc., as shown in Figure 2. The X-Z linear displacement robot includes an X-axis displacement unit, Z-axis displacement unit, and clamping unit. The Z-axis displacement unit and the clamping unit are responsible for the coring tube replacement, while the X-axis displacement unit is combined with the C-axis rotation of the fidelity chamber to align the WSC robot with the storage hole. To identify the storage status of the coring tubes, the storage holes are numbered according to their positioning in the polar coordinate system, which consists of the C-axis and X-axis.

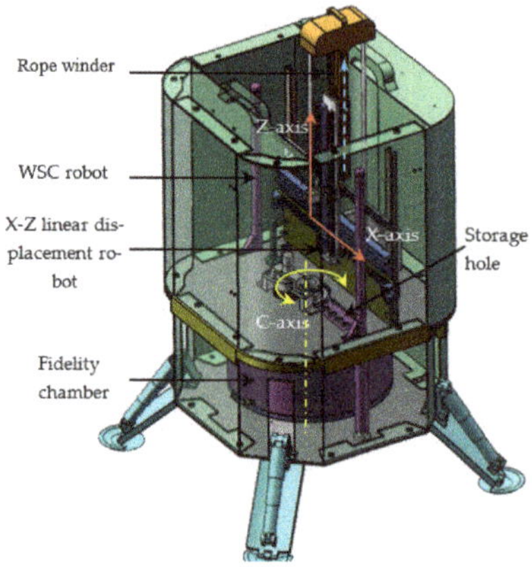

Figure 2. Design of the coring executor.

The coring executor coring process is as follows.

1. After the wire-line coring robot is placed on the moon, the exploding bolt works to separate the WSC robot from the coring executor, and the X-Z linear displacement

robot grabs the WSC robot and moves it to the center while loosening the cable of the rope winder;

2. The X-Z linear displacement robot releases the WSC robot, and then the rope winder slowly lifts the WSC robot down the through-hole by the cable. After dropping the specified amount of cable, the WSC robot begins coring work. When this coring phase is completed, the X-Z linear displacement robot grabs the WSC robot to fix the position;
3. The X-Z linear displacement robot and the fidelity chamber combine their movements to transport the WSC robot to the position corresponding to the number of this full coring tube. Then, the full coring tube is unloaded and installed into the empty coring tube by a Z-axis displacement unit. Repeat steps 2 and 3 until the desired mission target is completed.

2.2. *Wire-Line Self-Excavating Coring Robot*

The composition of the WSC robot is shown in Figure 3, including the pressure supply part, drilling part, and coring part. The pressure supply part fixes the WSC robot's position in the coring hole and provides drilling pressure. The drilling part provides rotational and impact functions to cut and break the lunar soil/rocks. The coring part stores the lunar soil/rocks coring samples and temporarily stores the debris generated in the coring. The WSC robot is modularly combined to realize the functions of each part. The modular design provides easy control of the size of the WSC robot and facilitates the functional testing of the prototype. The WSC robot is implemented mechanically with core actuators to reduce the energy supply burden, except for the modules that require an active drive.

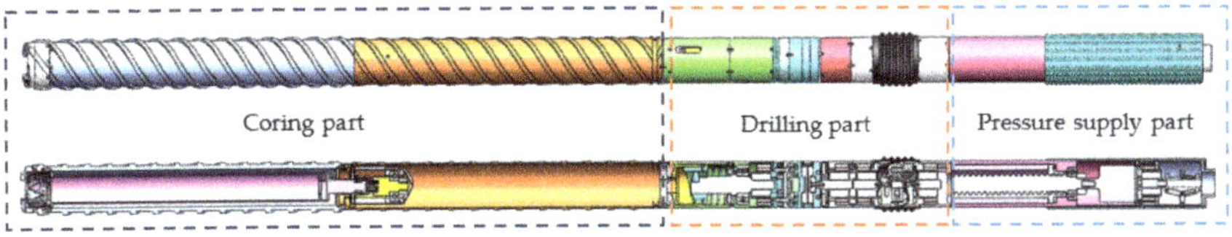

Figure 3. Design of the WSC robot.

The pressure supply part includes the anchor module which provides the support force in the hole, and the screw module to provide the drilling pressure, as is shown in Figure 4a. The anchor module is provided with three symmetrical crank slider mechanisms and anchor plates fixed on the sliders, where the crank is the same eccentric wheel. Therefore, the anchor plate can be driven by motors to synchronize the expansion, thus ensuring the positional anchoring of the WSC robot. To avoid anchor plate rebound during coring, a ratchet locking device is installed in the anchor module. The locking device is unlocked with the rope retrieval force so that the anchor plate can be retracted when the WSC robot is lifted. The locking device enables the anchor module to require less energy after deployment. Thus, the WSC robot can provide a higher energy supply for the drilling relative to other telescopic coring devices, such as the autonomous tethered corer.

The drilling part consists of the redirection module, the impact module, the rotation module, and a force sensor, as shown in Figure 5a. The redirection module has the ability to drive the WSC robot to shift direction actively in the hole so that the WSC robot can avoid extreme drilling situations, as shown in Figure 5b. The impact module generates the impact force through the spring energy storage mechanism. The application of the impact force can improve the drilling efficiency and reduce the torque for drilling the rocks. The force sensor is used to obtain real-time data on the axial force and rotational torque to make preliminary judgments on the current drilling situations.

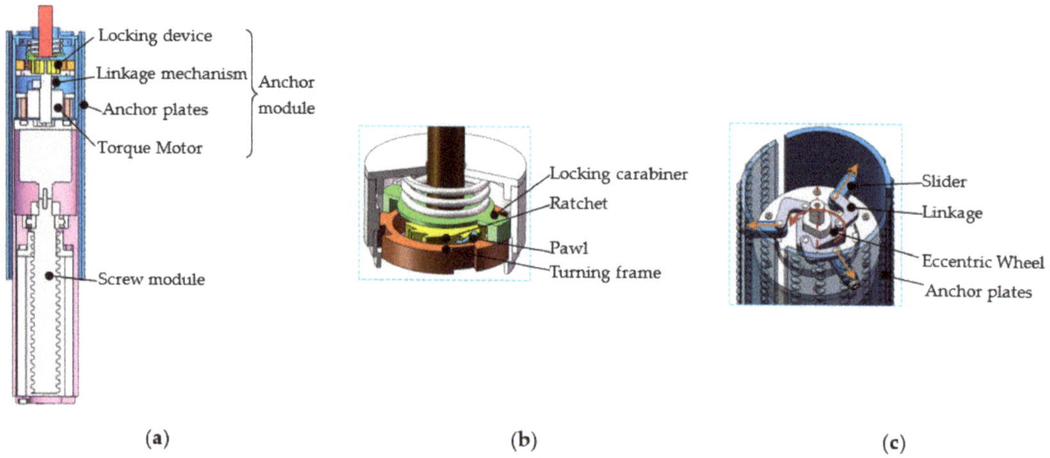

Figure 4. Design of the pressure supply part (**a**) Modules configuration (**b**) The locking device of the anchor module (**c**) Operation mechanism of the anchor module.

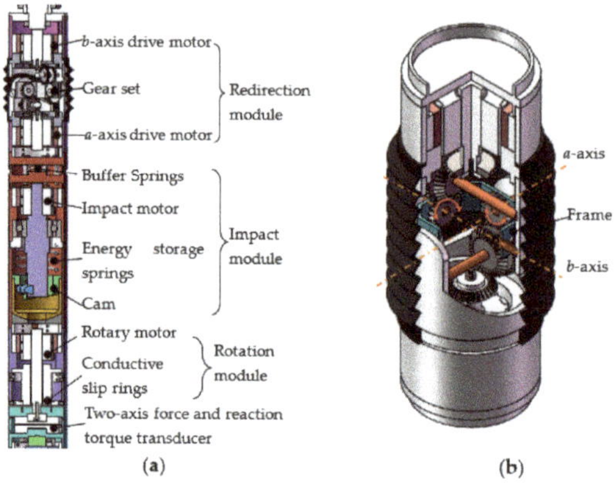

Figure 5. Design of the drilling part (**a**) Modules configuration (**b**) Operating mechanism of the redirection module.

The coring part can be divided into the debris-tolerant chamber, the connection module, the coring tube module, and the bit module, as shown in Figure 6. The coring part is a purely mechanical structure with the potential to be applied to other celestial bodies, such as Mars. Due to the load limitation of the aerospace mission, a consumable drilling fluid is not used to dispose of the debris that is generated during the coring process. Therefore, the debris-tolerant chamber is designed to temporarily store the debris. To dispose of the debris, the combination of the connection module and the debris-tolerant chamber enables the WSC robot to automatically discharge the debris after releasing the coring tube. Additionally, compared to other wire-line coring devices without waste chip handling, the setup of the debris-tolerant chamber significantly increases the length of the coring robot. However, debris increases the drilling resistance and leads to large amounts of debris in the subsequently collected samples. The connection module is designed with a heart-shaped slot and a spring, which enables the connection module to switch between the locked and unlocked states through a single application and unloading of the unidirectional Z-axis force. This state-switching function enables the WSC robot to replace coring tubes with unidirectional Z-axis forces (F_Z), as shown in Figure 7. Meanwhile, the connection module is connected to other modules of the WSC robot through bearings, and this approach can avoid the interference of the rotational motion to the sample. The mechanically triggered truncation device is designed in the coring tube module for the composite lunar soil/rocks sampling requirement. This device uses a trigger plate to determine the position of the lunar soil/rocks in the coring tube, which triggers the truncator to cut and store the sample. Finally, to protect the drilling hole wall, the bit module can be transformed by the friction between the drilling tool and the drilling surface. The transformation capability of the bit module can shrink the drilling tool before lifting the WSC robot to reduce the scraping of the drilling tool and the drilling hole wall.

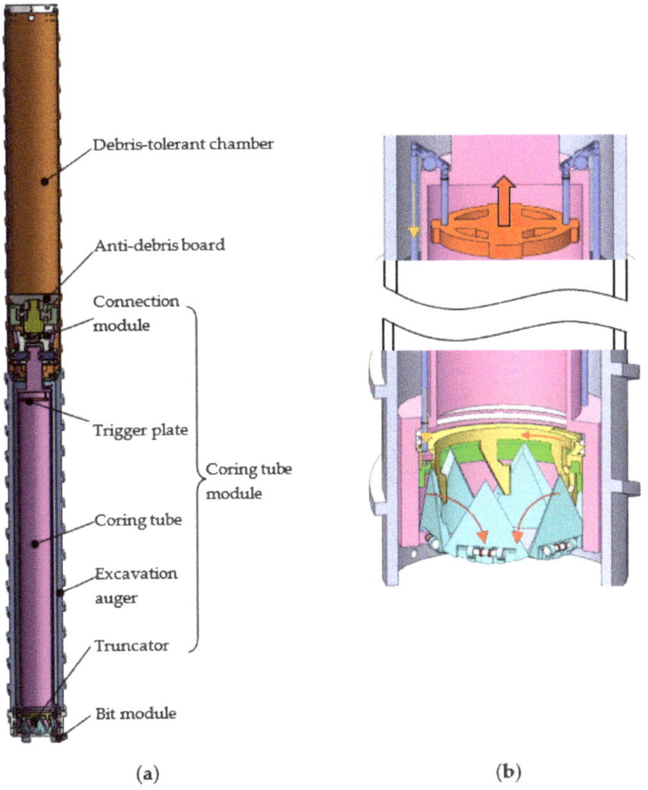

Figure 6. Design of the coring part (**a**) Modules configuration (**b**) Operating mechanism of truncator.

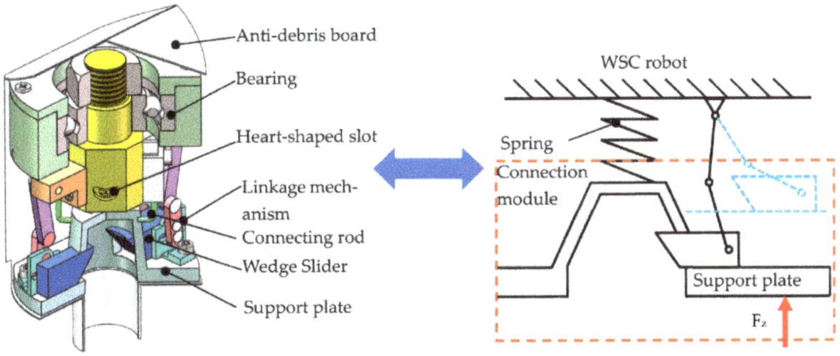

Figure 7. Design and operating mechanism of the connection module.

The single coring process of the WSC robot is as follows: after receiving the coring start signal from the coring executor, the anchor module is activated to anchor the WSC robot position. The screw module, rotation module, and impact module then work together to drill into the deep lunar rock. Finally, with the coring tube module automatically cut off and the storing of the lunar rock, the WSC robot is lifted back into the coring executor for coring tube replacement.

3. Dynamic Analysis of the WSC Robot

Part of the function modules in the WSC robot cannot be determined directly by the parameters of the original actuator, such as the anchor module and impact module. Therefore, the dynamic analysis of the impact module and the anchor module is targeted.

3.1. Maximum Support Force Analysis of the Anchor Module

The maximum support force is related to the drilling function of the WSC robot in the subsurface and is critical for the strategy of coring. The anchor module squeezes the drilling hole wall by expanding the anchor plates to provide sufficient friction to support the WSC robot underground. Thus, the higher the squeezing pressure, the stronger the support force of the WSC robot in the subsurface. However, the lunar regolith of the drilling hole wall can often slip when the squeeze pressure is excessive, thus preventing the anchor module from providing a stable positional fixation. Therefore, there is a limit to the support force provided by the anchor module.

For determining the maximum support force, the mechanical properties associated with the lunar regolith at different depths should be analyzed. According to NASA's analysis of the returned samples from the Apollo program, the relationship between the lunar regolith packing density ρ and depth z is [20]:

$$\rho = 1.92\frac{z + 12.2}{z + 18} \tag{1}$$

Additionally, the following relationship that exists between ρ and the lunar regolith pore ratio n is [21]:

$$n = 1 - \frac{\rho}{G\rho_w} \tag{2}$$

where G is the average specific gravity of the lunar sample, with a suggested value of 3.1 [22] and ρ_w is the density of pure water at 4 °C, which is 1 g/cm^3.

According to Prandtl's failure mechanism, the ultimate bearing capacity is related to cohesion and the angle of internal friction. Additionally, there is an exponential relationship between the lunar regolith pore ratio n and the lunar regolith cohesion c, as well as a linear relationship with the tangent of the lunar regolith angle of the internal friction φ. Thus, the expressions for c and φ can be obtained by fitting the data from Table 1 [23]:

$$\begin{cases} c = 10^{2.9331-6.0035n} & (R^2 = 0.9885) \\ \varphi = \arctan(3.0982 - 4.1088n) & (R^2 = 0.9519) \end{cases} \tag{3}$$

Table 1. Estimated values of cohesion and the angle of internal friction of the lunar regolith at different depths (Data from reference [23]).

Depths z (m)	Cohesion c (kPa)	Angle of Internal Friction φ (°)
0~0.15	0.44~0.62	41~43
0~0.3	0.74~1.1	44~47
0.3~0.6	2.4~3.8	52~55
0~0.6	1.3~1.9	48~51

Bringing Equations (1) and (2) into Equation (3) yields the expressions for c and φ with respect to z:

$$\begin{cases} c = 10^{2.93 - \frac{3.69z+247.72}{z+18}} \\ \varphi = \arctan\left(3.1 - \frac{2.53z+169.54}{z+18}\right) \end{cases} \tag{4}$$

A schematic diagram of the slip surface of the anchoring area that was obtained according to Prandtl's failure mechanism is shown in Figure 8, in which Zone I is the active Rankine zone, Zone II is the Prandtl zone, and Zone III is the passive Rankine zone. According to Prandtl's theory, the ultimate bearing capacity of the hole wall can be obtained as:

$$p_u = cN_c + qdN_q \tag{5}$$

where $N_c = \cot\varphi\left[e^{\pi\tan\varphi}\tan^2\left(\frac{\pi}{4}+\frac{\varphi}{2}\right) - 1\right]$, $N_q = e^{\pi\tan\varphi}\tan^2\left(\frac{\pi}{4}+\frac{\varphi}{2}\right)$, and q is the uniform load in the passive Rankine zone, which can be considered as 0.

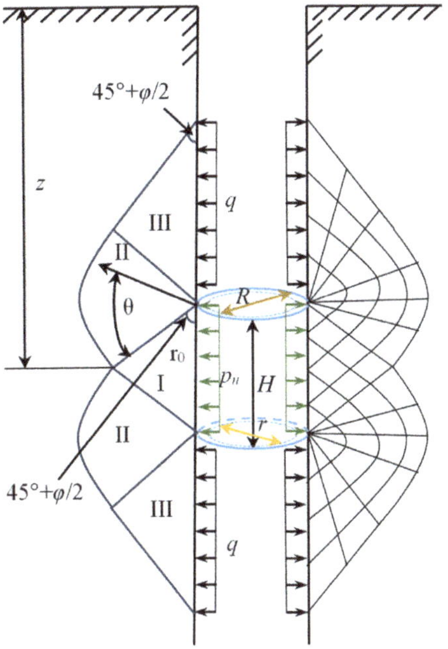

Figure 8. Schematic diagram of ultimate bearing capacity of drilling hole wall.

Since the anchor module is fixed in position by expanding the anchor plates, there are gaps after unfolding. Additionally, each anchor plate can still form a cylinder-like shape after the anchor module is unfolded. Therefore, the shape of the anchor module after unfolding is equated to an incomplete cylinder, and the missing part is represented by the equivalent rounded angle θ_m in the calculation, as follows:

$$\theta_m = 2\pi\frac{r}{R} \tag{6}$$

where r is the radius of the anchor module when it is not unfolded, and R is the length of the anchor plate unfolded from the center of the WSC robot.

Combining Equations (5) and (6) yields the maximum support force that the lunar regolith can withstand which is:

$$\frac{M_u}{R} + F_u \leq \mu_s RH\theta_m p_u \tag{7}$$

where μ_s is the lunar regolith friction coefficient;

H is the length of the anchor plate;

M_u is the drilling torque;

F_u is the drilling pressure.

If H is determined, the relationship between the theoretical maximum drilling pressure and torque with depth can be obtained separately according to Equation (7), as shown in Figure 9. According to Figure 9, the drilling pressure and torque that can clearly be provided by the current depth support. Since the pore ratio of the shallow lunar regolith increases rapidly with the increase in lunar regolith depth, the anchoring effect in shallow lunar regolith above 0~4 m still varies drastically with the depth. The pore ratio of deep lunar regolith is close to the limit value, and the anchoring effect of the anchor module tends to be stable. Therefore, the drilling power needs to be changed in real-time when the WSC robot is working on shallow lunar regolith, and the full drilling power can be exerted when the WSC robot is working on a deep lunar regolith. According to the design target, the operation at full power is available in the lunar soil layer below 4.7 m depth. However, since the specific dynamic environment of the lunar soil layer is unknown, operation at full power should be performed again in deeper, more stable lunar soil below 7 m. When the anchor module was first anchored in the lunar soil, the bit module had already been drilled to a depth of more than 1 m. At this moment, the support force is hardly able to support the WSC robot to continue drilling. The solidifying cylinder could be added to assist with drilling.

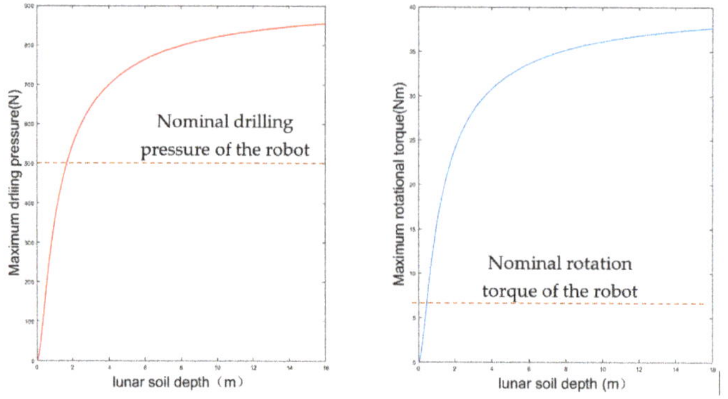

Figure 9. Maximum drilling pressure and rotational torque in relation to depth.

3.2. Dynamic Analysis of the Impact Module

The impact module converts the kinetic energy of the motor rotation into impact energy by the spring energy storage mechanism. To analyze the dynamics of the impact module, the single impact process can be divided into the energy storage phase and the release phase. For the energy storage phase, the simplified cam curve can be expanded along a straight line, as shown in Figure 10, where the structural parameters are the cam radius R_c, spring preload length l_0, cam stroke height h, and drive wheel radius R_d. For the release phase, a certain length of the gentle section without loading is set on the cam to ensure the effective release of the impact energy and that the proportion of the loaded segment is α. Among them, α, l_0, and h has a large impact on the impact work, so these parameters are used as optimization variables. For coil springs, based on the optimized design of cylindrical compression springs, the spring wire diameter d and the effective number of turns n are selected as optimization variables when the maximum energy storage in the restricted space is the optimization objective. The rest of the variables, such as the spring's mid-range D and spring shear modulus G_s, are constants. Subsequently, the maximum impact energy as the objective function can be expressed as:

$$f(\mathbf{X}) = \frac{1}{2}kh(h + 2l_0) + mg_{lunar}h + \frac{1}{2}m\left(\frac{\lambda h}{\alpha}\right)^2 \quad (8)$$

where $k = \frac{G_s d^4}{8D^3 n}$ is the spring stiffness;
g_{lunar} is the lunar gravitational acceleration;
λ is the impact frequency;
m is the mass of the impact hammer.
$\mathbf{X} = [\alpha\ l_0\ h\ d\ n]$.

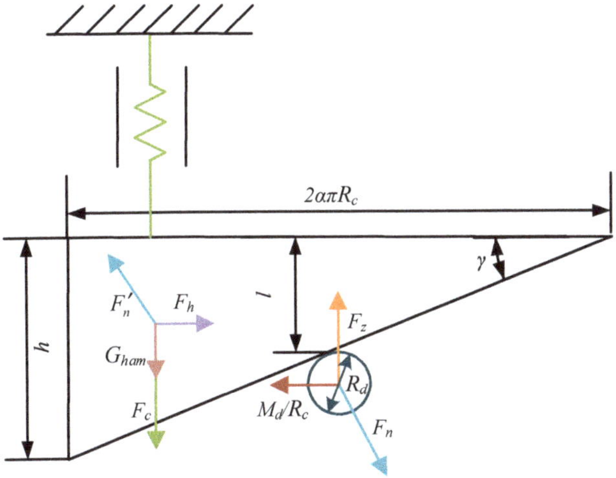

Figure 10. Simplified cam curve expanded along a straight line.

Based on spring design guidelines, the effect of the curvature factor K should be considered when the spring is subjected to a dynamic load, which can be expressed as:

$$K = \frac{4C - 1}{4C + 4} + \frac{0.615}{C} \quad (9)$$

where $C = \frac{D}{d}$.

Based on the effect of the curvature factor, d should satisfy the following constraints:

$$g_1 = \sqrt[3]{\frac{8KDF}{\pi[\tau]}} - d \le 0 \quad (10)$$

The allowable shear stress $[\tau]$ decreases with the increase in the spring wire diameter; however, it is defined as a constant to simplify the optimization process. For installation space constraints, on the one hand, it is necessary to consider that the spring deformation needs to be smaller than the theoretical full deformation. On the other hand, it is necessary to consider that the height after pre-pressing is less than the installation space of the impact module H_0. Accordingly, the installation dimensions are constrained as follows:

$$\begin{cases} g_2 = l_0 + h - \frac{D\pi n[\tau]}{KG_s d} \le 0 \\ g_3 = \frac{D\pi n[\tau]}{KG_s d} + (n + 1.5)d - h - H_0 \le 0 \end{cases} \quad (11)$$

For the energy storage phase, an analysis of Figure 10 yields the constrained relationship between the motor torque and the structure parameters during cam energy storage.

$$g_4 = [G_{ham} + k(l_0 + l)]\frac{h}{2\pi\alpha} - M_d \le 0 \tag{12}$$

where M_d is the nominal torque of the motor;

l is the current axial displacement of the roller, with the maximum value of h;

G_{ham} is the gravity of the impact hammer.

For the release phase, if the friction between the impact hammer and the guide wall is neglected, the equation of state for the release phase of the impact hammer is:

$$\ddot{l} = -\left(g_{lunar} + \frac{k(l_0 + l)}{m}\right) \tag{13}$$

The analysis of the motion of the impact hammer provides the following initial conditions for the motion of the impact hammer at the cam notch:

$$\begin{cases} l(0) = h \\ \dot{l}(0) = \frac{\lambda h}{\alpha} \\ \ddot{l}(0) = -\left(g_{lunar} + \frac{k(l_0+h)}{m}\right) \end{cases} \tag{14}$$

Substituting the initial conditions into Equation (13) for the solution yields the time from the release of the impact hammer to the return of the initial height as:

$$t_1 = \sqrt{\frac{m}{k}}\left[\arcsin\left(\frac{mg + kl_0}{k\sqrt{a^2 + b^2}}\right) - \arccos\left(\frac{b}{\sqrt{a^2 + b^2}}\right)\right] \tag{15}$$

where $a = \frac{mg_{lunar}}{k} + l_0 + h$,

$b = \frac{\sqrt{\frac{m}{k}}\lambda h}{\alpha}$.

Assuming that the impact energy takes time to be fully released and it is set to t_2, the constraint that ensures that the impact energy is fully released before loading is:

$$g_5 = 2\pi R_c\lambda(t_1 + t_2) + 2R_d - 2\pi R_c(1 - \alpha) \le 0 \tag{16}$$

According to Equations (8), (10)–(12), (16), and the inherent boundaries of each parameter, the numerical model of the constraint problem can be obtained as:

$$\begin{aligned} &\max f(\mathbf{X}) = \tfrac{1}{2}kh(h + 2l_0) + mg_{lunar}h + \tfrac{1}{2}m\left(\tfrac{\lambda h}{\alpha}\right)^2 \\ &s.t.\ g_1 = \sqrt[3]{\tfrac{8KDF}{\pi[\tau]}} - d \le 0 \\ &\quad g_2 = l_0 + h - \tfrac{D\pi n[\tau]}{KG_s d} \le 0 \\ &\quad g_3 = \tfrac{D\pi n[\tau]}{KG_s d} + (n + 1.5)d - h - \mathrm{H}_0 \le 0 \\ &\quad g_4 = [G_{ham} + k(l_0 + l)]\tfrac{h}{2\pi\alpha} - M_d \le 0 \\ &\quad g_5 = 2\pi R_c\lambda(t_1 + t_2) + 2R_d - 2\pi R_c(1 - \alpha) \le 0 \\ &\quad g_6 = \alpha - 1 \le 0 \\ &\quad g_7 = -\alpha \le 0 \\ &\quad g_8 = -l_0 \le 0 \\ &\quad g_9 = -h \le 0 \\ &\quad g_{10} = h - 50 \le 0 \\ &\quad g_{11} = 0.05 - d \le 0 \\ &\quad g_{12} = d - 1.5 \le 0 \\ &\quad g_{13} = 1.5 - n \le 0 \\ &\quad g_{14} = n - 200 \le 0 \end{aligned} \tag{17}$$

Since the length of the WSC robot was limited by the mission objectives, the working space reserved for the impact module was only 20 mm after the necessary equipment was designed. Additionally, the available installation diameter of the WSC robot was only 38 mm. Considering the working space and working environment of the WSC robot, the parameters were initially determined as follows: the nominal torque and rotation rate of the impact motor were 0.84 Nm and 600 rpm; the energy storage spring was made of oil-quenched and annealed spring steel wire with a shear modulus of 78.5 GPa and tensile strength of 1540 MPa; the mass of the impact hammer was predicted to be 190 g based on its 3D model; t_2 was set to 1 ms. If the energy consumption during impact loading, such as friction, is neglected, the global optimal solution of Equation (17) can be obtained by combining the optimization toolbox with the global optimization algorithm in MATLAB. The optimization results after rounding are shown in Table 2. The optimized theoretical single maximum impact energy can reach 3.7 J.

Table 2. Structural parameters of the optimized impact module.

Motor Torque M_d (Nm)	Cam Stroke Height h (mm)	Preload Length l_0 (mm)	Spring Stiffness k (N/m)	Proportion of the Loaded Segment α (%)	Impact Mass M (g)	Impact Frequency λ (Hz)
0.84	8.75	5.75	40,000	95	190	10

The finite element simulation of the impact process on lunar rocks was carried out in LS-DYNA with optimized structural parameters to verify the performance of the impact module. The lunar rocks model used the modified HJC constitutive model in LS-DYNA, and the parameter settings are shown in Table 3. Both the coring tube and the impact hammer use pre-defined isotropic elastic models of aluminum alloy and steel, respectively.

Table 3. HJC constitutive parameters of lunar rocks (Data from reference [24,25]).

Density ρ (kg/m^3)	Shear Modulus G (GPa)	Tensile Strength T (MPa)	Uniaxial Compressive Strength f_c (MPa)	Cohesive Strength A	Pressure Hardening B	Strain Rate Coefficient C	Pressure Hardening Exponent N
2164	4.437	1.107	70.27	0.79	1.6	0.007	0.61

The impact stress wave generated by the impact hammer is transmitted to the lunar rocks through the coring tube, and the stress wave transmission simulation effect is shown in Figure 11. The bit module is driven by the impact action to intrude into the lunar rocks and form an impact crushing pit at the contact point. At the same time, the lunar rocks around the bit module generate stress concentration in a short period of time, which leads to cracks inside. During the simulation, the impact stress wave is loaded to the lunar rocks at 0.16 ms, which causes the lunar rock to produce a crushing pit, as shown in Figure 12a. By this time, part of the impact energy in the coring tube has been consumed; however, another part of the impact energy still exists in the coring tube in the form of reflected stress waves. The reflected stress waves are repeatedly returned in the coring tube to enlarge the impact-crushing pit. During the simulation, the drill bit intrudes into the moon rock at a 1.2 mm depth after the initial impact loading and eventually to a 4.3 mm depth. However, the reflected stress wave in the actual experiment is usually consumed greatly during the reflection process, and the final intrusion depth does not surpass the initial intrusion depth too much.

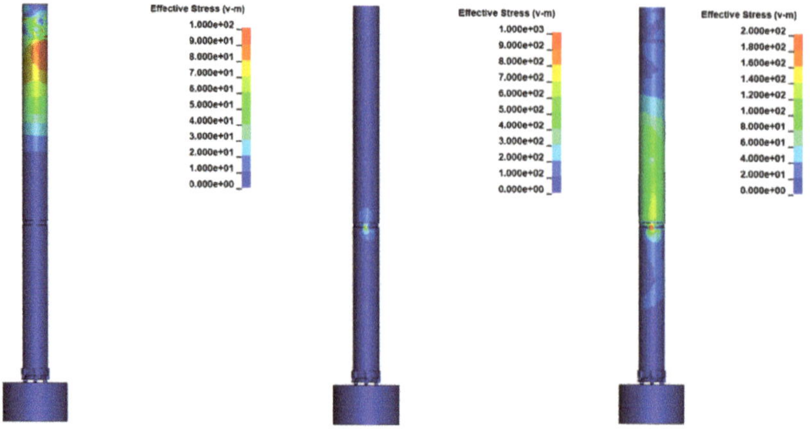

(a) (b) (c)

Figure 11. Stress waves during intrusion of lunar rocks by the WSC robot (**a**) Load phase (**b**) Transfer to connection point (**c**) Reflection phase.

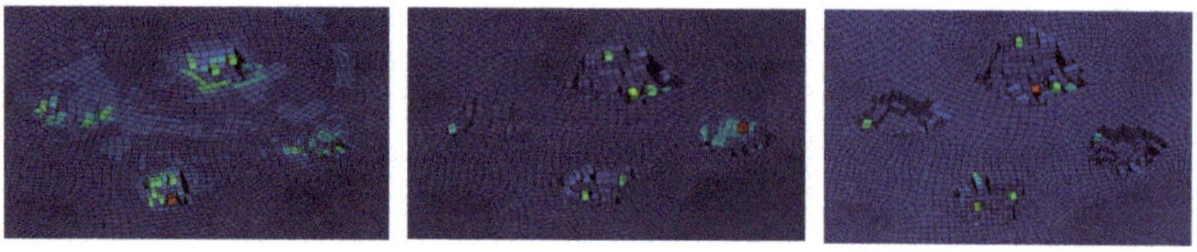

(a) (b) (c)

Figure 12. Lunar rocks crushing simulation results (**a**) 0.16 ms; (**b**) 1 ms; (**c**) 2 ms.

4. Conclusions

This paper designs a coring robot for deep lunar rocks based on a wire-line sampling device: the WSC robot. The WSC robot has functions, such as a subsurface anchor module and debris-tolerant chamber, which makes it possible to complete the whole coring process in the subsurface autonomously. The coring executor has the functions of changing the coring tubes and storing full sample coring tubes. Then, the dynamic analysis of the anchor module in the WSC robot can be carried out. A lunar regolith greater than 4 m is tight enough to support the full-power WSC robot according to the model of support force versus the depth of the lunar regolith in this paper. The support force provided by the lunar regolith at 0–4 m varies considerably with depth, and the support condition needs to be monitored in real-time to change the WSC robot power output. Finally, the impact function of the WSC robot is modeled and optimized, and the maximum impact energy based on the spring storage mechanism is determined to be 3.7 J. Then, this impact process is simulated, and it is determined that the WSC robot could effectively produce impact-crushing pits on the lunar rocks. Thus, the rock drilling capability of the WSC robot is initially verified, and the basis for the prototype is provided.

Author Contributions: Y.W. (Yufeng Wen) and G.Z. completed the main research tasks and wrote the manuscript. G.Z. revised the whole manuscript. H.X. proposed the initial ideas. M.G. and C.L. completed the derivation of the theory related to the soil mechanics. X.Z. and Y.W. (Yaohui Wang) assisted in the design of the mechanical structure. All authors have read and agreed to the published version of the manuscript.

Funding: The work described in this paper was supported by the National Natural Science Foundation of China (Grant Nos. U2013603, 52275454, 51827901), and the Shenzhen Natural Science Foundation (Grant Nos. 20200826160002001, JCYJ20220531103614032).

Institutional Review Board Statement: Not applicable.

Data Availability Statement: Not applicable.

Conflicts of Interest: The authors declare no conflict of interest.

References

1. Zhang, T.; Xu, K.; Yao, Z.X.; Ding, X.L.; Zhao, Z.; Hou, X.Y.; Pang, Y.; Lai, X.M.; Zhang, W.M.; Liu, S.T.; et al. The progress of extraterrestrial regolith-sampling robots. *Nat. Astron.* **2019**, *3*, 487–497. [CrossRef]
2. Bar-Cohen, Y.; Zacny, K. *Drilling in Extreme Environments: Penetration and Sampling on Earth and other Planets*; Wiley-VCH: Berlin, Germany, 2009.
3. Badescu, V.; Zacny, K. *Inner Solar System: Prospective Energy and Material Resources*; Springer: Cham, Switzerland, 2015. [CrossRef]
4. Zhang, T.; Wang, B.; Wei, H.; Zhang, Y.; Chao, C.; Xu, K.; Ding, X.; Hou, X.; Zhao, Z. Review on planetary regolith-sampling technology. *Prog. Aeronaut. Sci.* **2021**, *127*, 1–26. [CrossRef]
5. Qiao, L.; Chen, J.; Xu, L.; Wan, S.; Cao, H.; Li, B.; Ling, Z. Geology of the Chang'e-5 landing site: Constraints on the sources of samples returned from a young nearside mare. *Icarus* **2021**, *364*, 114480. [CrossRef]
6. Slyuta, E. Chapter 3—The Luna program. In *Sample Return Missions*; Longobardo, A., Ed.; Elsevier: Amsterdam, The Netherlands, 2021; pp. 37–78. [CrossRef]
7. Jerde, E.A. Chapter 2—The Apollo program. In *Sample Return Missions*; Longobardo, A., Ed.; Elsevier: Amsterdam, The Netherlands, 2021; pp. 9–36. [CrossRef]
8. Zhang, X.; Zhang, G.Q.; Xie, H.P.; Gao, M.Z.; Wen, Y.F. A Review of Sampling Exploration and Devices for Extraterrestrial Celestial Bodies. *Space Sci. Rev.* **2022**, *218*, 1–50. [CrossRef]
9. Zhang, Y.L.; Zhang, T.; Wei, H.Y.; Liu, J.B.; Wang, W.; Yuan, X.Y.; Pang, Y.; Guan, Y.S.; Hou, X.Y.; Xu, K. Advances in Extraterrestrial Drilling Technology to Discover the Secrets Hidden Inside Celestial Bodies. *Space Sci. Rev.* **2022**, *218*, 1–46. [CrossRef]
10. Liang, P.; Hou, X.; Zhang, K.; Zhang, K.; Deng, Z. The research and design of pneumatic multi-pipe deep lunar soil drilling device. In Proceedings of the 2016 IEEE International Conference on Mechatronics and Automation, Harbin, China, 7–10 August 2016; pp. 1379–1384. [CrossRef]
11. Bogatcbev, A.; Koutcberenko, V.; Malenkov, M.; Matrossov, S. Developments of Track Locomotion Systems for Planetary Mobile Robots. *IFAC Proc. Vol.* **2004**, *37*, 153–158. [CrossRef]
12. Magnani, P.G.; Re, E.; Ylikorpi, T.; Cherubini, G.; Olivieri, A. Deep drill (DeeDri) for Mars application. *Planet. Space Sci.* **2004**, *52*, 79–82. [CrossRef]
13. Cannon, H.N.; Stoker, C.R.; Dunagan, S.E.; Davis, K.; Gómez-Elvira, J.; Glass, B.J.; Lemke, L.G.; Miller, D.; Bonaccorsi, R.; Branson, M.; et al. MARTE: Technology development and lessons learned from a Mars drilling mission simulation. *J. Field Robot.* **2007**, *24*, 877–905. [CrossRef]
14. Li, P.; Zhang, H.; Jiang, S.Y.; Zhang, W.W. Analysis and Testing of Load Characteristics for Rotary-Percussive Drilling of Lunar Rock Simulant with a Lunar Regolith Coring Bit. *Shock. Vib.* **2017**, *2017*, 3012749. [CrossRef]
15. Szwarc, T.J. Thermal Modeling of Coring and Drilling Operations for Solar System Exploration Applications. Ph.D. Thesis, Stanford University, Stanford, CA, USA, 2013.
16. Marshall, J.P.; Hudson, T.L.; Andrade, J.E. Experimental Investigation of InSight HP3 Mole Interaction with Martian Regolith Simulant. *Space Sci. Rev.* **2017**, *211*, 239–258. [CrossRef]
17. Zhang, W.; Li, L.; Jiang, S.; Ji, J.; Deng, Z. Inchworm Drilling System for Planetary Subsurface Exploration. *IEEE/ASME Trans. Mechatron.* **2020**, *25*, 837–847. [CrossRef]
18. Zacny, K.; Bar-Cohen, Y.; Brennan, M.; Briggs, G.; Cooper, G.; Davis, K.; Dolgin, B.; Glaser, D.; Glass, B.; Gorevan, S.; et al. Drilling systems for extraterrestrial subsurface exploration. *Astrobiology* **2008**, *8*, 665–706. [CrossRef] [PubMed]
19. Bar-Cohen, Y.; Zacny, K.; Badescu, M.; Lee, H.J.; Sherrit, S.; Bao, X.Q.; Freeman, D.; Paulsen, G.L.; Beegle, L. Auto-Gopher-2-Wireline Deep Sampler Driven by Percussive Piezoelectric Actuator and Rotary EM Motors. *Adv. Sci. Technol.* **2016**, *100*, 207–212.
20. Heiken, G.H.; Vaniman, D.T.; French, B.M. *Lunar Sourcebook, A User's Guide to the Moon*; Press Syndicate of the University of Cambridge: New York, NY, USA, 1991.
21. Mitchell, J.K.; Houston, W.N.; Carrier, W.; Costes, N.C. Apollo soil mechanics experiment S-200. *Arch. Dermatol. Syphilol.* **1974**, *53*, 19740019219.
22. Duke, M.; Woo, C.; Sellers, G.; Bird, M.; Finkelman, R. Genesis of lunar soil at Tranquillity Base. In Proceedings of the The Apollo 11 Lunar Science Conference, Houston, TX, USA, 1 January 1970; pp. 347–361.
23. Mitchell, J.; Houston, W.; Scott, R.; Costes, N.; Carrier III, W.; Bromwell, L. Mechanical properties of lunar soil: Density, porosity, cohesion and angle of internal friction. In Proceedings of the The Third Lunar Science Conference, Houston, TX, USA, 1 January 1972; pp. 3235–3253.

24. Pham, K.D.; Zhao, W.; Zmuda, H.; Sun, H.; Jia, Q.; Cox, J.L.; Meyer, G.J.; Zhang, Y. Mechanical analysis about the spherical mobile robot on the moon environment. In *Sensors and Systems for Space Applications IV*; SPIE: Orlando, FL, USA, 2011. [CrossRef]
25. Yang, Z. *Research on Impact Crushing in Luna Soil Sampling Based on ANSYS/Ls-Dyna Numerical Simulation Master*; Harbin Institute of Technology Harbin: Harbin, China, 2019.

applied sciences

MDPI

Article

Innovative Design of a Conductive Center Pole for an Active Thermal Insulation and Coring System in Deep Rock

Bo Yu [1], Zhiqiang He [2,*], Jianping Yang [3], Zijie Wei [2], Cong Li [2] and Heping Xie [4]

1 School of Mechanical Engineering, Sichuan University, Chengdu 610065, China
2 State Key Laboratory of Hydraulics and Mountain River Engineering, College of Water Resource and Hydropower, Sichuan University, Chengdu 610065, China
3 College of Polymer Science and Engineering, Sichuan University, Chengdu 610065, China
4 College of Civil and Transportation Engineering, Shenzhen University, Shenzhen 518060, China
* Correspondence: 13281255182@163.com

Abstract: Intelligent drilling technologies, such as downhole signal and power transmission, can be used to measure key downhole data and obtain thermal insulation cores. This technology is of great significance for the accurate assessment of deep oil and gas resources, the reconstruction of oil and gas resource extraction systems, and the realization of efficient, intelligent and safe resource extraction. In order to meet the needs of underground communication and power supply for active thermal insulation coring, a new type of conductive center pole was innovatively designed. Using the theory of innovation problem solving (TRIZ) and axiomatic design (AD) to analyze the functional requirements of the conductive central pole, establish and solve the original design matrix. Based on the axiomatic design theory, the non-coupling matrix is decoupled by using the TRIZ solving tool, and the key indicators of the design scheme that meet the independent axiom are evaluated. In view of the contradictions and conflicts, the TRIZ solution tool was continually used to solve, optimize and obtain a design scheme with a higher comprehensive evaluation. Thus, the self-adaptive non-winding connection and power conduction of the conductive center pole was realized. Finally, the strength of the newly designed center pole was checked, and a physical prototype was made. Pre-research experiments on its conductivity and electrothermal conversion efficiency were carried out under different simulation environments to verify its conductivity. It provides innovative solutions to related problems in the field of deep insulation coring and intelligent drilling and provides effective technical means for related needs.

Keywords: insulation coring; intelligent drilling; conductive center pole; axiomatic design (AD); TRIZ

1. Introduction

In 2021, British Petroleum (BP) released the 2021 World Energy Statistics Yearbook, in which non-renewable resources, such as oil, natural gas, and coal, accounted for an extremely high proportion of energy consumption around the world, reaching 83%. Even in recent years, the whole world has emphasized energy saving and emission reduction, and put forward related concepts such as "carbon neutrality" and "carbon peaking" to reduce carbon emissions [1,2] The consumption of renewable resources, such as wind and solar energy, has reached a historical peak and only accounts for 6% of the total consumption. Figure 1 shows the proportion of energy consumption in all continents and regions of the world [3].

Especially for developing countries, their dependence on non-renewable resources, such as oil and natural gas, is even more serious. For example, China's consumption of non-renewable energy accounts for as high as 85%, which is higher than the world average. The proportion of energy consumption is shown in Figure 2. It can be seen that human beings are still highly dependent on the utilization of non-renewable resources, such as petrochemicals and oil and gas.

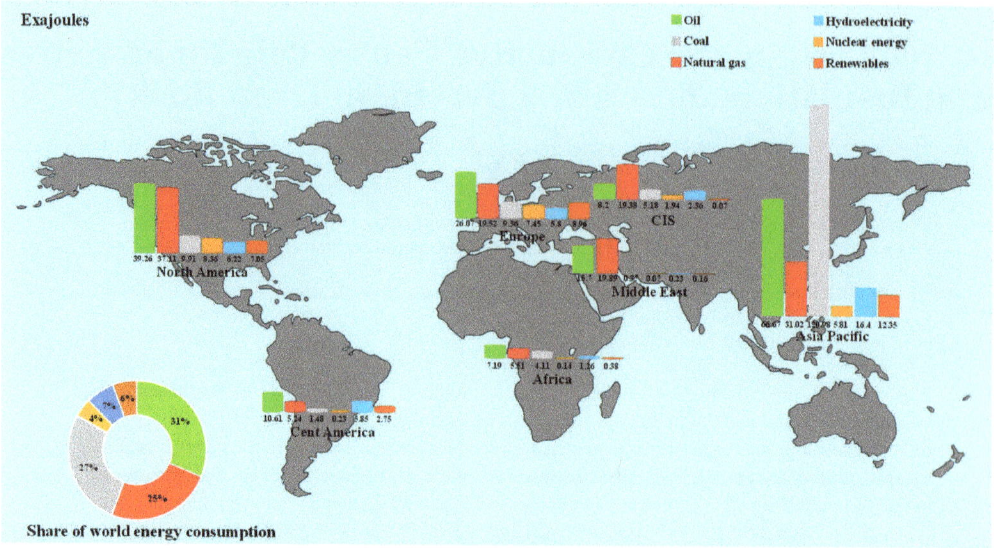

Figure 1. Percentage of energy consumption by continents and regions in the world in 2020.

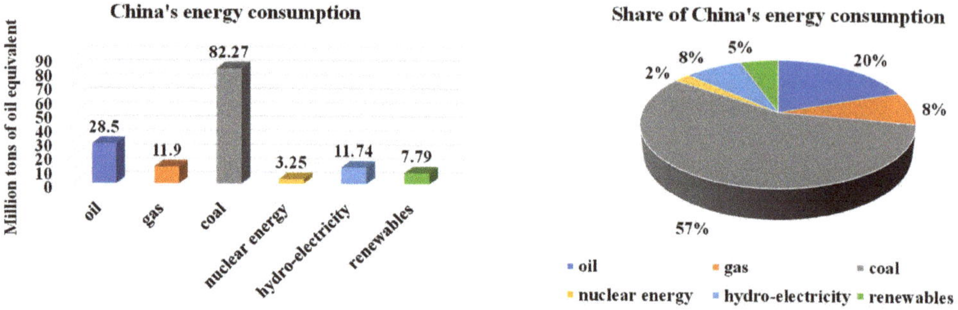

Figure 2. Proportion of China's energy consumption in 2020.

People's high dependence on petrochemical resources has led to the gradual depletion of minerals and oil and gas resources in the shallow parts of the earth, and the exploitation of resources needs to continue to go to the deeper parts of the earth [4]. Efficient exploration and accurate assessment of deep oil and gas resources are crucial for their exploitation [5,6]. However, the existing deep resource mining work lacks consideration of the real physical and mechanical parameters and model basis of the core in the deep in situ environment, resulting in failure to achieve safe, efficient and economical deep resource mining and utilization [7]. Therefore, obtaining fidelity cores with deep in situ environmental conditions is of great significance to the exploration and evaluation of deep oil and gas resources [7].

At present, the research and application of fidelity core technology at home and abroad mostly belong to the category of holding pressure, and the fidelity of temperature is rarely involved [8,9]. However, changes in in situ sample temperature will also have a significant impact on rock porosity, permeability, and mechanical properties. The conventional coring technology lacks consideration of insulation, leading to serious deviations in results, affecting the preparation and evaluation of deep resources. It also helps researchers understand the microbial life in the deep subsurface of the Earth [10–12].

To find out the laws of the Earth's oil and gas resource storage, it is necessary to overcome the influence of changes in the in situ sample temperature and other occurrences in the environment on the in situ properties of the rock during the coring process [13]. However, the extreme environment and complicated working conditions deep underground make it extremely difficult to achieve power and data transmission at the bottom of the hole, making it extremely difficult to achieve core temperature fidelity [9].

The research and development of key technologies and equipment for intelligent geological drilling at large depths is one of the necessary means to realize deep exploration [6] In this paper, aiming at the technical difficulties of in situ thermal insulation and coring in deep rocks, the mechanism and technical requirements for in situ thermal insulation and coring in deep rocks are analyzed, and innovative design methods are used to design and optimize the conductive center pole. Based on the independence axiom of axiomatic design and integrating TRIZ conflict resolution theory, the innovative design process of a downhole drilling conductive center rod is established. By analyzing the boundary conditions of the use environment, the design requirements of the conductive central rod are obtained, and the non-winding and effective contact power transmission of the underground conductive central rod is realized. In addition, it is not limited by the assembly position during the assembly of the central rod, and can be operated in the casing of the coring device, so as to realize the effective and stable connection of the power channel during the rotation of the central rod.

The conductive center pole will provide energy for the deep insulation system, establish deep underground information and power channels, realize intelligent and digital mining, and ensure the safety, speed and efficiency of the drilling process [14].

2. Related Works

At present, the international community only involves thermal insulation and coring in in situ low-temperature environments, such as combustible ice coring, while high-temperature thermal insulation and coring in deep hard rock is a blank in research. The core samplers with thermal insulation function include the pressure temperature core sampler (PTCS) designed by Japan Petroleum Corporation [15]. Multiple autoclave corer (MAC) and dynamic autoclave piston corer (DAPC) used in R.V.SONNE cruises developed by the German OMEGA project [16]. The pressure and temperature preservation system (PTPS) developed by China First Ocean Research Institute [17]. The hole bottom freezing core sampler (FCS) developed by Jilin University [18]. The insulation and pressure-maintaining sampler developed by Beijing Institute of Prospecting Engineering [19]. The gravity piston fidelity sampler of Zhejiang University [20] Changsha Mine Research Institute developed a deep-sea hard rock fidelity core remover [21]. The GW194-70BB thermal insulation pressure-maintaining coring tool and the coal-bed methane thermal insulation, pressure-maintaining and shape-preserving coring tool developed by the PetroChina Great Wall Drilling Engineering Technology Research Institute [22,23]. The heat preservation method of each core remover is shown in Table 1.

Except for the main types of core removers mentioned above, other core removers do not have the function of heat preservation. At present, most thermal insulation cores only use passive thermal insulation, and few use active thermal insulation. The most representative one is the pressure temperature core sampler developed by Japan, which has both active and passive heat preservation. Its structural principle is shown in Figure 3. The core remover mainly uses heat insulation materials and liquid nitrogen between the core lining pipe and the inner pipe to realize passive heat preservation. At the same time, a battery is used to drive the Peltier refrigeration sheet and cooperate with the low-temperature drilling fluid to remove the heat from the hot end, maintain high-efficiency thermoelectric conversion in the well, and realize active heat preservation. However, due to its complex structure, difficult processing, and high cost, its active insulation technology has only been tested indoors and has not been applied in engineering [15].

Table 1. Main thermal insulation method of core remover.

Name of Core Sampler	R&D Country or Institution	Insulation Method
PTCS	Japan	Active insulation
MAC	Germany/R.V.SONNE cruises	External cooling device
DAPC	Germany/R.V.SONNE cruises	External cooling device
PTPS	First Ocean Institute	Passive insulation
FCS	Jilin University	Dry ice, low-temperature alcohol
TKP-1	Beijing Institute of Prospecting Engineering	Passive insulation
Gravity piston fidelity sampler	Zhejiang University	Passive insulation
Deep-sea hard rock fidelity core sampler	Changsha Mine Research Institute	Passive insulation
GW194-70BB type heat preservation pressure core tool	PetroChina Great Wall Drilling Engineering Technology Research Institute	Passive insulation
Coal-bed methane thermal insulation, pressure-maintaining and shape-preserving coring tool	PetroChina Great Wall Drilling Engineering Technology Research Institute	Passive insulation

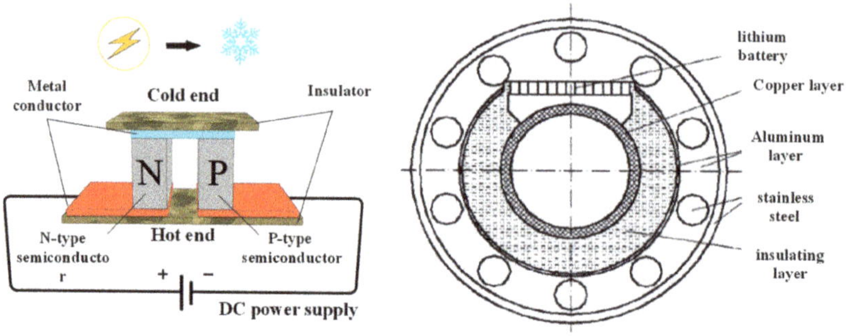

Figure 3. Schematic diagram of active and passive heat preservation of PTCS.

Since the in situ temperature of combustible ice is not much different from the ambient temperature, the use of passive heat preservation and pressure-maintaining coring technology can achieve combustible ice acquisition [24]. However, for deep hard rock, the in situ temperature is as high as hundreds of degrees Celsius, which is very different from the ground environment temperature. The heat loss during the coring process is serious, so it is necessary to take active heat preservation for real-time heat compensation to maintain the in situ temperature of the core.

Underground power supply and signal transmission technology are the prerequisites for realizing active thermal insulation and coring, but this is still a difficult problem internationally [25]. At present, most of the downhole signal and data transmission are realized through the drilling fluid pulse transmission method, electromagnetic wave transmission method, acoustic wave transmission method, optical fiber transmission method, and wired transmission method [26,27]. Downhole current transmission is realized by embedding cables inside the drill pipe, which greatly improves the reliability and power transmission capacity. This method was first proposed by Intelliserv Corporation of the United States, and is called smart drill pipe [28]. Wired drill pipe transmission technology includes the induction and wire butt method. As shown in Figures 4 and 5, respectively [26,29].

However, the smart drill pipe is mainly for the measurement of the environmental parameters of the drill bit and the bottom hole and cannot conduct and supply electrical energy to the core remover in the drill pipe, let alone realize the temperature measurement and temperature control of the core. In addition, the commonly used wired connection methods in smart drill pipes also have problems such as inability to align electrodes, poor contact, and low connection reliability [26].

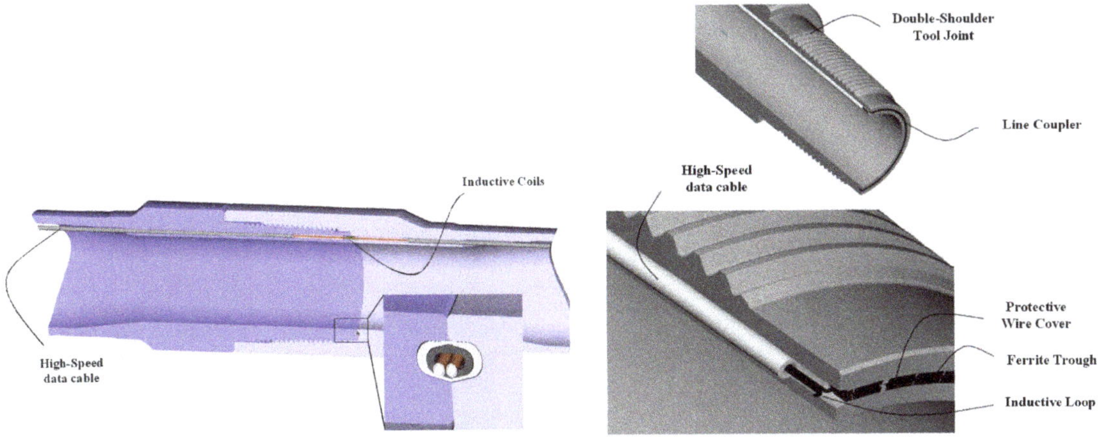

Figure 4. Principle and structure diagram of the induction transmission technology.

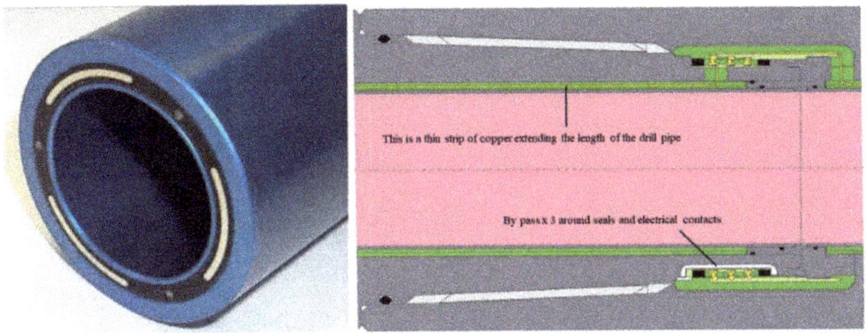

Figure 5. Structure diagram of the wire butt method.

Referring to the design principles of smart drill pipes, and the use innovative design methods we designed and optimized the conductive structure of the center pole of the core remover to realize a self-adaptive non-winding connection and power conduction of the conductive center pole. Finally, a physical prototype was made for relevant experimental verification to meet the signal and power requirements for in situ insulation and coring operations of deep rocks.

3. Overdesign

3.1. The Position and Workflow of the Center Pole

When taking the core, the core remover is in the center of the drill pole. First, the drill bit and drill pole are used to drill holes. After reaching a specified depth, the core remover is lowered inside the drill pole. The mud pump provides power to the coring device to realize the deep in situ coring operation.

By arranging wires in the center pole, electrical energy is provided for the heating system at the bottom of the hole, realizing active insulation and core removal in situ. One of the main difficulties is to realize the electrical conduction at the connection position. The conductive process is shown in Figure 6.

With reference to the conduction mode of the smart drill pipe at the connection position, there are often problems such as unaligned electrodes, poor contact, and wire entanglement. Therefore, an innovative design is made for the conductive center pole in view of the above problems.

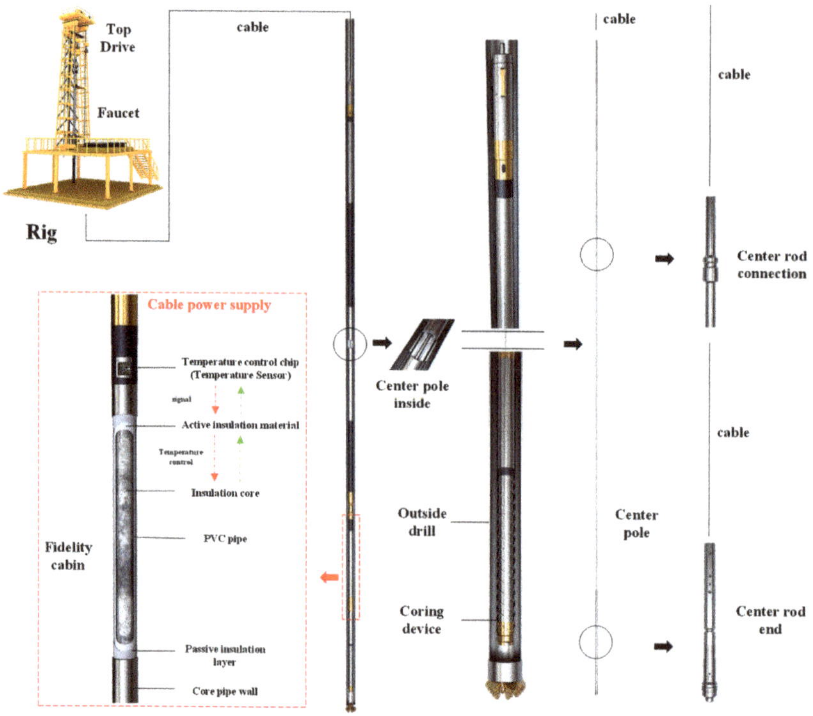

Figure 6. The position and workflow of the center pole.

3.2. Center Pole Size and Assembly Requirements

The center pole is formed by connecting multiple sections of slender poles, and the interface at the connecting position is a circular ring with an outer diameter of 30 mm and an inner diameter of 20 mm, as shown in Figure 7. The center pole is small in size and compact in structure.

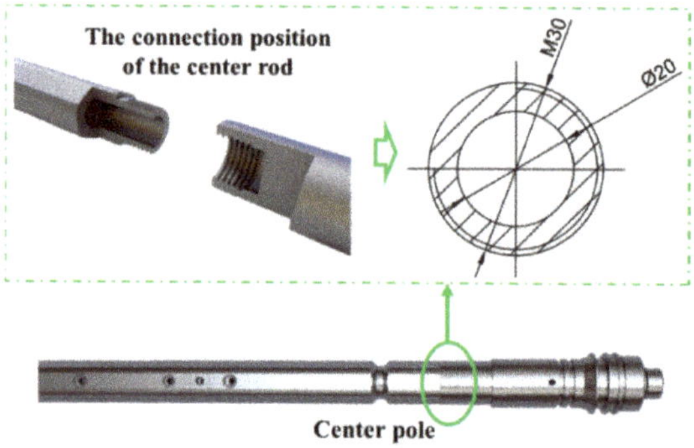

Figure 7. Sectional size of the connecting position of the center pole.

The center pole must strictly observe a certain assembly sequence during the assembly process, so assembly and wiring cannot be completed in advance. Additionally, it is required to realize the conduction of electrical energy at the same time after the screw connection of the central pole is completed.

4. Detailed Design of the Conductive Center Pole Based on the Innovative Design Method

4.1. Innovative Design Strategy and Process of the Conductive Center Pole

After clarifying the size and assembly requirements of the center pole, the innovative design method was used to carry out a detailed structural design according to its functional requirements. The TRIZ invention problem-solving theory was proposed by Rich Altshuller in 1964 [30,31]. The theory is composed of 39 engineering parameters and conflict matrices, 40 invention principles, four separation principles, and physical contradictions. It is believed that the essence of innovative and invention is the process of resolving contradictions [32,33].

Technical and physical conflict are the main research contents of the TRIZ theory. When we want to improve one feature in the technical system and cause another feature in the system to deteriorate, it is a technical conflict. When there are opposite requirements for a certain feature of a system, it is a physical conflict. To solve a technical conflict, the improved and deteriorated engineering parameters are defined with 39 technical parameters, and the invention principle of resolving the conflict is found in the classic conflict matrix, as shown in Figure 8. When there is a physical conflict in the technical system, four separation principles (space separation, time separation, separation of the whole and its parts, and conditional separation) and 40 corresponding invention principles are mainly used to solve the problem, as shown in Table 2.

Deterioration parameter / Parameters to be improved	1 The weight of a moving object	2 The weight of a stationary object	3 The length of a moving object	4 The length of a stationary object	22 Energy loss	30 Harmful factors acting on objects	39 productivity
1 The weight of a moving object			15,8,29,34		6,12,34,19	22,21,18,27	35,3,24,37
2 The weight of a stationary object				10,1,29,35	18,19,28,15	2,19,22,7	1,28,15,35
3 The length of a moving object	8,15,29,34				7,35,9	1,15,17,24	14,4,28,29
4 The length of a stationary object		35,28,40,29			6,28	1,18	30,14,7,26
33 operability	25,2,15,13	6,13,1,25	1,17,13,12		2,19,13	2,25,28,39	15,1,28
39 productivity	35,26,24,37	28,27,15,3	18,4,28,38	30,7,14,26	28,10,29,5	22,35,13,24	

Figure 8. Classical conflict matrix.

Table 2. Correspondence between the separation principle and the invention principle.

Separation Principles	Invention Principles
Space separation	1,2,3,4,7,13,17,24,26,30
Time separation	9,10,11,15,16,18,19,20,21,29,34,37
Separation of the whole and its parts	12,28,31,32,35,36,38,39,40
Condition separation	1,5,6,7,8,13,14,22,23,25,27,33,35

Axiomatic design is a design decision method proposed by Professor Nam P. Suh of the Massachusetts Institute of Technology in 1990 [34,35]. Axiomatic design divides product design into the user domain $\{CAs\}$, functional domain $\{FRs\}$, physical domain $\{DPs\}$, and process domain $\{PVs\}$, and each domain can be represented by matrix mapping. Product design mainly refers to the process of mapping and solving the functional domain $\{FRs\}$ and physical domain $\{DPs\}$ of the designed product [36]. Nam Suh used mathematics to formalize his work in axiomatic design. The following equation articulates any solution to a given design problem.

$$\{FR\} = [A]\{DP\} \tag{1}$$

Among them, $[A]$ is the design matrix, which represents the relationship between the functional requirements and design parameters. When the design matrix $[A]$ is a diagonal matrix or a triangular matrix, the elements in $\{FR\}$ are independent from each other to meet the product design requirements, which is also called the independence axiom [37].

The specialty of axiomatic design lies in the systematicness of overall design and process decomposition, which can provide designers with logical and rational thinking methods and tools. TRIZ's specialty lies in its technical innovation and the localization of conflict resolution. Based on the discussion of design theory and TRIZ theory, the technical process of the product design is formed according to the independence axiom of axiomatic design and the integration of TRIZ's conflict resolution principle.

We analyzed the functional requirements of the conductive center pole, established the functional requirement vector $\{FR\}$, used the TRIZ solution tool to perform preliminary solutions, and obtained the original design matrix $[A]$. Then, we used the conflict matrix and object field analysis method in TRIZ to solve and optimize the contradictions and problems in the design [38,39]. Finally, a comprehensive evaluation was made from six aspects: "structural design", "installation and assembly", "material properties", "independence", "functionality", and "manufacturability" to obtain comprehensive selection solutions and generate the corresponding design schemes. Then, we evaluated the generated scheme according to the initial functional requirements, and obtained the final feasible design scheme.

The innovative design process of the conductive center pole is shown in Figure 9.

4.2. Analysis of the Functional Requirements of the Conductive Center Pole

Thermal insulation in the deeper parts of the ground has high requirements for the design of power and signal transmission mechanisms. The conductive function is integrated into the center pole, and the conductive module is required to be connected and screwed with the center pole to complete the conduction of electricity.

The structure and performance design of the new conductive center pole needs to meet the following requirements:

1. The conductive module can realize the alignment of the positive and negative electrodes after the center pole is rotated and docked.
2. The conductive module can realize the contact between the positive and negative electrodes after the center pole is rotated and connected.
3. Avoid entanglement of the wire during the screwing process of the center pole.
4. The whole operation process meets the requirements of insulation and 150 °C temperature resistance.

A vector of the functional requirements is established, as follows:

$$\begin{bmatrix} FR_1 \\ FR_2 \\ FR_3 \\ FR_4 \end{bmatrix} = \left\{ \begin{array}{c} \text{Align the electrodes at both ends} \\ \text{Electrode contact at both ends} \\ \text{The wire is not entangled} \\ \text{Insulation and high temperature resistance } (150\ ^\circ\text{C}) \end{array} \right\} \tag{2}$$

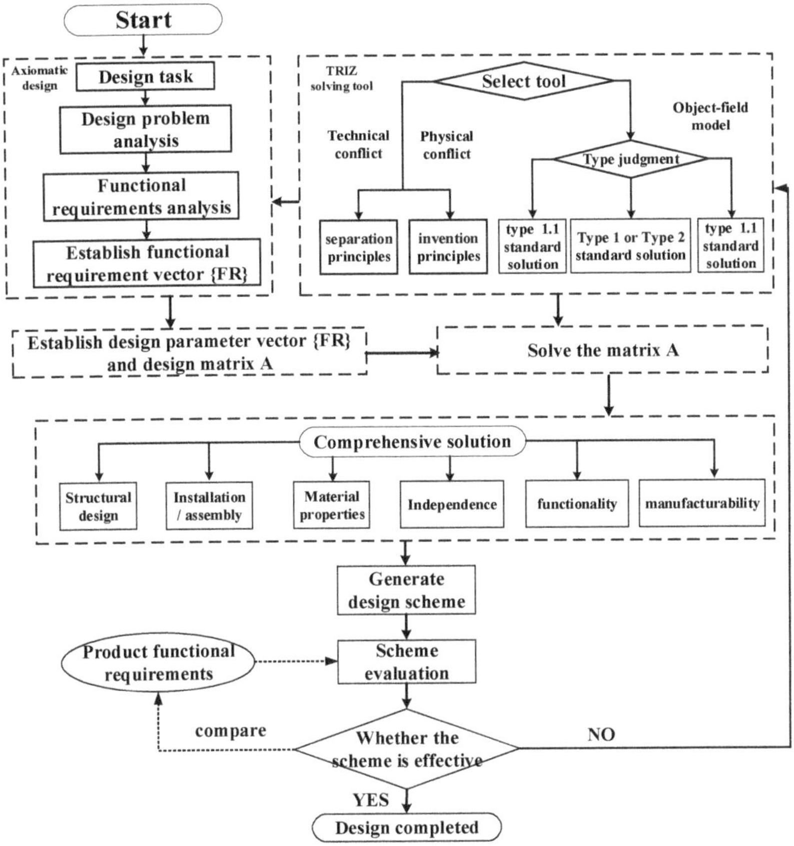

Figure 9. The innovative design process of the conductive center pole.

4.3. Establishing the Design Parameter Vector and Design Matrix of the Conductive Center Pole

Solving the design parameter DP_1: In order to ensure that the two poles of the conductive module can be accurately aligned after the center pole is screwed and docked, the corresponding position of the center pole can be marked after the center pole is screwed. Additionally, the electrode channel corresponding to the conductive module can be arranged at the marked position, and increase the probability of electrode alignment by increasing the contact area.

Solving the design parameter DP_2: In order to ensure that the two poles of the conductive module can fully contact and achieve conduction after the center pole is screwed together, the length of the connecting thread of the center pole should be measured in advance, and the placement position of the conductive module in the center pole should be designed according to the distance after screwing.

Solving the design parameter DP_3: In order to ensure that the wire is not twisted during the screwing and installation process of the center pole, an anti-rotation structure can be designed between the conductive module and the center pole to avoid the relative rotation of the conductive module and the center pole during the screwing process, which may cause the wire to be twisted.

Solving the design parameter DP_4: To ensure the insulation and temperature resistance of the conductive module, high-temperature-resistant resin and conductive copper phase materials can be used. The high-temperature resin is small in size and difficult to machine, so must be manufactured by 3D printing.

The expression of the design parameter vector can be obtained as follows:

$$\begin{bmatrix} DP_1 \\ DP_2 \\ DP_3 \\ DP_4 \end{bmatrix} = \left\{ \begin{array}{c} \text{Mark the position in the circumferential direction of the center rod} \\ \text{Measure and set the length of the thread} \\ \text{Design anti} - \text{rotation structure} \\ \text{Use high temperature resistant resin} \end{array} \right\} \quad (3)$$

Through the expression of the design parameter vector, the initial conceptual design diagram of the conductive center pole can be obtained, as shown in Figure 10.

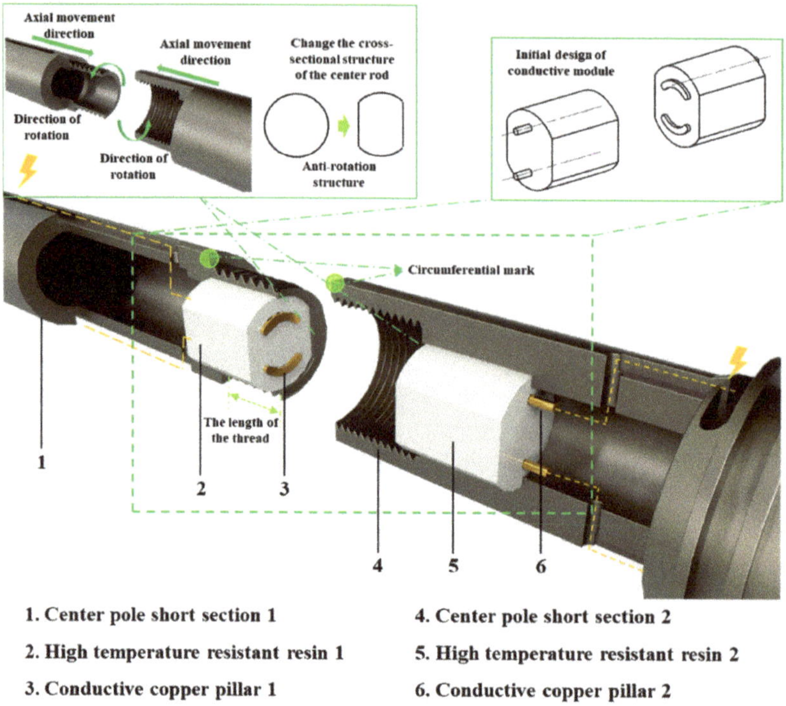

Figure 10. Conceptual design drawing of the conductive center pole.

Set the elements in the design matrix A to X. It can be seen from the mapping relationship between the functional requirement vector $\{FR\}$ and the design parameter vector $\{DP\}$ that the connection of the conductive module is related to the position of the center pole circumferential mark, the thread length, and the angle of the anti-rotation structure. Therefore, the design parameter DP_1 is related to the design parameters DP_2 and DP_3, and the design parameter DP_2 is related to the design parameter DP_1 and DP_3. The design matrix A is as follows:

$$A = \begin{Bmatrix} 1 & 1 & 1 & 0 \\ 1 & 1 & 1 & 0 \\ 0 & 0 & 1 & 0 \\ 0 & 0 & 0 & 1 \end{Bmatrix} \quad (4)$$

In the design matrix A, 1 means that there is a correlation between the design parameters, and 0 means that there is no correlation between the design parameters. This matrix is a coupling matrix and does not satisfy the independence axiom design. The associated design needs to be optimized and decoupled to form a triangular or diagonal array that meets the design requirements.

4.4. Design Matrix Decoupling Based on TRIZ

To decouple the design matrix A for the conductive module structure of the center pole in Figure 10, the position and length of the center pole need to be calibrated after the center pole is tightened to ensure that the conductive module can be screwed together with the center pole to complete the alignment and contact of the electrodes. However, whether the conductive module can be conducted is related to the position of the electrode in the circumferential direction, the distance in the axial direction, and the relative position of the anti-rotation structure. It is necessary to ensure the alignment of the electrodes and to ensure that the electrodes are in full contact and are not affected by the angle of the anti-rotation structure, that is, to eliminate the influence of elements A_{12}, A_{13}, A_{21}, and A_{23} in matrix A. Furthermore, the required effects or effects that need to be eliminated must be established according to functional requirements.

Ideally, to realize the conduction of the conductive module in the center pole, it is necessary for the conductive module to completely align its electrodes and ensure sufficient contact at the same time after the connection is completed. In order to avoid wire entanglement during the installation, an anti-rotation structure was designed to make the conductive module and the center pole move in-sync, remaining relatively static. However, the conductive modules in the two sections of the center pole move with the center pole, resulting in a relative rotation, which causes the electrodes of the two sections to move relative to each other, making it difficult to ensure alignment.

This problem is the alignment of the two conductive poles, which belongs to the physical conflict in TRIZ. When the two sides of the key subsystem conflict only appear on one side of a certain space, the space separation method can be used to resolve the physical conflict. Mann of the University of Bath in the United Kingdom proposed that there is a corresponding relationship between the separation principle for resolving physical conflicts and the invention principle for resolving technical conflicts. There are multiple invention principles corresponding to one separation principle, and more ideas for solving problems are provided [40]. The corresponding relationship is shown in Table 2.

The solution to spatial separation includes 10 principles of invention. To solve the problem of electrode alignment in the conductive module, the invention principle seven "nesting" and the invention principle 17 "space dimension change" can be used. "Nesting" refers to embedding an object in another object or allowing something to pass through the cavity of another object. "Space dimensionality change" refers to changing one-dimensional linear motion into two-dimensional plane motion or three-dimensional space motion. With the help of these two principles, and considering the rotational movement of the conductive module, the electrode can be designed as a combination of a ring and a dot. The dot-shaped electrode is placed in the center of the circular ring electrode, and the electrode at the other end is the dot-shaped electrode at the corresponding position, which avoids the problem that the two electrodes cannot be aligned due to the rotational movement. The structure before and after the improvement is shown in Figure 11.

This design ensures that when the center pole drives the conductive module to rotate, the electrodes at both ends can always be aligned in the circumferential direction and the center position and are not affected by the center rod's circumferentially calibrated position and the angle of the anti-rotation structure. Therefore, A_{12} and A_{13} in the design matrix A can be eliminated, and the alignment before contact can also be satisfied, that is, A_{23} can also be eliminated. Matrix A is improved to matrix B, as shown below:

$$B = \begin{pmatrix} 1 & 0 & 0 & 0 \\ 1 & 1 & 0 & 0 \\ 0 & 0 & 1 & 0 \\ 0 & 0 & 0 & 1 \end{pmatrix} \quad (5)$$

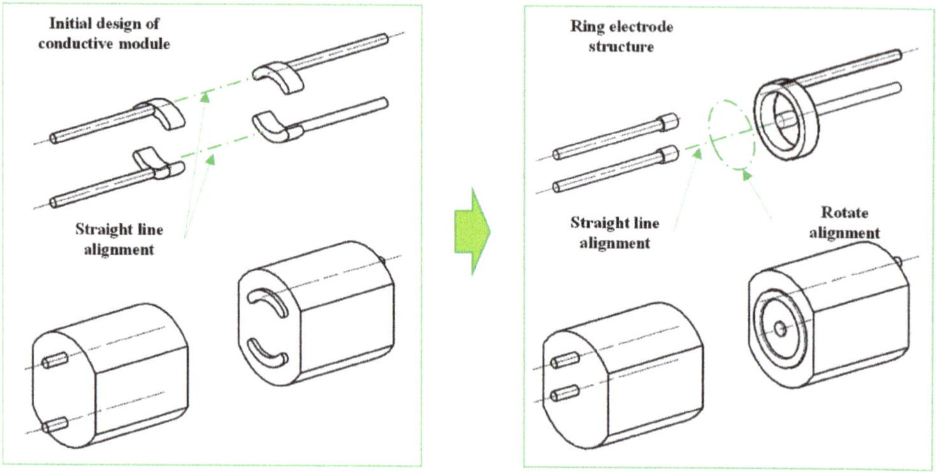

Figure 11. Improved conductive module structure.

However, whether the electrode can contact is still related to the circumferential calibration position of the center pole, that is, the angle of rotation of the center pole, so A_{21} is still 1. It can be judged by the independent axiom that the improved matrix B is still a coupling matrix, and the design scheme still needs to be improved. Since the contact of the conductive module is related to the screwing angle of the center pole and the thread wear condition, when the center pole is completely screwed, it may cause insufficient contact or excessive squeeze. The object–field model between the center pole and the conductive module can be established for analysis, as shown in Figure 12. S_1 represents the conductive module, S_2 represents the center pole, and F_1 represents the electrical conduction.

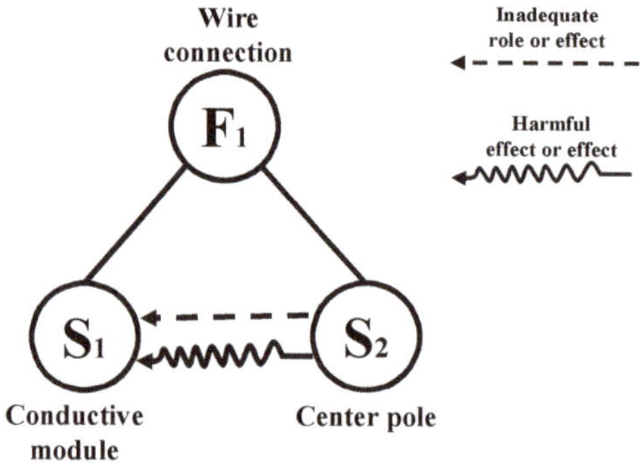

Figure 12. Object–field model of the conductive module.

Due to the insufficient contact or excessive squeezing of the conductive module, this object–field model belongs to the ineffective complete model and the harmful complete model. According to the general solution of the object–field model, the useful effect can be improved by adding another substance S_3 and another field F_2. Considering that the degree of electrode contact can be adjusted by itself, a spring that can provide a telescopic function is introduced as S_3, and the elastic force field is F_2. The improved object–field model of the conductive module is shown in Figure 13.

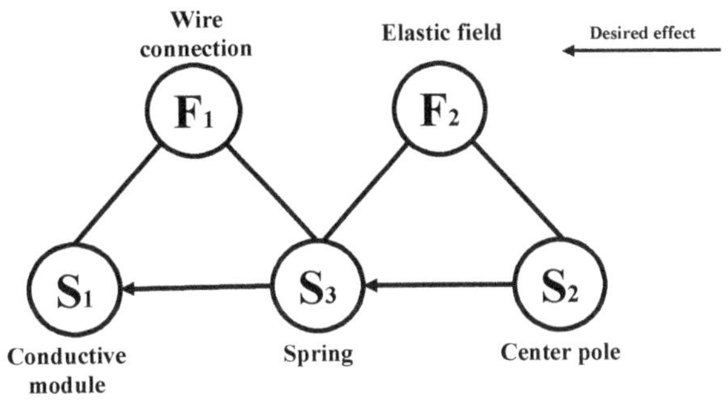

Figure 13. Improved object–field model of the conductive module.

By adding a spring mechanism between the center pole and the conductive module, and introducing an elastic force field, the problem of insufficient or excessive contact between the conductive modules is solved.

The functional behavior structure diagram to realize the conductive function of the center pole can be obtained, as shown in Figure 14 [41].

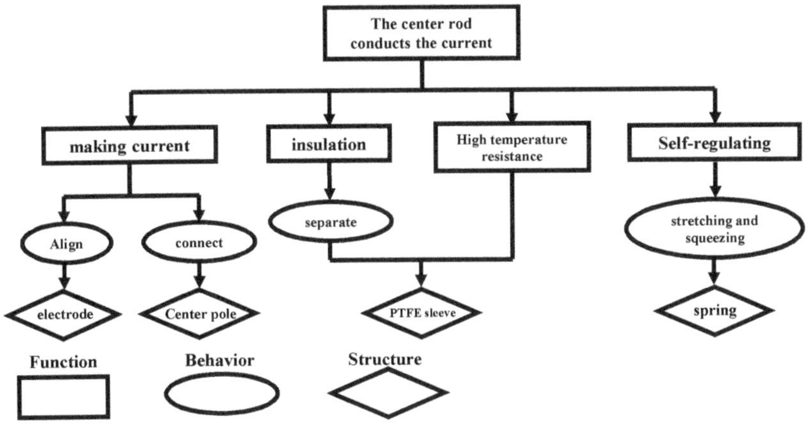

Figure 14. Functional behavior structure diagram of the electrified center pole.

By adding a spring mechanism between the center pole and the conductive module, the adaptive adjustment of the electrode contact is realized. The conductive center pole is shown in Figure 15. The space and positioning structure for placing the spring mechanism are designed inside the center pole, the spring is installed on the positioning structure, and the conductive module is placed on the spring. During the screwing process of the center pole, the two electrodes always remain aligned. A certain length of spring is selected to provide the initial pre-pressure to ensure contact, and after the screwing is completed, the position of the two electrodes is automatically adjusted by the compression spring to make them fully squeeze in contact without excessive squeezing, ensuring the safe conduction of electricity.

In this design, the contact of the electrode can be adjusted by a spring, and the contact of the electrode can be achieved even if the fixed-length thread and the circumferential position of the center pole are not set, that is, A_{21} can be 0. After design matrix B is improved, it becomes matrix C, as shown below.

$$C = \begin{pmatrix} 1 & 0 & 0 & 0 \\ 0 & 1 & 0 & 0 \\ 0 & 0 & 1 & 0 \\ 0 & 0 & 0 & 1 \end{pmatrix} \quad (6)$$

The design matrix C is a diagonal matrix, which satisfies the independence axiom design.

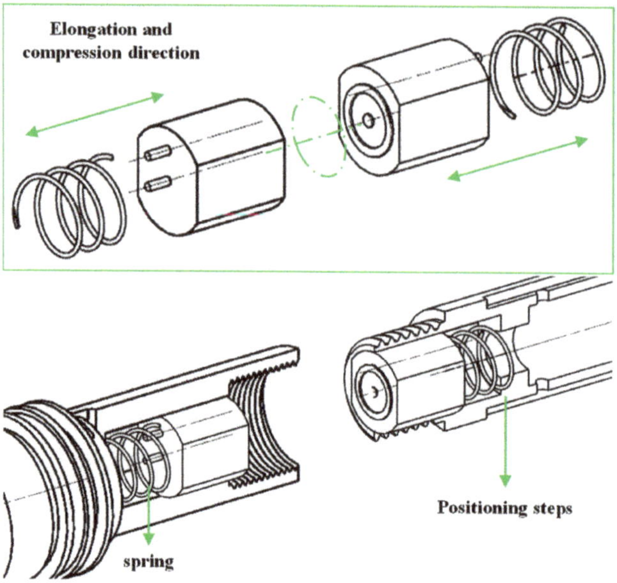

Figure 15. Conductive center pole.

4.5. Optimized Design of the Conductive Center Pole

According to the design of the conductive center pole in Figure 15, the design of the conductive center pole can meet the basic installation and conductivity requirements. However, its "independence", "functionality" and "installation and assembly" still need to be improved. In terms of "installation and assembly", a spring mechanism has been added, and an elastic force field has been introduced, which can solve the situation of insufficient or excessive contact of the conductive module. However, the internal space requirement for the center pole has increased, and the increased spring mechanism reduces the overall assemblability. In terms of "independence" and "functionality", although the electrode alignment and contact of the conductive module are not affected by the rotational angle of the center pole and the thread length, this structure has high requirements for the relative position between the two electrodes. Because the two electrodes are on the same conductive module, if one electrode comes into contact earlier than the other electrode, the first electrode in contact will push the conductive module to squeeze the spring, causing the conductive module to move as a whole, while the other electrode will not contact. The contact of the electrodes will form mutual interference. As shown in Figure 16.

In order to solve the problem of mutual interference of electrode contact, it is necessary for the two electrodes to have the ability to move and adjust independently, but the conductive module belongs to a hole with a fixed shape, and there is a physical conflict here. The division principle in the invention principle in Table 2. can be used to divide the electrodes so that they can be aligned and contacted, respectively. The preliminary segmentation is shown in Figure 17.

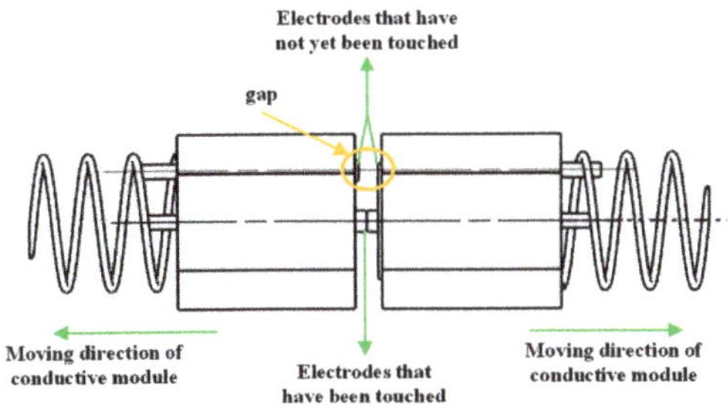

Figure 16. Interference of electrode position.

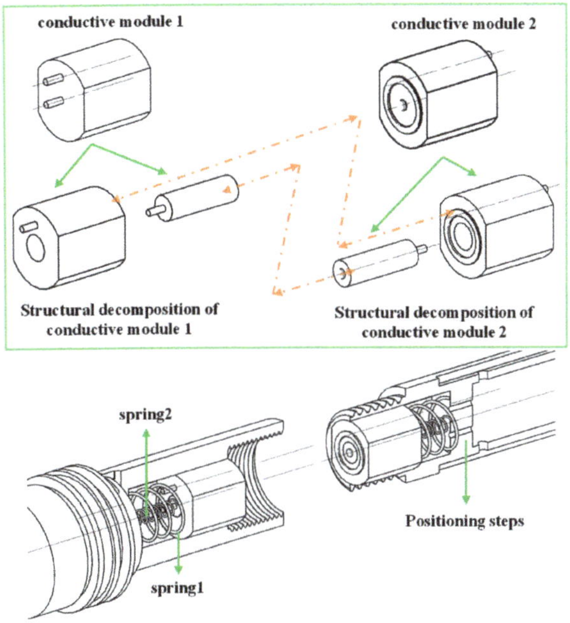

Figure 17. Structural separation of the conductive modules.

To optimize the "overall assemblability." of the conductive module, it is necessary to simplify the shape of the spring and the conductive module to reduce the difficulty of assembly and avoid interference with the center pole. However, the internal complexity of the corresponding system will increase, and its manufacturability will also deteriorate.

In engineering design, one design parameter of the system is improved, while another parameter is aggravated, that is, technical conflict [30,31]. To solve the technical conflict, it is necessary to transform the actual problem into the conflict problem model. The relationship between the technical parameters and the invention principle is found through the conflict matrix table, and the final solution is obtained according to the invention principle.

Using the technical conflict resolution theory, the corresponding technical parameters and invention principles in the classic conflict matrix were found, as shown in Table 3.

Table 3. Technical conflict matrix of conductive center pole assembly.

Optimized Parameters	Deteriorating Parameters	Invention Principles
Shape (9)	Manufacturability (32)	01,32,17,28
	System complexity (36)	16,29,01,28

To simplify the shape of the conductive module, while avoiding the deterioration of its manufacturability and system complexity, inventive principle 1 (segmentation: divide the object into mutually independent, detachable and installable parts) can be used as a solution. This solution integrated the spring structure into the conductive structure to make the overall shape more concise and easy to assemble, while retaining the expansion and contraction function of the spring. Even if the initial segmentation operation is performed, as shown in Figure 17, the relative position of the two electrodes in the axial direction cannot be guaranteed before the central rod is tightened, and they are prone to misalignment. So the segmentation operation in Table 3 needs to be performed again. This separation needs to maintain the shape of the conductive module, including the spring structure and can meet the independent adjustment of the two electrodes. The structure of the separated components is shown in Figure 18.

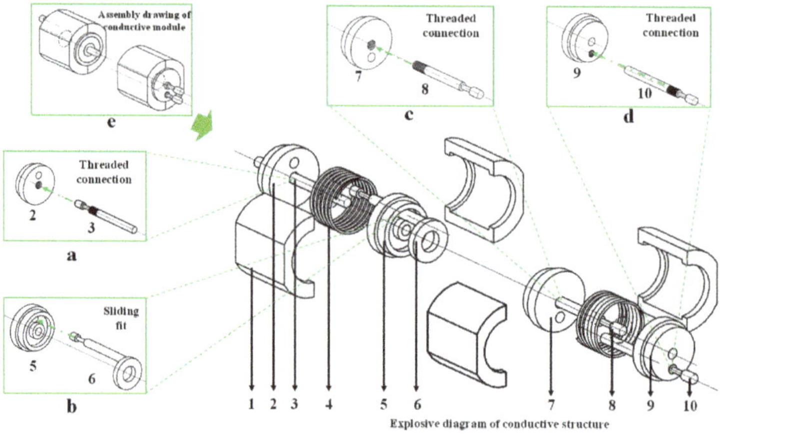

1. Insulation anti-rotation sleeve
2. Insulated base
3. Straight conductive copper nail
4. Spring
5. Ring insulation base
6. Ring conductive copper nail
7. Insulated base
8. Straight conductive copper nail
9. Insulated base
10. Straight conductive copper nail

a. Center fixed electrode
b. Annular sliding electrode
c. Center sliding electrode
d. Eccentric fixed electrode
e. Conductive structure assembly

Figure 18. The final optimization design of the conductive center pole structure.

As shown in Figure 18, the four electrodes at both ends are separated in the axial direction so that they can move independently without interfering with each other. The insulating base 2 and the straight conductive copper 3 must be threaded together to form an independently movable electrode unit, as shown in Figure 18a. The ring-shaped insulating base 5 and the corresponding ring-shaped conductive structure 6 are assembled to form an independently movable electrode unit, as shown in Figure 18b. The insulating base 7 and the straight conductive copper 8 must be threaded together to form an electrode unit that can move independently, as shown in Figure 18c. The insulating base 9 and the straight conductive copper 10 must be threaded to form an electrode unit that can move independently, as shown in Figure 18d.

The spring structure is integrated with the conductive module to make it both functional and simple in appearance. The original conductive module structure is divided to form a split structure, and the spring and the four independently moving electrodes a, b, c, and d shown in Figure 18 are placed inside the conductive module. Additionally, the split and step structures are placed in the insulating seat to form an assembly fit to realize the limit and movement guidance. Finally, its function integration and appearance simplification are carried out. The simplified conductive structure and overall shape are shown in Figure 18e.

The final design of the conductive center pole is shown in Figure 19.

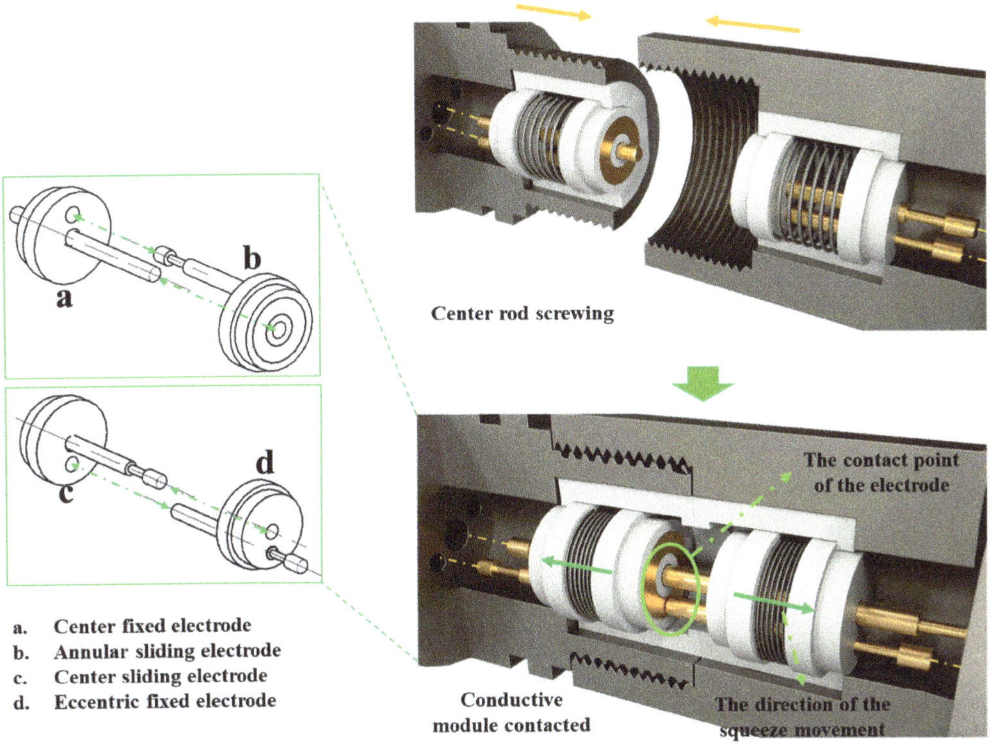

Figure 19. The final design of the conductive center pole.

The electrode unit a and the electrode unit b are matched with each other, the electrode unit c and the electrode unit d are matched with each other, and the conduction and self-adaptive adjustment of the electrode are realized by a spring.

The optimized conductive center pole integrates the spring structure, solves the contact interference of the two electrodes, and optimizes its "installation and assembly", "independence" and "functionality".

4.6. Design Comprehensive Evaluation and Analysis

According to the functional requirements and the comprehensive solution from Figure 9. The overall design scheme was evaluated from six aspects: "structural design", "installation and assembly", "material properties", "independence", "functionality" and "manufacturability".

The design schemes of the above three conductive center poles are summarized and evaluated through the analytic hierarchy process [42,43], as shown in Table 4. Scheme A is improved on the basis of the original scheme (Figure 10) by changing the electrode contact from surface contact to point contact, which solves the problem that the electrodes cannot be aligned when the conductive structure rotates with the central rod. Scheme B separates the conductive structure on the basis of Scheme A, and adds a spring structure at the middle electrode. The problem that the conductive structure in Scheme A is excessively squeezed and contacted after the central rod is rotated is solved. Scheme C is improved on the basis of Scheme B. The electrode is separated again, and the spring is integrated into the conductive structure, which increases the overall installation of the conductive structure.

Table 4. Comprehensive evaluation of the optimized conductive center pole.

Scoring Item and Weight	Design Scheme			Schematic Diagram
	Scheme A	Scheme B	Scheme C	
Structural design (0.1309)	0.4931	0.3342	0.1727	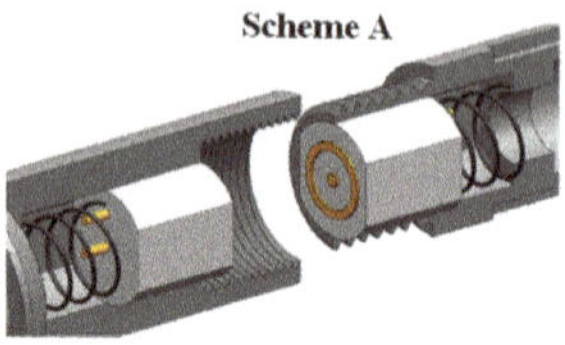
Installation and assembly (0.2032)	0.2413	0.1235	0.6352	
Material properties (0.0343)	0.3333	0.3333	0.3333	
Independence (0.2051)	0.1572	0.3193	0.5235	
Functionality (0.3231)	0.1616	0.3025	0.5359	
Manufacturability (0.1034)	0.4025	0.3291	0.2684	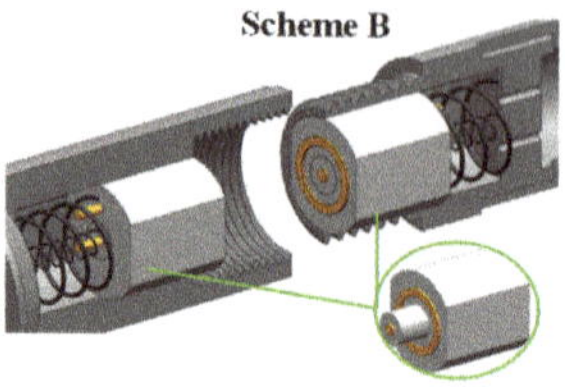
Comprehensive score	0.2511	0.2776	0.4712	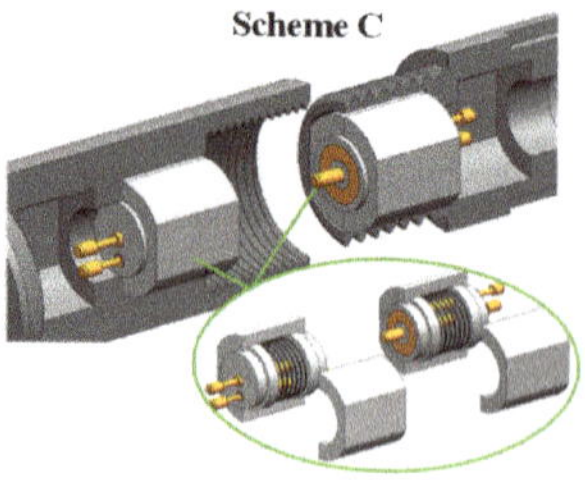

5. Strength Check of the Conductive Center Pole

In order to assemble the conductive module, it is necessary to expand the hollow inside the center pole, which causes the pipe wall at the threaded part to be thinned. The cross-section of the threaded connection is shown in Figure 20.

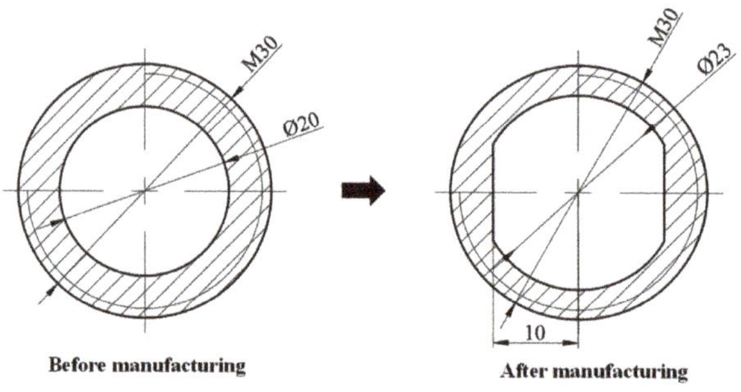

Figure 20. The cross-section of the threaded connection.

Therefore, it is necessary to check the strength of the threaded connection structure of the center pole after processing and thinning to ensure that the center pole can complete the lifting of the core remover.

During the operation of the core remover, it is always in a vertical working state. After the core is completed, the center pole needs to vertically lift the corer with a weight of about 350 kg. The threaded connection strength when the central pole is subjected to an axial load, and the tensile strength of the structure at the weakest part of the central pole need to be identified and resolved [44].

The connection of the center pole adopts an M30 standard thread, the pitch P is 2 mm, and the minor diameter d_1 of the thread is 27.835 mm. The center pole is made of 304 stainless steel, its yield strength R_{eL} is 310 MPa, and its tensile strength R_m is 620 MPa. In the case of a static load, the safety factor S_S of the bolt connection is taken as 4. To ensure the reliability of the threaded connection, it is required that the residual pre-tightening force of 1.3 times the working load is retained when the center pole is tensioned.

$$\sigma = \frac{1.3(1.3F_0 + F_0)}{\frac{\pi}{4}d_1^2} = 17.1 \text{ MPa} \quad (7)$$

The allowable strength is:

$$[\sigma] = \frac{R_{eL}}{S_s} = 77.5 \text{ MPa} \quad (8)$$

The strength check value is far less than the allowable strength, and the strength of the threaded connection meets the needs of use.

The tensile strength of the thinned part of the center pole must be checked. The cross-sectional area of the threaded connection of the center pole is A_s, and the area of the hollow is A_d.

$$A_s = \pi d_1^2 - A_d = 215.9 \text{ mm}^2 \quad (9)$$

$$\sigma = \frac{1.3F_0 + F_0}{A_s} = 37.29 \text{ MPa} \quad (10)$$

Taking the safety factor S_s as 4, the allowable tensile stress is $[\sigma_s]$.

$$[\sigma_s] = \frac{R_m}{S_s} = 155 \text{ MPa} \quad (11)$$

The tensile strength value is much smaller than the allowable tensile strength, which meets the operation requirements of the center pole pulling and lifting.

6. Experiments and Results

6.1. Continuity Performance Test

A physical prototype of the designed conductive center pole was made, as shown in Figure 21. Since it only needs to verify the action and conduction performance of the key structure of the conductive module, on the basis of retaining the key features and dimensions of the center pole, it has been reduced in the length direction. The lengths of the two test center poles are 200 mm and 133 mm, respectively, and the connection between the center poles is an annulus with a diameter of 20 mm and an M30 threaded connection.

The resistance of the connected conductive center pole was measured using a multimeter, as shown in Figure 22.

It was measured that one end of the connection resistance was 0.3 Ω, and the other end was 0 Ω, and its conduction performance was good. The electrothermal conversion efficiency of the center pole conductive module in actual use still needs further experimental verification.

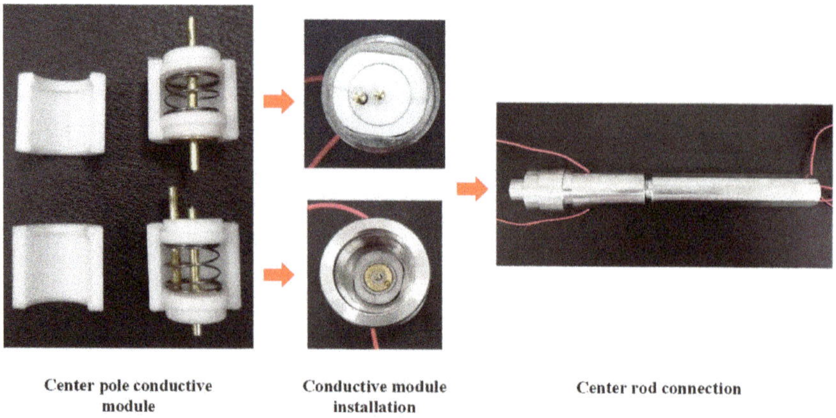

Figure 21. Physical prototype of the conductive center pole.

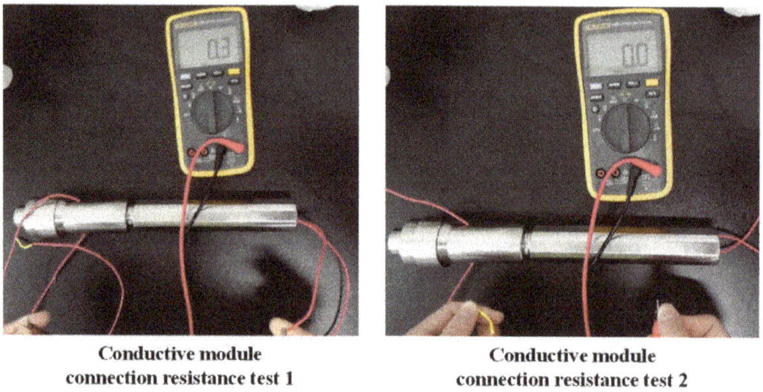

Figure 22. Conductive center pole resistance test.

6.2. Heating Performance Test of the Conductive Center Pole at Room Temperature

A conductive center pole and a conventional wire were used to power the carbon nano-material heater and heat the thermal oil, respectively, to compare its electrothermal conversion efficiency. The experimental platform is shown in Figure 23.

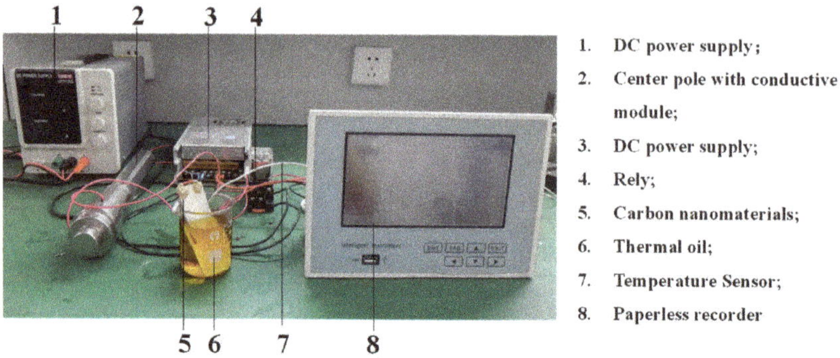

Figure 23. Comparative heating performance experiment.

Using a 12 V DC power supply to supply power to the load, 100 mL of thermal oil was heated with a heating target temperature of 90 °C, and kept at a constant temperature for 10 min after reaching the target temperature. The results of the experiment are shown in Figure 24. The thermal oil was heated to 90 °C through the conductive center pole and the conventional wire, which took 8 min and 8 min and 35 s, respectively.

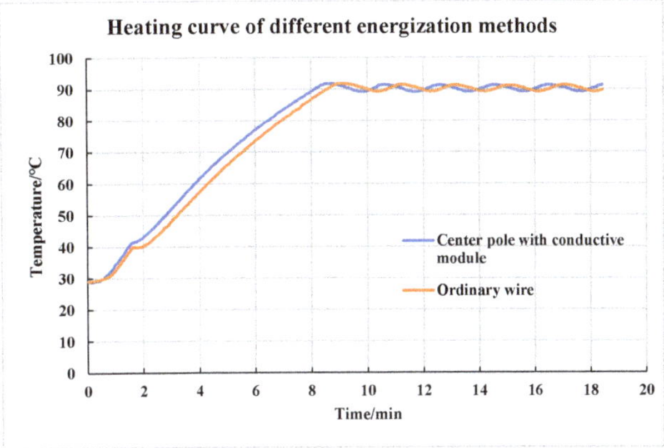

Figure 24. Heating curve of the different energization methods.

6.3. Heating Performance Test of the Conductive Center Pole at High Temperatures

The oven was used to simulate an in situ high-temperature environment of 150 °C to verify the working performance of the conductive center pole in a high-temperature environment. The conductive center pole was placed in a high-temperature oven, and the rest of the connected electronic components were placed outside the oven to ensure normal operation. The principle of the experimental system is shown in Figure 25.

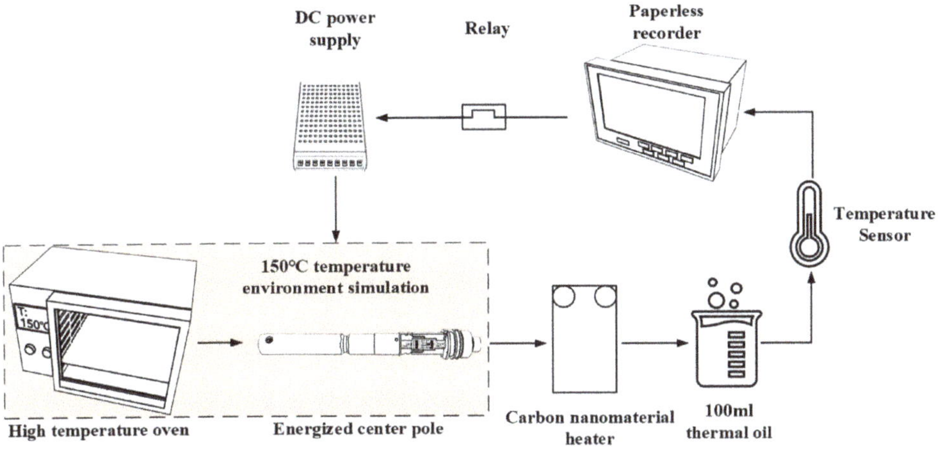

Figure 25. High-temperature test experiment of the conductive center pole.

The physical experiment platform is shown in Figure 26.

The results of the high-temperature-resistance test of the conductive center pole are shown in Figure 27. Heating the same thermal oil to 90 °C took 2 min and 45 s longer in a high-temperature environment than at room temperature, taking 10 min and 45 s in total. On the one hand, it is considered that due to the increase in temperature, the resistance of the wires in the center pole increases, and the loss of power consumption increases. On the other hand, the uniformity of the temperature distribution of the thermal oil is poor, and the position of the temperature sensor has great influence on its readings, which ultimately makes the heating curve of the two environments different.

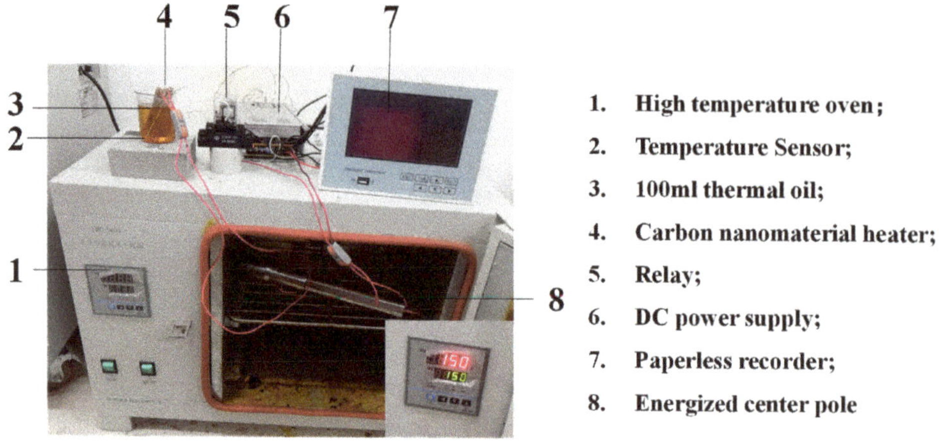

Figure 26. The physical experiment platform.

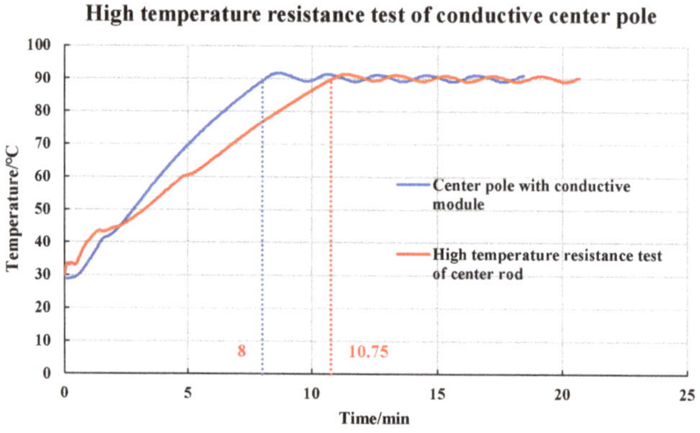

Figure 27. The results of the high-temperature-resistance test of the conductive center pole.

6.4. Long-Term Effectiveness and Stability Test of the Energy Supply Transmission and Signal Transmission of the Conductive Central Rod

In order to verify the long-term effectiveness and stability of the conductive central rod in the process of power and signal transmission, the long-term work and temperature and pressure signal transmission test experiments were added on the basis of the above experiments.

In the long-term energy supply stability test, the conductive central rod is used as the current-carrying middleware. The twisted conductive central rod is connected in series with the heating load, and the heating load is powered by a 0–30 V adjustable DC power supply. The heating medium is heat conduction oil, and the heating target temperature was set at 100 °C. When the target temperature was reached, the temperature was maintained by a paperless recorder and relay. The whole experiment process was set to maintain the temperature for more than 100 h. The experimental results are shown in Figure 28, which verify that the conductive central rod, as a current-carrying middleware, can stably supply power for a long time and meet the dynamic response when the voltage and current change.

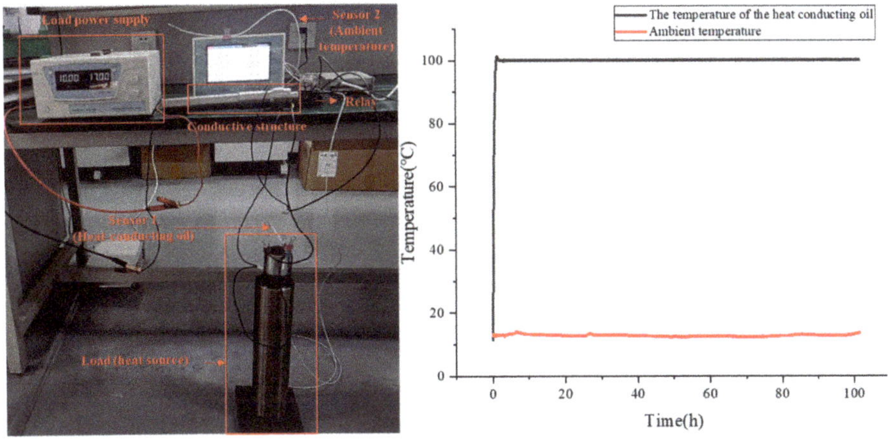

Figure 28. Long-term experiment and results of the stability of the energy supply by the conducting central rod.

In addition, the signal transmission performance of the conductive central rod was verified by experiments. First, the signal transmission of the PT100 temperature sensor was tested. The temperature sensor was connected in series with the conductive central rod, and the heat conducting oil was used as the object of temperature measurement. The different temperatures of the heat conducting oil at different times were measured and recorded. The experimental results are shown in Figure 29. The temperatures measured by the temperature sensor in series with the conductive central rod and the standard temperature sensor have a high consistency. Due to the different placement positions of the sensors, the measured temperatures have slight differences, but basically meet the engineering application requirements.

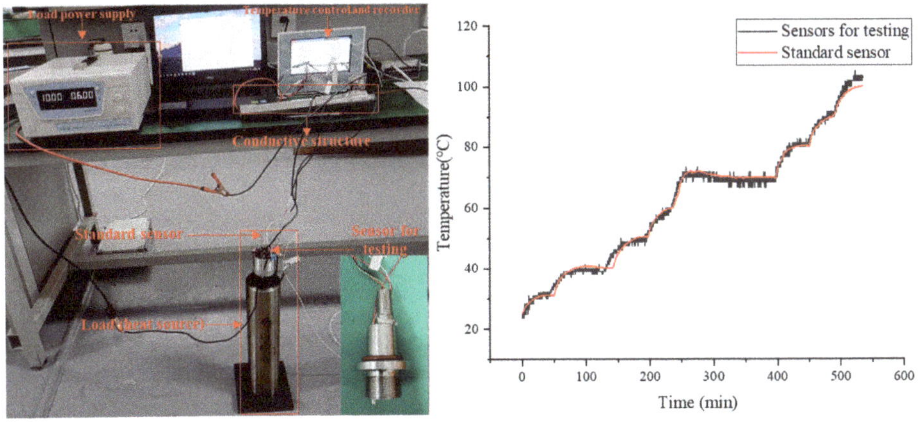

Figure 29. Comparison experiment and results of the temperature sensor testing.

Later, the pressure sensor signal transmission was tested. The pressure sensor was connected in series with the conductive central rod, and connected with the hydraulic station for pressurization and pressure data acquisition. In the experiment, the hydraulic source pressure was raised from 0 MPa to 63 MPa within 200 s, and the pressure data collected by the test pressure sensor was compared with the standard pressure data of the hydraulic station. The experimental results are shown in Figure 30. The two pressure data have good consistency and can meet the engineering application requirements.

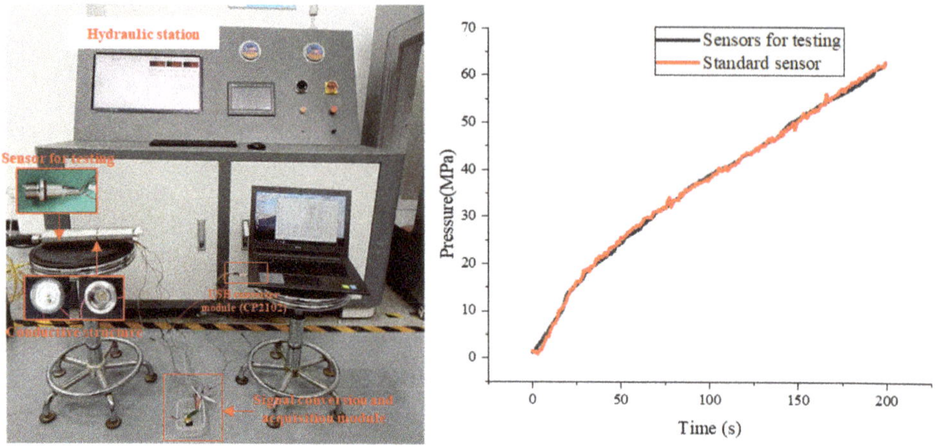

Figure 30. Comparison experiment and results of the pressure sensor testing.

The signal transmission experiment of the temperature sensor and pressure sensor verified the stability and reliability of the conductive central rod as the signal-transmission middleware, which has certain application prospects in the field of deep in situ measurements.

7. Conclusions

In this paper, based on the requirements of the in situ insulation and coring of deep rocks, and based on energized smart drill pipe technology commonly used in the logging field, an innovative conductive center pole was developed. The conductive center pole meets the power supply and lifting strength requirements for the in situ insulation and coring of deep rocks. With a small size, high-reliability connection and self-adjustment function, it can realize the non-winding energization and communication between the center poles.

- According to the requirements for the in situ insulation and coring of deep rocks and referring to the design of smart drill pipes in logging, the overall design of the conductive center pole is proposed.
- The innovative design process of the conductive center pole is proposed, the functional requirements of the conductive center pole were analyzed, and the design matrix A was established and solved.
- The TRIZ solving tool was used to obtain a preliminary design scheme, and to further optimize the scheme to obtain a scheme with a higher comprehensive evaluation.
- The strength of the conductive center pole of the new structure was verified, and a physical prototype was made to conduct comparative experiments in a realistic environment to verify the feasibility of its function and structure.
- In addition, the feasibility of its application in the field of energy supply and signal transmission was verified through long-term heating experiments and sensor data acquisition tests.

The conductive center pole technology proposed in this paper is of great significance for the realization of underground power supply and communication. The effectiveness of the integrated application and the design processes of the axiomatic and TRIZ design methods were verified. The preliminary research experiments were carried out in an ideal indoor environment. It performed well in the installation and resistance tests, and could realize a normal energy supply to the load under high-temperatures, which verified its characteristics of a non-winding and stable connection. It provides technical support for the accurate assessment of oil and gas resources and the realization of intelligent, efficient and safe digital drilling. It is also provides an innovative approach for the in situ insulation and coring of deep rocks. Follow-up work will continue to focus on experimental tests under high-temperature and high-pressure and practical engineering applications.

Author Contributions: Conceptualization, B.Y.; methodology, B.Y.; writing—original draft preparation, B.Y.; writing—review and editing, Z.H.; software, Z.H.; resources, J.Y.; investigation, Z.W.; data curation, C.L.; supervision, H.X.; funding acquisition H.X.; projection administration H.X. All authors have read and agreed to the published version of the manuscript.

Funding: This research was founded by the National Key R&D Program of China, grant number 2022YFB3706605, National Natural Science Foundation of China, grant number 52274133, National Natural Science Foundation of China, grant number 51827901.

Institutional Review Board Statement: Not applicable.

Informed Consent Statement: Not applicable.

Data Availability Statement: The data used to support the findings of this study cannot be shared.

Conflicts of Interest: The authors declare that they have no competing financial interests or personal relationships that could appear to have influenced the work reported in this paper.

References

1. Lin, W.; Wu, J. Discussion on the roadmap of China's energy transition framework under the goal of carbon neutrality. *Price Theory Pract.* **2021**, *6*, 9–12. [CrossRef]
2. Xie, H.; Ren, S.; Xie, Y.; Jiao, X.M. Development opportunities of the coal industry towards the goal of carbon neutrality. *J. China Coal Soc.* **2021**, *46*, 2197–2211. [CrossRef]
3. bp.com. *Statistical Review of World Energy*; Whitehouse Associates: London, UK, 2021. Available online: https://www.bp.com/en/global/corporate/energy-economics/statistical-review-of-world-energy.html (accessed on 21 June 2022).
4. Xie, H.; Gao, F.; Ju, Y. Research and development of rock mechanics in deep ground engineering. *Chin. J. Rock Mech. Eng.* **2015**, *34*, 2161–2178. [CrossRef]
5. Xie, H.; Gao, M.; Zhang, R.; Chen, L.; Liu, T.; Li, C.; Li, C.; He, Z. Study on concept and progress of in situ fidelity coring of deep rocks. *Chin. J. Rock Mech. Eng.* **2020**, *39*, 865–876. [CrossRef]
6. Xue, Q.; Zhang, J. Advances in intelligent automatic drilling technologies and equipment. *Explor. Eng. (Rock Soil Drill. Tunn.)* **2020**, *47*, 9–14. [CrossRef]
7. Xie, H.; Gao, F.; Ju, Y.; Gao, M.Z.; Zhang, R.; Gao, Y.N.; Liu, J.F.; Xie, L.Z. Quantitative definition and investigation of deep mining. *J. China Coal Soc.* **2015**, *40*, 1–10. [CrossRef]
8. Li, C.; Xie, H.; Gao, M.; Chen, L.; Zhao, L.; Li, C.; Wu, N.; He, Z.; Li, J. Novel designs of pressure controllers to enhance the upper pressure limit for gas-hydrate-bearing sediment sampling. *Energy* **2021**, *227*, 120405. [CrossRef]
9. Yu, B.; Zhao, W.; Chen, L.; Gao, M.; He, Z.; Wan, H. Innovative design of active insulation system for in-situ fidelity coring in deep strata. *Chin. J. Eng. Des.* **2020**, *27*, 407–415. [CrossRef]
10. Kashefi, K.; Lovley Derek, R. Extending the Upper Temperature Limit for Life. *Science* **2003**, *301*, 934. [CrossRef]
11. Borgonie, G.; García-Moyano, A.; Litthauer, D.; Bert, W.; Bester, A.; van Heerden, E.; Möller, C.; Erasmus, M.; Onstott, T.C. Nematoda from the terrestrial deep subsurface of South Africa. *Nature* **2011**, *474*, 79–82. [CrossRef]
12. Teske, A.P. The deep subsurface biosphere is alive and well. *Trends Microbiol.* **2005**, *13*, 402–404. [CrossRef]
13. Lupton, N.; Connell, L.D.; Heryanto, D.; Sander, R.; Camilleri, M.; Down, D.I.; Pan, Z. Enhancing biogenic methane generation in coalbed methane reservoirs—Core flooding experiments on coals at in-situ conditions. *Int. J. Coal Geol.* **2020**, *219*, 103377. [CrossRef]
14. Yan, T.; Xu, R.; Liu, W.; Sun, W.; Hou, Z.; Shao, Y. Research and development of intelligent drilling technology in China. *J. Northeast. Pet. Univ.* **2020**, *44*, 15–21+6. [CrossRef]
15. Abid, K.; Spagnoli, G.; Teodoriu, C.; Falcone, G. Review of pressure coring systems for offshore gas hydrates research. *Underw. Technol.* **2015**, *33*, 19–30. [CrossRef]
16. Abegg, F.; Hohnberg, H.-J.; Pape, T.; Bohrmann, G.; Freitag, J. Development and application of pressure-core-sampling systems for the investigation of gas- and gas-hydrate-bearing sediments. *Deep Sea Res. Part I* **2008**, *55*, 1590–1599. [CrossRef]
17. Zhu, H.Y.; Liu, Q.Y.; Wong, G.R.; Xiao, X.H.; Zhu, X.H.; Jiang, Z.L.; Zhang, D.Y. A Pressure and Temperature Preservation System for Gas-hydrate-bearing Sediments Sampler. *Pet. Sci. Technol.* **2013**, *31*, 652–662. [CrossRef]
18. Wang, Y.; Guo, W.; Sun, Y.; Jia, R.; Liu, H.N.; Xue, J. The Development of Wire-line Sampling Drilling Tool for Gas Hydrates by Hole Bottom Freezing with Development of Wire-line Sampling Drilling Tool for Gas Hydrates by Hole Bottom Freezing with Liquid Nitrogen as Ex-ternal Cold Source. *Drill. Eng.* **2013**, *40*, 1–3. [CrossRef]

19. Liu, X.; Zhao, Y.; Liu, H.; Ruan, H.; Chem, Y.; Shen, L.; Wu, H.; Liang, Q. Comparative Study on Sampling Tools for Insulation and Pressure-holding of Marine Gas Hydrate. *Equip. Geotech. Eng.* **2018**, *19*, 11–15. [CrossRef]
20. Li, S.; Cheng, Y.; Qin, H. Development of pressure piston corer for exploring natural gas hydrates. *J. Zhejiang Univ. (Eng. Sci.)* **2006**, *40*, 888–892. [CrossRef]
21. Wan, B.; Huang, Y.; Qian, X. Deep-sea hard rock fidelity corer. CN Patent CN 200958379Y, 10 October 2007.
22. Yang, L.; Sun, W.; Luo, J.; Wang, G.; Wang, J. Study and application of GWY194-70BB heat and pressure preservation coring tool. *Oil Drill. Prod. Technol.* **2014**, *36*, 58–61. [CrossRef]
23. Wang, X.; Zhou, D.; Yang, L.; Gao, W.; Sun, S.; Su, Y. Development and Field Application of a Coalbed Methane Coring Tool with Pressure Maintenance, Thermal Insulation, and Shape Preservation Capabilities. *Pet. Drill. Tech.* **2021**, *49*, 94–99. [CrossRef]
24. Katz, B.J. Hydrocarbon shows and source rocks in scientific ocean drilling. *Int. J. Coal Geol.* **2003**, *54*, 139–154. [CrossRef]
25. Xing, D.; Qi, L.; Zhao, J.; Wang, Y. The design of computer controlled ground information transmission down platform in drilling. *MATEC Web Conf.* **2020**, *309*, 04017. [CrossRef]
26. Lurie, P.; Head, P.; Smith, J. Smart Drilling with ELECTRIC DRILLSTRING. In Proceedings of the SPE/IADC Drilling Conference, Amsterdam, The Netherlands, 19–21 February 2003. [CrossRef]
27. Hu, Y.; Li, X.; Huang, Y.; Liu, Y. Design of Downhole Automatic Power Supply Device based on TPS2121. *Pet. Drill. Tech.* **2020**, *48*, 76–81. [CrossRef]
28. Yang, J.; Zhu, G.; Zhang, H.; Li, X.; Tian, H.; Guo, X. Noteworthy advanced international petroleum engineering technology. *Oil Forum* **2012**, *31*, 36–44. [CrossRef]
29. Jellison, M.; Hall, D.; Howard, D.; Hall, H.T.J.; Long, R.C.; Chandler, R.B.; Pixton, D.S. Telemetry Drill Pipe: Enabling Technology for the Downhole Internet. In Proceedings of the SPE/IADC Drilling Conference, Amsterdam, The Netherlands, 19–21 February 2003. [CrossRef]
30. Jiang, J.; Li, Y.; Li, L.; Zhou, C.; Huo, Y.; Li, Q. An Innovation Design Approach for Product Service Systems Based on TRIZ and Function Incentive. *Complexity* **2021**, *2021*, 5592272. [CrossRef]
31. Chou, J.-R. A TRIZ-based product-service design approach for developing innovative products. *Comput. Ind. Eng.* **2021**, *161*, 107608. [CrossRef]
32. Li, M.; Ming, X.; He, L.; Zheng, M.; Xu, Z. A TRIZ-based Trimming method for Patent design around. *Comput.-Aided Des.* **2015**, *62*, 20–30. [CrossRef]
33. Liu, A.; Lu, S. Functional design framework for innovative design thinking in product development. *CIRP J. Manuf. Sci. Technol.* **2020**, *30*, 105–117. [CrossRef]
34. Jahanmir, S.; Saka, N.; Tucker, C., II; Kim, S.-G. Axiomatic Design. In *Advances in Multidisciplinary Engineering*; ASME Press: New York, NY, USA, 2016.
35. Li, X.; Qiu, S.; Ming, H.X.G. An integrated module-based reasoning and axiomatic design approach for new product design under incomplete information environment. *Comput. Ind. Eng.* **2019**, *127*, 63–73. [CrossRef]
36. Benavides, E.M. Axiomatic design. In *Advanced Engineering Design*; Woodhead Publishing: Sawston, UK, 2012.
37. Kulak, O.; Kahraman, C.J.I.S. Fuzzy multi-attribute selection among transportation companies using axiomatic design and analytic hierarchy process. *Inf. Sci.* **2005**, *170*, 191–210. [CrossRef]
38. Delgado-Maciel, J.; Cortés-Robles, G.; Sánchez-Ramírez, C.; García-Alcaraz, J.; Méndez-Contreras, J.M. The evaluation of conceptual design through dynamic simulation: A proposal based on TRIZ and system Dynamics. *Comput. Ind. Eng.* **2020**, *149*, 106785. [CrossRef]
39. Liu, A.; Wang, Y.; Teo, I.; Lu, S. Constraint management for concept ideation in conceptual design. *CIRP J. Manuf. Sci. Technol.* **2019**, *24*, 35–48. [CrossRef]
40. Li, Z.; Tate, D.; Lane, C.; Adams, C. A framework for automatic TRIZ level of invention estimation of patents using natural language processing, knowledge-transfer and patent citation metrics. *Comput.-Aided Des.* **2012**, *44*, 987–1010. [CrossRef]
41. Sadeghi, L.; Dantan, J.-Y.; Mathieu, L.; Siadat, A.; Aghelinejad, M.M. A design approach for safety based on Product-Service Systems and Function–Behavior–Structure. *CIRP J. Manuf. Sci. Technol.* **2017**, *19*, 44–56. [CrossRef]
42. Saaty, T. That is not the analytic hierarchy process: What the AHP is and what it is not. *J. Multi-Criteria Decis. Anal.* **1997**, *6*, 324–335. [CrossRef]
43. Chen, C.; Tao, Y.; Li, Y.; Liu, Q.; Li, S.; Tang, Z. A structure-function knowledge extraction method for bio-inspired design. *Comput. Ind.* **2021**, *127*, 103402. [CrossRef]
44. Gong, H.; Liu, J.; Feng, H. Review on anti-loosening methods for threaded fasteners. *Chin. J. Aeronaut.* **2021**, *35*, 47–61. [CrossRef]

MDPI AG
Grosspeteranlage 5
4052 Basel
Switzerland
Tel.: +41 61 683 77 34

Applied Sciences Editorial Office
E-mail: applsci@mdpi.com
www.mdpi.com/journal/applsci